A Land I Will Show You

Tim Milnes

ISBN (Print Edition): 978-1-54398-758-4

ISBN (eBook Edition): 978-1-54398-759-1

A Land I Will Show You

TIM MILNES

Timothy Joseph Milnes was born on May 25,1956 in Juneau, the Territory of Alaska, (a fact he enjoyed pointing out.) He died an untimely death in a tragic car accident near his home on May 2, 2017. He was married to Mary Louise Shalz for 38 years. He lost his first son as an infant, but had 5 adoring children who put up with his complaints, his woes, and enjoyed his humor. He had a bachelors degree in Theology and a master's degree in Pastoral Ministry from Seattle University. He had a sociology degree and a teaching certificate from Evergreen State College, Olympia, WA. He also completed a certificate in Spiritual Direction from St. Placid's Priory, Olympia, WA. He taught religious education at Bellarmine Preparatory High School, Tacoma WA for over 30 years. He was a youth minister at St. Michael's Catholic Church, Olympia, WA for 2 years. He also volunteered teaching adult religious education at various parishes and played guitar for hospice clients. He was a talented guitar player and had many other hobbies over his life time. Writing started as a hobby and became a passion. Given the chance, he would have pursued writing as a full- time career. He loved to read and write poetry. He had written a multitude of poems which have been collected at the end of this book. His previous work, as an author, was an unpublished autobiography for his master's program entitled Gabrielle's Rose.

ACKNOWLEDGEMENTS

from Mary Lou Milnes

First of all, I need to apologize to anyone who should be recognized but did not because I can't remember. Sadly, Tim is not here to write this acknowledgement. I have to go by the seat of my pants, so bear with me.

On behalf of Tim, I would like to thank all of you for your patience in my getting this book published. I would like to thank Book Baby for helping me do this and to Sr. Laura Swan OSB for recommending them. She also did the initial transcribing of this book.

I want to thank a dear friend of Tim's, Mark Hart, who read and critiqued his books and poetry over the years. He also encouraged me to include Tim's poetry at the end of this novel.

I also would like to thank The Puget Sound Writers Guild which Tim belonged to. He loved the guild and greatly appreciated the critiquing and work you contributed to his writing.

I would especially like to thank Mary Vanek for her grammatical editing of Tim's book. (She admitted that sometimes her editing was "a little bit more than grammatical.") Sadly, she did not live to see this published, but is rejoicing with Tim that I'm finally getting it done.

I would, most especially, like to thank Rie Montané for painstakingly retyping Tim's manuscript with the corrections and getting it onto a flash drive because we could not find his original work saved on his computer.

A huge thank you to my kids: David, Esther, Bekah, Rachel, Joel, Remara, and James. I am especially grateful to James for all his tech support for his poor tech illiterate mother. Without your love and support, I couldn't have done this. And to the little imps that make my life worth living: Elizabeth, Isaiah, and Kellen.

To Tim, you have a beautiful piece of work here that I know you were so proud of. Thanks for sharing the process you went through in writing this book. I was so impressed with the research you did to make everything as accurate as possible. I am proud of you!

Finally, a word to any authors out there from the wife of an author: Do your chores before you disappear into writing your book!

PART I

Go forth…

Genesis 12:1

ONE

Juneau, Alaska, July 1980

Marianne turned the key in the lock and opened the door into her future. Her new attic apartment at the top of the Highlands on the north edge of town and looked west across the silver waters of Gastineau Channel a mile or more to the line of mountains comprising the backbone of Douglas Island. It took an effort to take it all in, but Marianne smiled at the beautiful view.

Marianne glanced at her watch—she'd arrived this morning on the ferry. She had plenty of time to get her things settled and go for a walk to Basin Road this afternoon.

In the hard discipline of her suffering, she had learned orderliness. Everything had its place. She spent thirty minutes bringing boxes up the long stairway into her living room. She placed her rosary and her favorite drawing of the Virgin Mary on the end table next to a wooden rocking chair. Next came her colored pencils and painting supplies, which she set for now on two shelves of a bookcase next to a fireplace on the wall opposite the window, putting the books she'd brought there as well.

She quickly made up her bed, put her clothes in the dresser and closet, unpacked the dishes, and set out her toiletries in the bathroom just off her bedroom. Food that she'd bought on the way here from the ferry terminal went into the fridge and cabinets. By then it was past lunchtime. She turned on her radio and set about making a sandwich and small salad.

When the first notes of the Everly Brother's "Let It Be Me" flowed from her radio, Marianne set her knife on the kitchen counter, sat herself at the dining table and cried. It had been their song in 1964, the year of the loveliest relationship of her life before it had crashed down in an act of violence and subsequent misunderstanding that she didn't fully understand to this day. She cradled her chin and cheek in the palm of her right hand, laughing at the silliness of her tears. But she knew there was a lot more behind them than a broken relationship between two seventeen year olds.

Marianne noticed a man sitting on his deck across the narrow dead-end street looking her way—she waved down at him, and he waved back.

Wiping at her damp cheeks as the song ended, she returned to cutting tomatoes and cucumbers for a lunch salad, her thoughts lingering a moment longer in 1964. Marianne opened the Juneau Empire she'd bought. Food was expensive, apples at forty-five cents a pound, two pounds of bacon going for $1.89. An article said food prices were expected to rise over two percent this month alone. On a darker note, tensions were rising between Iran and Iraq—not that anybody she knew really seemed to care. War. Her hands shook a bit—her body reacted on its own sometimes. Marianne wondered about her plan for later in the day, to return to the raised area behind Second Bridge. She believed it was the right thing to do, but what if she couldn't deal with it? What if she were attacked again? She took a breath, recognizing the craziness of that thought.

An hour later she put on a light sweater and headed down the narrow streets that eventually dropped onto 12th Street and the rest of the town. She cut through Evergreen Bowl and took the trail that led up its steep backside. Two large ravens wove through the trees with surprisingly loud thwaps of their wings. A third trailed, its caw-caw bringing to mind someone gargling with pebbles. Coming out on 7th Street, she was only a couple blocks from

Basin Road and all at once felt an ache in her heart. Eager to see it, Marianne decided to walk two blocks down Gold Street to the Cathedral.

She walked up its stairs and into the church. Taking a deep breath, she closed her eyes. It smelled exactly the same, a hint of incense combined with melting candle wax, old wood, and the aging carpet. Walking along the vestibule, she turned right and passed through the open double-doors into the church proper, before the narrow stair that led up to the choir loft.

To her left several candles were burning. It's so small she thought, remembering that it was the smallest Roman Catholic Cathedral in the world. She walked slowly up the central aisle, looking around. The same statues of Mary and Joseph filled two corner niches. The communion rail was gone, the old altar replaced with a simple table, not the more complex one from before Vatican II. She genuflected and entered a pew on the left. It was cool and quiet. A nice place to pray. She pulled out the kneeler and knelt down with her eyes closed. The first thing that came into her mind was the persecuted poor in El Salvador.

Ten minutes later Marianne emerged, blinking her eyes in the brightness of the day. A bit of anxiety troubled her stomach. Stop doubting and just go, she thought. She moved quickly up Harris Street a couple blocks to a short stairway that provided a shortcut to Basin Road. Halfway up the stairs, she had the sensation of being watched. It's just my imagination, Marianne thought. She took a few more steps, but finally unable to help herself, she turned quickly around.

There was a large, dark haired man on the street below her, his body facing her direction, but his face turned to the right down the hill. Had he looked away as she turned? She thought maybe he had, but couldn't be sure. He came the rest of the way up the street, glanced her direction at the corner then quickly away. In a few steps he entered the Alexander Apartments.

Marianne's body reacted on its own for a second time that day with an adrenaline-pushed surge of her pulse hard to ignore. She walked to the top of the stairs, looking up for a few seconds toward the peak of the Knoll three hundred feet above her.

In a couple minutes she was wandering high above Gold Creek on Basin Road, which wound behind Juneau and around the back of the Knoll into a narrow valley. Michael had always said, "Let's go Back Basin," and this became their private name for the valley. Hard packed dirt, the road was used mainly as a trail. Few cars ever came this way.

As she walked along First Bridge, a long wooden structure that clung to the steep backside of the Knoll, her pace slowed. At the end of the bridge, she stopped. In a couple hundred meters, just before Second Bridge, she would be there, and now she felt a deepening uncertainty.

Marianne pulled the clean air deep into her lungs and slowly exhaled. She took another slow breath and released it just as slowly. She looked across the ravine through which Gold Creek flowed, up and up to the base of Mt. Juneau's massive cliffs. Marianne could see three black bears in the large clearing at the bottom of the cliffs, probably a mama and her two cubs. It looked as if the cubs were playing with each other. She smiled.

Marianne turned back to the dark forest behind her. She had many good memories here before her unknown attacker had changed everything. In all her thoughts on her return to Juneau Marianne had not realized how much Michael would be present to her, the way a pleasant dream surfaces with a half-remembered feeling of peace.

They had come this way many times. In this moment she remembered them returning from the top of Mt. Juneau, tired and arm-in-arm, chatting the whole time of nothing and everything.

Marianne raised her left hand to her brow, and felt the small scar there. Now, she thought, really. Now is the time. She continued along the dirt road, head down, unaware of the person coming toward her until the last second, and she gasped and jerked to a stop. He was a little taller than her with darker skin—almost certainly a Tlingit. A memory flashed in less than an instant, even as the man was apologizing.

"Oh, hey, sorry about that. Didn't mean to scare you."

"No," Marianne laughed shakily, "My fault, really, I was looking down, lost in thought. Should have been watching where I was going. Don't worry about it."

The man nodded his head, "Okay, but still, sorry for scaring you." He looked at her strangely for a second, making her feel uncomfortable, then went on his way. She turned for a moment, noticing his long hair. Some memory had been stirred. She'd thought of Johnny Williams for an instant—was that him? But he'd been taller, hadn't he? And his hair had been a typical crew-cut of the mid-Sixties. Although he could have grown it out. After all, her own hair was longer than she'd worn it in high school. She shook her head, letting it go.

Marianne had long ago given up searching her memory for what happened that day. Maybe it was better anyway, given how badly she'd been beaten and that there was nothing that could be done now. And then she was there.

A few steps from Second Bridge which appeared utterly unchanged. The small road down which she'd walked 16 years ago was gated, overgrown with brush. Mt. Roberts and Mt. Juneau rose steeply to either side of the narrow valley just as they had then. The creek rushed by with the same ruckus. Marianne closed her eyes, breathing in the humid feel and smell of the rainforest which she had so loved. Prompted by the familiar smell, memory flowed without her willing it.

It was a late April day, and she was excited for so many reasons—being a senior, thinking about next year at college. And Michael. She knew they were young, but she loved him so much. He was full of positive energy, was smart, funny, and she liked the way he looked at her. He was easy to be with and had such a deep faith. They were going to go to the same college, Seattle University. They talked of their life together, all their lovely dreams.

She touched her lips, remembering Michael's first hesitant kiss last June out on the beach at the end of the Million Dollar Golf Course. Then a rainstorm had come in, and they'd run to his car and kissed a little more. They'd come a long way since then, she thought, and laughed quietly to herself. And here she was, waiting for him near Second Bridge. She looked at her watch; twenty minutes early. How embarrassing.

And then she went blank. Her next memory was of coming to consciousness, her body wracked by pain. She was in the woods, in an elevated section back a ways from the bridge, lying under the trees among devil's club and wild blueberries, face down in a deep depression formed where a large tree had blown over in a windstorm. Her left arm was jammed up against a big jagged stone. Green moss covered everything. When she raised her head, she saw red in the moss. Her blood, she realized after a moment. She stumbled as she went to stand, jeans around her ankles. And her underwear.

Blank again. In her next memory, she was down on her knees, trembling, hiding. From him. Michael was walking away, back toward Juneau. Later she stumbled out of the forest and down to Gold Creek. She hurt everywhere. Rinsed the blood off her face and arms. The cold water woke her up. She began to cry, sobs wracking her body.

She remembered no more. Evidently a couple had come across her, shivering as she made her way toward home. She told her mom she had taken a terrible fall off some rocks and down a steep slope. It was three weeks before she told the truth.

Everything she had believed about life had cracked and come apart like a calving glacier. Shame froze her as if she were encased in ice. Her belief in Michael's betrayal simply overwhelmed her ability to understand and function. She needed to talk to someone but could not bring herself to do so.

Sometime during the third week, there was a brief touch of memory, the only one she would ever have. Someone had come up behind her. She had not seen him. When she came to consciousness and saw Michael walking away, in her confusion she'd thought it was him who had done raped and beaten her. For three weeks she had thought that. As this new memory surfaced, she realized it could not have been Michael—the man's ugly voice was not his at all. And he was so big, much bigger than Michael.

She hated that she'd believed that of Michael. He loved her. In a blizzard of self-recrimination, shame piled on shame, an accumulation that finally gave way in an avalanche of self-loathing that nearly buried her. It took her a few days, but finally she called Michael. She'd rushed to meet him, had blurted out something, but here again memory was blurry, telling him she'd been raped, and "I thought it was you, but now I know it wasn't, and I am so sorry but please, please forgive me."

A raven cry broke her reverie. Her heart fluttered like an injured bird. It was an eight to ten foot climb up a deer trail to the flattish area where the attack had occurred. Halfway up she slipped on the damp earth, getting mud on the knees of her jeans and her both hands. Taking a deep breath, Marianne grabbed a couple of small bushes and pulled herself up.

She stopped to steady herself, wiping off her hands, wandering back into the forest until she finally found where she'd been dumped. After sixteen years the fallen tree looked like an elevated trail, long, rounded, moss covered. Devil's Club rose like arms reaching from the depression where she'd lain, their central berries still green. She reached out and touched one of the large leaves. Picked a few berries and tossed them out onto the surrounding forest floor. Everything seemed so far in the past. Then she trembled, tears forming.

Marianne sensed the presence, perhaps heard the soft fall of a foot. Fear jolted in an adrenaline surge and she cut off a cry as she turned. A man was visible out on the road—the same man from before. She slipped down into the depression where she had been dumped in sixteen years earlier, peeking through the large leaves of Devil's Club. The man had stopped on the bridge and was looking around.

TWO

The man walked slowly away, looking around. Marianne watched until he disappeared around a far corner. She rose and, resisting the urge to run, made her way straight to the road, quickly heading back toward town. Approaching First Bridge, she looked back. The man was not in sight, and Marianne relaxed, laughing quietly at the thought that if he were to appear now, she could outrun him to town.

Her hands shook only the slightest bit from the residue of the adrenaline rush. Marianne could only shake her head. She'd been here only a few hours and already felt quite a bit of anxiety. She wished she had been able to spend more time at the place of the attack. It had been strange standing there, more like looking into someone else's life than being at the spot that had marked such a turning for her. I'll have to go back, she thought, but not today.

Marianne took a quick, deep breath, and looked up again at the cliffs of Mt. Juneau. A long waterfall plummeted down from the heights above the cliffs, and the Black Bears were still visible near where the falls hit the rising lower slopes. Glancing once more back toward Second Bridge, she walked to the guard rail that edged the dirt road. She had loved this place once. Except for the road, she could be a million miles from anywhere. The air was clean and the creek filled the narrow valley with a lovely noise. All around mountains shot steeply to the sky, their steep ridges reminding her of high gothic arches. Nature's church.

Attracted by a noise, she looked back toward Second Bridge. Two girls on bikes, maybe ten years old, coasted down the slope just this side of the bridge, their laughter bringing a smile to her face. It looked as if they had decided to race as they started pumping their pedals furiously. As they came closer, one of the girls hit a bump, and her chain came off. Unbalanced, her bike swerved toward the edge of the road, near where Marianne stood. The guard rail ended just uphill from her, and the girl was headed straight for it. Without thinking, Marianne ran and positioned herself between the bike and the end of the guard rail. She put her arms out in an attempt to stop the girl who crashed into her a second later.

The handlebars hit her hard in the hips, and the girl's forehead hit her cheek. Marianne went down hard, and lay stunned on the road. The girl was on top of her, crying as she pulled herself up. There was a cut on the girl's arm, and her jeans were ripped at both knees. As Marianne recovered her wits, she saw that her own hand was cut, and her cheek hurt a lot. She moaned as she sat up. Blood dripped to the ground. Marianne pulled her handkerchief out of her jeans pocket and pressed it to her hand. She held back a hiss at the sharp sting.

The uninjured girl spoke out in an excited voice, "Joanie, are you all right? Look, your arm is cut." She looked at Marianne. "Oh, your hand is cut too. You stopped Joanie." Joanie was sitting now on the ground, still crying and holding her arm. Afraid it might be broken, Marianne stood up, wincing at the pain in her hip, and took two steps to the pair, willing herself to be calm.

"Wow," Marianne said to Joanie, "you really plowed into me. Can I look at your arm?"

Marianne saw no obvious break. The cut on the girl's arm didn't look too bad.

The girl gave Marianne a small smile. Marianne said, "You are so brave, Joanie. Where do you live?"

"I live on Starr Hill, on Kennedy Street."

"Do you think you can walk?"

The girl shook her head and started crying again. Marianne scooted over next to her, putting her arm around her.

Trying to think through her own pain, she asked the other girl her name and then asked, "Irene, do you live nearby?"

"Yeah, I live on Eighth Street. It's real close."

Marianne was relieved—Eighth Street was no more than three or four minutes away on a bike.

"Is your mom or dad home?"

"My mom's home."

"Do you think you can go get her?"

"I'll go get her."

As Irene went to her bike, Marianne told her, "Ride home at a normal speed."

Marianne watched her ride off, then turned her attention back to Joanie. To distract her she asked, "What grade are you in?"

Joanie tried to answer but couldn't for a minute through her ragged breath.

Guessing a grade higher than Marianne thought the girl was in, she asked, "Are you in fourth grade?"

Joanie looked at her with a small smile. "No, I'm in third grade. But my mom says I'm real smart, and read like a sixth grader."

"What's your favorite book?"

"I love Anne of Green Gables best."

"Oh, I like her too. She's kind of sassy."

The girl smiled again, and the two carried on the conversation. She did not hear the man's approach, until he spoke.

"Is everything okay? You both look hurt."

Marianne looked up into the man's dark eyes, her heart beating harder. The man came to them and kneeled down. Marianne positioned herself between him and Joanie.

He looked at the pair for a few moments and said. "Looks like you have it under control. Can I help the two of you back to town?"

Marianne interjected quickly. 'No, we're fine. This girl's friend has gone to get her mom. She'll be here in just a minute."

Irene was pedaling back to them but was alone. She was panting as she rode up.

"Mom's not home—she left me a note. She went grocery shopping. I tried Mrs. Brewer's house, but she wasn't home either."

Marianne asked Joanie, "Do you think you can walk now?"

"Maybe, I hit my knee really really hard. It hurts too."

The man walked over. "Let me carry her."

Marianne looked at him, took a breath.

Irene spoke to the man. "I saw you yesterday with Evie Williams."

"I'm her brother. My name's Johnny. What's yours?"

As the girls told him their names, Marianne relaxed. So it was Johnny Williams, Michael's best friend in high school. This man had once done her a deep kindness. Then she realized with a start that it was her turn. She looked up at him. "Johnny, you may remember me—I'm Marianne Greene."

He helped her up with his hand. "I know. It took me a couple minutes to place you, but then I came back to find you. Didn't expect this, though."

Marianne laughed, then winced. "My hip and stomach are going to be sore tomorrow." That said, the four made their way slowly along First Bridge and back to town, Johnny carrying Joanie, Irene walking next to them, and Marianne limping along on the other side, pushing Joanie's bike.

When they arrived at Irene's home, her mom was there. She called Joanie's mother right off, who immediately left work to come get her daughter.

They left before Joanie's mom arrived. Out on the street, Johnny said, "That cut looks serious. Would you like me to run you out to the hospital?"

"Yes, I'd appreciate that."

"We have to go to my mom's house to get my sister's car—do you remember Evie?"

"I remember her well. I really liked her." She wondered if he didn't have his own car. Was he living with his mother?

They walked down Basin Road's shaded curves, homes to the right, trees covering the steep slope of the Knoll on the left. Turning left at Starr Hill, they walked up the steep cement anged at all." Stepping back, she noticed Marianne's hand and dirty pants, a look of concern coming over her.

After that things proceeded swiftly, and within a couple minutes she and Johnny were on their way to Bartlett Regional Hospital, four miles away.

As they drove through town, Johnny was quiet. Marianne looked out the window as they came to Egan Drive, thinking of the day when Johnny had come across her at the top of the Knoll.

Her hand hurt, and she felt tired all at once.

They left town and within two minutes arrived at the drive up to the hospital. As they came to the parking lot, Johnny pulled into a slot, turned to her with a huge sigh, and started to speak. "Marianne, —."

He looked disconcerted.

"Johnny, what is it?"

"Where are you living? What I mean to say is, are you living alone?" He stopped, looked a little quizzical, and continued. "I mean, I don't . . . ."

Marianne laughed at the personal nature of his questions, but stopped quickly at the serious look on his face.

"I live up in the Highlands. My brother David came up with me to help me get settled, he's leaving in a couple days."

Johnny had looked relieved, and said, "Well, let's get you inside. Get that taken care of."

He had been kind enough to wait for her, and less than an hour later, they were on the way back to her home, her hand stitched and bandaged.

He turned up the long, narrow road to her attic apartment. There were no other houses until the top, where one home sat across a paved parking area from where Marianne lived. Johnny looked around as they stopped in front of her apartment.

"Thanks," she said as she opened the door and started to get out. "I'm sore all over, and really tired. I just want to take a hot bath and a nap.

"Marianne, wait," he said quickly. She turned to him, the car door half open.

"Listen, I know you want to get inside. Can we meet tomorrow? I mean, there's something I'd like to talk about."

She was puzzled, and taken aback by the intensity in his eyes. "I . . ." she started to say, but he cut her off.

"I'd tell you now, but I'd like to have a little more time to talk."

Marianne remembered that day on the Knoll, how good a friend of Michael's he was and decided this was a man she could trust. They arranged to meet tomorrow after her meeting with Sister Kris.

THREE

Johnny jerked up unexpectedly, turning on the lamp on his bed stand. He rose and went to his dresser, picking up and holding the one item he had brought with him from the village of Angoon, his home these last 12 years. It was an old Tlingit knife, a gift from this great-uncle Walter Williams, the closest thing to a father and mentor from Johnny's tumultuous childhood. His own father, Albert, had been distant, something caught in the fog of too much Tokay wine, and although never mean, he'd never acted as if Johnny were important to him. But he'd worked most of the time and never abandoned the family.

It was 2:33 in the morning. As he held the knife, he remembered the dream-become-nightmare which had awoken him.

He moved with the silence of his ancestors through the forest. Ahead of him was a grizzly, which he knew was aware of him. He placed his feet carefully, sliding around trees, twisting his way through a denseness of the huge Devil's Club, scarcely more than a sigh of wind across the landscape. He heard the grizzly moving away, but was implacable in his slow pursuit, straight up toward the rim of Mt. Robert's long ascending ridge.

Emerging above timberline from the last vestiges of the forest, Johnny saw the bear disappear over another rounded ridge above him. Johnny ran smoothly up the switchbacks which led to the upper slopes of the mountain, his breath easy and contained.

Cresting the ridge, the view was disorienting---where Gastineau Channel should have lain two thousand feet below, was a shallow green valley, rimmed by low hills a half mile away. Danger was all around, and he flattened himself to the ground, drawing his M60 machinegun around. He heard a rustling and pulled himself back into the jungle. Two Phantoms flew low overhead, their roar drowning out all else. As the sound dimmed, he heard people close by although he could not see them. His trigger finger twitched with fear. As the people drew abreast him, he leapt up, already squeezing the trigger burst even as his mind registered "children." They fell screaming to the ground as he screamed . . . .

He'd waked himself up with his yell, sweating in his bed. He did not sleep again for hours.

At nine o'clock a knock on his door roused him. His sister Evie came slowly into the room, two cups of coffee in her hands. She set one down on his bed stand and moved to the nearby chair. Johnny sat up, reaching for the cup. He took a grateful sip, looking over at his sister.

"Thanks, I need this."

"I heard you yell out again last night. That's three nights in a row. Did you get back to sleep?"

"After a while," he said flatly.

"Johnny, do you dream like this every night?"

He took another sip, sighing in pleasure. "If I'd known you could make coffee this good, I wouldn't have stayed away all those years."

"Johnny . . . ?"

He glanced again at her. Her hair was long and black and straight, eyes an expressive dark brown. Even some white guys had wanted to date her in high school. He'd been surprised when he returned after twelve years from the village of Angoon to find she was every bit as tall as he was at 5'9", but slim where he was stocky. He knew this fact, but it always took him aback.

"Ah, it's never possible to get you off track—you're worse than a mama grizzly when you want something, you know that?" Evie joined him in a laugh.

"I used to get the dreams all the time, but it got better. What I mean to say is the war was fading. The dreams started up again three nights ago, when I got back. Christ, Evie, I'm jumpy. Those damn tourist helicopters drive me nuts. They don't have the deep thwap, thwap of the Hueys, but still they send me right back to . . ." He left the sentence uncompleted.

"What are you? What's your dream about?"

Johnny lowered his head a moment, quietly asking as he had a million times for forgiveness. He shook his head briefly. "No, Evie, you don't want to know. It's just that the war has pulled me back in."

Evie did not respond for a few moments. Then her eyes and voice hardened somewhat. "I know why you're here, Johnny. It's Vince Murdoch, isn't it?"

Smart, he thought. "I need to get dressed."

"All right, I'll be out in the hall. I'm not going anywhere, Johnny."

In less than a minute she was back in the room. "You're here because of Vince."

Johnny sighed. "Yes, I am here because of that bastard. Fifteen years, and now he's out."

"You don't even know that he's coming back to Juneau."

"He's back. Rock told me on the phone about a month ago that Vince was getting out. Where else is he going to go?"

Evie thought a moment. "Okay Johnny, but what's the plan? I mean, are you here to, well, you think he's going to do something to us?"

Johnny approached his sister whom he'd always protected. Or tried to. But racism had been everywhere, and had hit her hard. He reached out and gently touched the scar on the right side of her forehead, remembering. It had been his senior year in high school. He'd come home from Cross Country practice to police cars, lights flashing. His father was rushed away in an ambulance, Evie being helped down the stairs by their mom and an EMT, a bandage on her forehead. Some months later, Vince was found guilty of aggravated assault on Evie and her dad, and then of second degree manslaughter of their dad who had died—his head hit a rock when he fell unconscious to the ground.

There was other stuff Vince had been guilty of. Albert Williams had been a security guard at the old freighter dock and had caught Vince stealing equipment one night. Vince had a gun. He attached Albert for revenge and attacked Evie because she was there. And how he's out, Johnny thought as he took his fingers away from Evie's scar.

Evie reached out and took his hand. "Johnny, please don't do anything foolish. You were always the one who used his fists to defend me and the other Tlingit children from the meanness of the white kids. You fought for us all. I have always been so grateful to you, but," her eyes teared up, "you can't do anything to him. You'll end up in jail. Or worse."

"You can't ask me to do nothing. He's evil. You saw his eyes when they took him from the court to jail. Don't you remember his threats?"

"That was fifteen years ago, Johnny. I didn't hear him the same way you did."

Under her steady gaze, he looked away. "Johnny," she whispered, "look at me. The war is still inside you. Please, please, please, let it be."

"Hey you two," their mom yelled up from below, "if you want your food hot, better get down here."

Evie looked frustrated as Johnny led the way downstairs.

Fifteen minutes later the three of them sat around the dining room table, their plates empty of the breakfast they'd just shared—toast with home-made raspberry jelly, an egg with small flakes of seaweed mixed in and a piece of Dryfish. Ronalda's home on Starr Hill looked out over much of the older parts of Juneau. The view from the large dining room window was the best in the house. It was a partly cloudy day, the mountain peaks of Douglas Island three miles away appearing and disappearing as the clouds moved across and between them.

"Johnny," said Ronalda, their mom, "I wonder if you can give Rock a ring—borrow his boat and catch some salmon? I'd like to have Rock and his mom over for dinner Saturday, and maybe a couple other people."

"Yeah, sure Mom, I'll go tomorrow or Friday."

"And maybe," her voice taking on a humorous pleading tone, "some end of summer blueberries?"

Johnny sighed. He loved to fish, but at this time of the year, as his mom well knew, any ripe blueberries would be found only high up on the north-ern sides of the mountains. He wondered if any of his secret berry picking places still existed above Basin—it had been twelve years since he'd been back there. With a slight edge in his voice, he joked. "Would you like me to trap a grizzly as well?"

His mom reached out and playfully slapped his shoulder. He still felt a little irritated that he had to head up Mt. Roberts, but thought the irritation was probably just fatigue.

A few minutes later, carrying several plastic bags for the berries, he was ready to go. As he stepped down the outside stairs and started up Starr Hill to the beginning of the Mt. Roberts trail, Evie came bounding down the stairs. "I'll come with you," she said breathlessly.

In an eruption of irritation, he turned on her. It exploded out of him so fast, before he even willed it. "Damn it, Evie, just leave it alone, will you? The only reason you're coming is to pester me with your questions. What the hell are you going to do when Murdoch comes around, huh? What?"

She recoiled as if he'd struck her, the shock on her face hitting him like a bucket of glacier water. He turned away and took several deep breaths, turning back then to apologize. She was sitting on the bottom stair, tears.

"Christ, Evie, I'm so . . ."

"You looked." She had to stop and take a breath between each word, and then it came out like a torrent. "Just like Vince did when he attacked me and Dad. I remember it like it was yesterday." He reached toward her, but she pushed his hand away, turning and walking off down the hill. As he watched her with dismay, he noticed a couple neighbors observing him. He started to yell at them to mind their own business, but then heard the door to his mom's house open.

"I heard yelling. Johnny? Where's Evie? What did you do?"

What did you do, he thought. Always it's me, always me. Well, who the hell else was there to beat up those effing racist morons who picked on Evie? He heard the irrationality of his thoughts, but he could no more stop them than he could stop avalanche. Wordlessly he turned from his mom, heading up to the top of the hill and Mt. Roberts trail, anger preceding him like a concussive force. He thought of Vince.

Let him come.

He hiked fast, which eventually tired him out. He found two old picking patches that were brimming with berries. He picked from long habit, reaching and feeling with his fingers as he gathered a small bunch of three or four berries, gently plucking them together from the bush. The routine calmed him down. He was shocked by his unexpected reaction, and ashamed of how he'd treated Evie. It was three and a half hours before he returned home. Evie sat on the stairs, reading a book. Waiting. As he approached, she looked up at him. The look of compassion on her face undid him.

"Johnny, you can't do this. You need help. You need to see someone."

He sat down next to her. "Evie, I'm so sorry. It all just came out. I know, I know. You're right."

They sat in quiet communion for a few moments. His every intention was directed toward undoing the twisted knot of anger, fear, and reactive forces that had led to that instant when his little sister had become someone to push away with implied violence.

She reached out and squeezed his hand. In that moment, on the stairway next to Evie, it all seemed possible.

FOUR

Marianne had taken some aspirin and went to bed. She woke up sore and groaning. In her bathroom mirror she looked at a face with a nice bruise just below her right eye. She took an extra-long hot shower before picking up her brother up at the airport.

He came through the doors with a smile on his face. He was tall and lanky, and hugged her enthusiastically.

Marianne laughed, happy to see him. "David, you'd think it had been a year since you'd seen me, not a week." She reached up and ruffled his hair, which was blond and thick like hers. Unlike her, he had dark brown eyes and their mom's narrow nose.

"What happened to you?" he asked with concern in his voice.

"I got in the way of a moving bike to keep a girl from smashing tin the end of a guard rail."

He shook his head. "You know little sister, there are immutable scientific laws that show why such interference doesn't end or the person on foot."

She lowered her head and smiled, proud of her brother, who was a Chemistry professor and Track Coach at the University of Puget Sound in

Tacoma. "I believe you should leave Physics to the physicists, Mr. Smarty Chemistry pants."

David laughed out aloud. "Well, I'll brew us up some coffee back at your place, and you can explain to me how you got so banged up independent of the laws of physics."

A half hour later they sat down in her living room with the promised coffee.

Marianne laughed in a self-deprecating way. "Oh, David, I feel like I fell off a mountain."

"How're your stitches?"

"My hand doesn't bother me much, it's just the rest of me that hurts. I feel like I fell off a mountain. Or worse, one fell on me."

David looked around. "Really looks nice here, you moved in quick. Why did I even come up here?"

"You know as well as I, to keep Mom and Dad happy."

David shook his head. "You sure got Dad riled up, and Mom is worried sick about you. I think I get it, that you feel stagnant, and want to try something new. I'm not sure I see why you returned her rather than going to Portland or Seattle or back to San Francisco."

Marianne shook her head. "David, I don't know what more I can say that I haven't already said. It's an intuition I have, and I'm going to follow it. There's something I need to reclaim, and it needs to happen here."

David looked at her with a half-sad smile and such love in his eyes that she got up, crossed the room and hugged him, kissed him on the cheek and said, "I never would have made it through those darkest days without you. You waited a semester to start college just to be with me. The whole family was great, but you were my anchor. I can never thank you enough."

"Little sister, you had so much courage. I'm proud of you, and even if I don't fully understand, I support your decision."

At that moment the phone rang. "Hello," Marianne answered.

"Marianne, this is Teresa Snyder at the hospital. John Depuis, the head of staffing who is meeting with you tomorrow? Something has come up, and he is wondering if you could come in this afternoon instead of tomorrow for your introductory meeting."

Marianne thought quickly. She would have to cancel her meeting with Sr. Kris, but that

should be easy enough to reschedule.

"I don't see why not. What time are you thinking?"

"He could meet at 3:30, if that works for you."

"Sure I'll be there."

"Good, I'll let him know. See you then, and thanks for your flexibility."

She and David chatted for a half hour, then he left for a run. As always before drawing, Marianne sat down for a few minutes to pray. Collecting her drawing notebook and three pencils, she quickly sketched in the figure of the Virgin Mary holding her infant. It was the look in the Virgin's eyes that Marianne strove to get right. She lost herself in the experience and put her pencil down a half hour later, pleased with the result. Mary looked down at Jesus, her eyes half closed, her face turned slightly away from the viewer, imbuing the drawing with a private moment between mother and child. In some mysterious process that never ceased to amaze Marianne, the compassion and love in Mary's eyes exceeded her creative effort.

With a start Marianne realized that she had not drawn a boy, but a baby girl.

Marianne heard the humming of the fridge. In the distance a siren wailed. The house creaked. A single tear moistened each eye, a baptism of love and loss that marked her path through life more certainly than having been raped. Marianne realized her deftly trained hands had drawn from the deepest well of her suffering without awareness or without asking permission.

Marianne looked at the face of her baby girl, born 36 weeks after she'd left Juneau sixteen years ago.

Johnny walked across town and over the new bridge to Douglas Island, turning south along the road to Douglas. He stopped in the middle of the bridge, happy with the familiar—the noise of small planes coming and going, the view down the eight-mile length of Gastineau Channel. He glanced back to town, his eyes rising up and up to look at the long ridge that ran east from the peak of Mt. Juneau. He and Mike had hiked it a couple times. For the first time in years he missed their friendship, but this memory was followed immediately by bitterness as he remembered what Mike had done.

Johnny thought about how badly he treated Evie earlier. In the week he'd been back his old short temper seemed to have returned. That and the dreams. He'd not expected either one.

He did not think is mom was really glad he was back. She almost certainly knew why he'd returned. Vince goddam Murdock. And now a new complication. Marianne Greene. How strange that she was back in Juneau just at this time. Why had she come?

More than Mike, and if Mike was to be believed, more even than Marianne, he knew the plain vile truth. Johnny was almost certain that Vince Murdock was the one who had raped her.

With that thought he headed down the stairs to his aunt's house. His cousin Rock almost knocked him off his feet in a bear hug.

"Johnny, it is good to have you home. I hope you stay. All these years you have been gone I felt only like a half-me."

In that moment, Johnny realized the folly of having run from his family. He'd fractured his love for Evie and set himself apart from his cousin and friend, Rock. In the years of his lonely exile he'd opened a chasm between his daily life and his source of love and support that would have served him and his family better.

"Damn it's good to see you, Rock. I'm not planning on going anywhere."

After a few minutes visiting with his Aunt Chicken, he and Rock headed down to the stony beach.

Rock said, "The boat's gassed up and ready. Where you going?"

"Probably a run between Oliver Inlet and Green Cove. Mostly, I just want to get out on the water. Mom wants to invite you and your parents to dinner on Saturday."

"You better catch something then."

"Love to, but I gotta stay and help Mom with some cooking and delivering. His dark eyes narrowed. "Ricky Johnson got busted up pretty bad last night. Couple of teenagers found him after midnight in the lot down past City Cafe. He says he doesn't remember much. Never saw the guy. Wonder about that. It's bad though—he'll not work for a few weeks. Broken jaw, just beat to shit. Gotta do all that and then get home before Linda does—my turn to cook."

Rock helped Johnny carry the open air eighteen foot Lund to the water. Johnny got in, started the powerful outboard and with a roar and a wave headed south.

He closed his eyes for a few seconds, feeling the air as it moved across his face and whipped up his hair. He loved the salt-tang sea smell, the vibration of the tiller in his hand and the gentle bouncing of the skiff in the small waves. In three minutes, he was racing past Douglas. A thousand people or so lived in the small town, but few Tlingits, he thought bitterly. The city of Douglas had deliberately burned the winter village homes of the T'aaku Kwáan the summer after his sophomore year in high school. Almost everyone had been down on the T'aaku Heéni, the great river, for the summer, hunting, fishing, picking berries and putting everything up for winter.

All along his route south he looked over land that had been stolen from his people—Lingít Aaní, Land of the People.

"*You must never forget who you are, Johnny and Evie. Raven brought the sun for all people, not just the Lingít Aaní. You can accept things from White culture, but you must remember what your mother sang to you when she carried you before you were born. Everything breaths with its own life. Even the rocks. Too many forget, you must not.*"

With those words, Uncle had begun teaching him and Evie how to carve. Raven first, then Eagle, then the other animals, telling and retelling stories thousands of years old all the while.

"*Keep these stories alive—learn them, tell them, sing them, carve them.*"

And he called them by their Tlingit names.

"I'm sorry, Uncle." he thought. "I will do better to be your worthy nephew."

He reached the south end of the island and headed across Steven's Passage toward Deishu Áak'w, Oliver Inlet. He knew its Tlingit name only because Uncle had brought him here many times. About a hundred yards off shore he dropped his two lines and began slowly trolling west toward Young Point. And started thinking again about Marianne.

How do you tell a woman you think you know who raped her? After all these years, was it wise to even tell her? To not tell her? In other circumstances he would have talked with his sister, Evie,about this, but he knew in the end trying to avoid his duty was like a grouse hiding in the bushes. If the hunter is patient, it does no good to hide.

Johnny feared for Marianne, that Vince would discover she was back in town and . . . and what? Was she in danger? During Johnny's sleepless hours last night he had thought and thought on this, and his answer was no different now. He could not leave her ignorant.

But what would he say?

"Raven had white feathers, unblemished, before he brought the sun. It was the love of his grandfather for him that allowed Raven to steal the sun and escape out the smoke hole with it and release it to the sky, bringing light to all people. But the smoke turned his feathers black. You cannot always act with perfect innocence, Johnny, and cannot control what changes will occur."

Uncle told him those words after Mike had betrayed him. He had tried to make sense of what Mike had done. Now Johnny saw their value. He could not control Marianne's reaction, but she must be told. Didn't need Evie to see that.

A couple hours later he landed his third King, a generous haul. He thanked the salmon as he tightened up his gear. It was time to return to Juneau and meet Marianne. Motoring east toward the entrance to Gastineau Channel he glanced up Taku Inlet at the far end of which flowed the great Taku River. He always looked with longing and sadness at T'aak'ux'a Aan, Point Bishop. It had been the summer village for his ancestors, and Uncle remembered living there as a small boy before the move to the Indian Village in Juneau.

Johnny could never look up the river without remembering the most vivid dream of his childhood, when all the people of the T'aaku Kwáan lined both sides of the river, welcoming and thanking the first salmon of the year. He'd been six or seven years old and had drifted in and out of sleep several times, always returning to the dream each time. When he was finally fully awake, the dream had felt more real than his waking life. It lived in memory like a true name, imprinting his life with simultaneous gratitude and melancholy.

Forty minutes later he ran the Lund up on the beach and pulled it up above the waterline. Rock must have seen him. He was there to help within a few seconds.

Rock looked in the boat. "Nice catch."

"Take your pick," Johnny said as they lifted and then walked the boat up toward his Aunt's house.

"Is Aunt Toots going to want to smoke these? I could do it tomorrow after work" asked Rock.

Johnny smiled at the family's nickname for his mom. "No, she 'll be baking when you come over Saturday, and I'd bet a whole summer's catch she's going to give one to the Johnson's after what you said earlier about Ricky."

Rock shook his head. "Ricky's as big as me. And tough. Don't know who'd think to take him on."

Like the sudden appearance of a grizzly from behind a berry bush, Johnny startled into clarity, but kept the thought to himself.

Vince Murdock would.

"Johnny," his Aunt Chicken called down from the small deck of her house. "Your mom called and needs you to come home right away. A pipe is leaking, and she can't get it turned off."

Damn he thought, I'll need to get to the hardware store and won't have time to see Marianne. He shook his head, frustrated that he would have to wait to talk to her. Vince surely doesn't know about Marianne yet. She just got here. And Marianne said her brother was around for a few days. There's time. Johnny would see her real quick today and set up another time to meet.

Marianne sat back into the pew, trying to listen down below her thoughts, wishes, desires. She found it difficult to wait on God.

"If it's clarity you want, become a math teacher," Sister Kris had written her once. Darn if she wasn't right.

It was partly because of Sister Kris that she was thinking of becoming a nun. Marianne had told her parents nothing about this thought. It was the second reason she'd chosen to leave Salem. She needed to get away from her family to think clearly about her life. They loved her, but for too long now, they'd subtly treated her like an invalid. Sister Kris, with whom she'd kept up a sixteen year friendship through letters, had eased the transition to Juneau by helping her find the apartment. She also, Marianne smiled in bemusement, had convinced her to volunteer at the Gift Shop in the basement of the Cathedral.

She closed her eyes and tried to pray for her family, but she could not clear her mind from the drawing of her baby girl. She felt the loss keenly today, as if the intervening years had been swept aside, and she once more allowed the nurse to take her daughter from her arms and from the room, through door that opened to another name, another life, another universe not hers but one that pulsed with her blood.

"Jesus help me."

A noise brought her up from her prayer, and she opened her eyes, looking around the darkish interior of the church. She heard a squeak and the barest whisper of a footstep. Did the church doors open? Her pulse raced, and she consciously relaxed by taking a slow deliberate breath. She looked back. No one was in the church. She heard nothing further.

Marianne tried one last time to pray for her family, especially for her dad. She remembered as always Archbishop Romero, who had been assassinated a few months ago. Looking up at the crucifix in the front of the church, she pondered the longing that had developed for her to go to El Salvador and help the poor. Much of the time, when Marianne considered the level of violence ther, she wished this inner pull would disappear. And how could she go to this dangerous place when some days she stressed out over the simplest things?

Unbidden came the thought: I do not want to be a martyr.

Marianne checked her watch and saw it was time to meet Johnny. When she'd agreed to meet at the hospital earlier today, she had forgotten about her plans with Johnny. They could reschedule. On her way out of the church, she dipped her hand in the holy water and made a sign of the cross. She left the church and turned right at the street, then right again at the corner, heading up a half block to her car. Johnny was just coming down the hill.

"Marianne, I'm sorry, got to head home. Plumbing emergency." Johnny shook his head and sighed. "So, I can't go to coffee."

"Well, I start work tomorrow, and actually have an unexpected meeting myself in about a half hour, so I couldn't go either." She laughed, and continued, "I have to work the next three days, can it wait?"

Johnny pursed his lips, saying, "Mmm, yes, it's okay. How about I call you next week?"

"I don't have my phone number yet. I'm off Wednesday through Saturday. I'm volunteering in the Cathedral Gift Shop Wednesday afternoon. Why don't you come by then? I'm there from one to five."

Marianne was facing uphill to Johnny and as she finished speaking, she noticed a quick movement up in the narrow path between the cathedral and St. Anne's Hospital. Johnny followed her gaze.

He asked, "What?"

She shook her head. "It's nothing. For a moment I thought I someone watching us, but when I looked again, no one was there."

Surprising her, Johnny turned and jogged up the hill to the point across from the narrow walkway. He came back, shaking his head.

"Nope, didn't see anyone."

They said their good-byes and Marianne headed to her car, puzzled. She had sounded uncertain to Johnny, but was actually quite sure she'd seen the head of a man in a baseball cap peeking around the corner of the church at them.

FIVE

Vince Murdoch dreamed. He rose from deep water and emerged onto a narrow beach lying at the base of a cliff. A cave opened in front of him, head high in a narrow cleft set into a rocky protrusion which bulged from a higher cliff. It was edged by ferns and small bushes up the sides and above its arched top to just below the ridge of the headwall. He walked toward it, attracted to its dark fecund mystery, longing to enter. As always, Vince woke up, just as he was approaching the entrance.

He spent a few moments remembering. But the chance of insight disappeared into a moaning stretch and a wince at the sharp pain in his right hand. Ahh, the fight last night. He smiled at a different thought. Freedom. The word rolled around his mind like a piece of sweet candy in his mouth. It was day twenty-three of freedom after sixteen years of being locked up.

And already he was bored. That was the biggest reason for yesterday's fight with Ricky what's-his-name. The guy acted like a jerk. They'd bumped, some of his beer had spilled, and the guy had acted like it was nothing. A couple hours later the asshole had left the bar right before him, stumbling into a dark and empty parking lot a couple of blocks past the Juneau Café. It had been too easy—they hadn't seen him coming up behind him.

Down those long years of incarceration, he'd imagined only happiness when thinking about being free. Now, a question loomed like the shadow of a standing ten-foot grizzly. What to do? Can't beat the shit out of someone every night.

Vince got up. His mom was long gone to work. Jesus Christ, it was already 12:30 in the afternoon. Well, fighting is hard work.

And Ricky-Dipshit had had a gun. Not no more, he thought. Not no more. There it was, right on top of his dresser. He headed over to put it in a drawer when the phone rang.

"Hey."

"Vince, this is Baby Thomas down at Schulter's. So, I talked with Roger, like I said. He said he'd be willing to give you a chance. Can you come down today?"

"Oh, man, Baby Thomas, thanks a lot. I owe you big."

"We go back, Vince. You don't owe me. We're good. Roger wants to see how handy you are at body work. A wreck came in. He's gonna have you bang on some dents."

"It's been a while on the body side of cars, but I'll probably do okay. When ought I come down?"

"Right now?"

"Works for me. I'm walking so see you in a half hour."

"Vince, Roger's a great guy. Don't screw this up."

Roger was a great guy, and, a few hours later Murdoch shook his hand and headed the half mile back to town. It'd felt great to hold a hammer in his hand, work up a sweat. And he'd done pretty good. Now he had a job, money coming in. Feeling celebratory, he stopped at the 20th Century Market and got himself two Mountain Bars and a six-pack of Rainier. A couple blocks later he came to Gold Street and headed left up the hill, noticing at the last moment a woman with long blond hair entering the church.

Vince recognized her. Oh, how he remembered. The memory of her kept him going many nights during his imprisonment. Marianne…? Well, last names don't mean shit. He made his way slowly and quietly up the stairs to the double entrance doors of some church. With a patience born from the monotony of prison, he eased the door open and entered a narrow hall with red carpet. It smelled musty, and he scrunched his nose. Church. What the hell happens in these places?

A few quiet steps and he arrived at the open double doors which led, at a right angle, into the church itself.

He pulled the baseball cap low. Leaned into the opening. She was alone, kneeling in a pew near the front of the church. He stared at her blond hair, the way it fell past her shoulders, watching as she ran her hand through it, pulling it behind one ear. He could see her exposed neck. White smooth skin. Wanted to run his hand through her hair. He remembered the fear in her whimpers. Vince hardened and looked past her to the crucifix, feeling contempt. Let's see if you can protect her, Jaysus fucking Kayrist. Let's see if you help your little goody-two-shoes prayer bitch. Holding back a snort took a bit of effort.

After a few moments she sat back into the pew. Startled by her movement, Murdoch eased away from the door and stood stock still. Heard nothing, considered looking in again. Changed his mind. Turned back toward the entrance, the floor giving out a tiny squeak. Quickly out the front door. The light of the day seemed brighter. He felt the racing pulse in his neck.

Murdoch stood for a minute on the sidewalk. Getting a job had felt good, but this was an excitement he hadn't felt since before jail. Raw desire surged through him. He heard the church doors open and quickly walked past another church building and left up into the wise walkway between it and the now closed St. Ann's school, stepping into the deep recess of its main doors. Then, impulsively not caring if she saw him, he stepped back out and down toward the street. She was walking away toward Gold Street. Murdoch ran to the other end of the church and turned left, moving quickly through the narrow dirt walkway between the church and the old St. Ann's Hospital. Breathing hard and ragged, heart pounding, he came to the end of the church wall in time to see her cross the street and head his direction up the hill. As she neared what was evidently her car, Murdoch received a bigger jolt of adrenaline than when he'd first seen Marianne. Johnny goddamn Williams walked up to her and greeted her.

Anger shook him.

Back in his apartment a few minutes later, Vince grabbed a beer and sat down on his mom's couch. Adrenaline kept him keyed up as he remembered Marianne looking his way. He'd jerked his head back and quickly walked away.

Johnny goddamn Williams. Now there was a last name he remembered. He'd beat up his dad, who'd later died. Vince hadn't exactly intended that, beat his sister too. He and Johnny fought, a real war. Both hurt bad. Then the trial which landed him in prison for sixteen years. Theft, and he'd had his piece.

Assault, three times. Some other goddamn shit. And the big one. Manslaughter.

Murdoch flexed his right arm. Johnny, want to fight now?

He visibly jerked at the knock on the door.

He opened it to two cops. "Sir, I'm Detective Monagle and this is Officer Jonas from the Juneau Police Department. We're looking for Vince Murdoch. Are you him?"

Vince nodded, thing of the .45 he'd taken off Ricky last night, sitting now on top of his dresser. He wasn't sure if the bedroom door was open or closed.

"We'd like to speak with you," Monagle continued.

Trying not to look nervous, Vince asked, "What about?"

"Can we come in?"

A deep breath. He was pretty sure the door was closed. "Sure, come on in." Vince turned and led them toward the living room. Shit, his door was open. Another couple steps and the dresser would come into view. He turned on the cops and said in a pleasant voice, "This is good. What do you need?"

"Relax, Mr. Murdoch, we just want to know where you were last night at 11:00."

Murdoch decided he needed to stay close to the the truth. "I was at City Tavern, drinking with a couple of buddies."

The second cop looked down and asked him with an edge in his voice, "What happened to your hand?"

Murdoch glanced at it." I got a job at Schulter's today. I was doing some body work and mashed it against a car body." He laughed. "What's this about?"

"Can we sit down?"

"Right here is good."

"Who were you with?"

"A couple of buddies." He gave the cops their names. " I left before they did. Came home."

"Can anyone verify when you got home?"

Murdoch realized that his mom had already been asleep when he'd arrived. He had no idea when she'd headed to bed. "This is my mom's place. She was asleep when I got home. I walked around some before I came home. I don't really know when I came in."

Both officers looked skeptical. Murdoch continued, "Look, man, I got a lot to think about. I got a job. I'm just trying to figure stuff out. I new Mom'd be mad if I came home reeking of beer, so I walked it off."

"Where'd you go? Anyone see you?"

"All over. Up Main, down the stairs to Willoughby. Just wandered. I seen some people. Didn't know anyone. I came back on Goldbelt," he finished. "So what's up? Don't you gotta tell me?"

"So no one saw you?"

"Like I said." Murdoch noticed the second cop looking around, starting to inch this way past him.

"Hey, " he said, looking at him. "Is that it? I had some beers, walked home, went to bed."

"You mind if we look around?"

"Yeah. I do. If that's it, you gotta go." Christ, if that cop took one more step, he could see the gun.

The cop took that step.

"Hey, man," he said loudly, getting the cop's attention. "You got no more questions, that's it. I ain't done nothin'. You gotta go."

He was right and the officers knew it.

"Keep yourself clean, Mr. Murdoch. A man got beat up badly last night and there's some thought it was you. We know who you are, and this town isn't so big we can't watch you." With that the uniformed pair left.

Murdoch immediately headed into his room and picked up the .45. He needed to hide it. Was there anywhere to really hide it of the cops came back with a warrant? Then he smiled. It took twenty minutes of careful work and it was done. He stood back, looking. He doubted anyone would find it. He liked his chances.

Earlier he'd taken out a couple frozen trout. He was no cook, but he could fry trout and make up a salad. When his mom got home, the trout were sizzling in a frying pan, salads were on the table, and she thanked him as she hung up her coat. He told her about his job as they ate. She was elated at his news. Later they sat together in the living room, watching tv.

She turned to him and said, "Vinnie, do we have to watch *Charlie's Angel's*? I don't like the show. The women prance around half-naked all the time."

He baited her. "You don't like women's bodies?"

"Of course they are fine, but there's no modesty any more. I don't want to watch it."

Murdoch shook his head, got up and turned off the television. He turned to her. "You're so narrow. Ain't nothing wrong with women."

She was silent a moment, then responded quietly, "There's nothing wrong with women, but prancing around like that. I think that television shouldn't show bodies like that. It's not good for people. There should be affection between people."

Meanness rose up. He felt an urge to strike out. "What's good for me? How would you know? You show more affection to that damn cat than you ever did to me."

She took a step back, her eyes large. "Why do you say that? Vinnie, I love you, I gave up everything for you."

Murdoch turned away. She was partly right. He could still remember her— finally standing up to his dad, threatening to call the cops if he didn't leave. That had taken some balls. Yeah, his mom had balls. It fit. And he needed her, at least right now. He willed himself to calm down.

"Sorry. "

"Vinnie, look at me." She went to him, reached to touch his face and drew back. "Vinnie, I know what you did, but I still love you. You can make a life. You have a job now. You can start over."

She hesitated, then added, "Mrs. Browning from across the street told me the cops were here today, in the building."

Vince's anger surged and his neck muscles contracted with tension. Keeping his voice low he said, "That old hag has always had her nose out of joint. It's none a' her business." Once again Vince put a lid on his anger and sighed theatrically. "But yeah, they were here. Some guy got beat up last night down South Franklin, they wanted to know if I did it. I told 'em the truth, I didn't. They left. No biggie."

Later, after she'd gone to bed, Vince nursed second beer. It rained hard, so his view was distorted by the wet, unpredictable patterns on the window. His thoughts circled around Marianne, Johnny, and seeing the two of them together. Were they fucking? The thought of her under him was revolting.

He thought back to that day up Basin Road, when he'd seen her alone, preening like some bitch-princess who owned the world. He'd attacked her without forethought. Someone could have been walking by, but Basin was usually pretty quiet. Still, he knew he'd been lucky - for all the other shit he'd been set up for, no one knew about the rape.

Well, time for the one-man-band, he thought with a laugh and headed for bed.

He dreamed. Immersed in water, which roiled around him. With no transition he stood in what might have been an eddy in a creek. In front of him lay the cave opening, scarcely more than a narrow crack. It lured him - he needed to see what was inside. He took a step, another … and woke to a new day, light streaming through his window. He decided that whatever he did about Williams, and whatever he might do to Marianne, he would lay low for a while. Let the cops relax. No more fights. Let some time pass. He had a job. Maybe he'd leave them alone. Maybe not.

SIX

Johnny pounded down the stairs into the space between his mom Ronalda's dining room and kitchen.

"Don't run, Johnny," she said in an habituated but amused voice.

He answered, "Never happen again, Mom," and they both laughed. She pushed a loose strand of her dark graying hair back, looking at him for a moment longer. Did he see worry? She went back to kneading bread as he poured himself a cup of coffee.

"That's good coffee, Mom. So. I was wondering, could I borrow the truck some evening this week?"

"Not until the weekend. Aunt Chicken has it tomorrow—she wants to tow Rock's boat out to Wooshdeix' Altyé, fish the Bread Line. I thought you'd be fishing with him. What do you want it for?"

Johnny was surprised he was hesitant to tell him mom. Was he getting nervous? "Mmm. I'd like to take someone out to dinner."

His mom raised her eyes, a smile dancing across her face. She raised her eyebrows.

"Okay," Johnny said, "You might remember her, Marianne Greene. She only lived in Juneau less than two years. I ran into her a few days ago. She's just moved back, and, well, what I mean to say is, she doesn't know anyone, and I thought to take her to dinner."

Ronalda furrowed her brow, wiping her hands on her apron. "Was she a friend of Mike's?"

"Yeah, that's how I got to know her." Johnny heard the sullenness in his voice.

"Didn't something happen to her? Was Mike her boyfriend? You say she left town?

"Well, they did break up, just a high school thing, but you know Mike, Mr. Drama, everything all Mike, all the time," he said with a deliberate hint of derision in his voice.

"You might speak of someone who was once a friend a bit more kindly, Johnny. Especially given what happened to him." At the quizzical look in his eyes, she continued, "You never heard, then. His wife died in a car accident. There are stories he was involved somehow, but you can't catch salmon with rumors."

Johnny was silent for a few moments. Ronalda sounded irritated. "Whatever happened between the two of you? One moment you're the best of friends, the next you act like he never existed."

"Not everyone you think's a friend is a friend, Mom. It's that simple. So," he continued, bringing the conversation to a close, "Sounds like I could use the car Friday or Saturday? I'll let you know which evening works best." Assuming she says yes, he thought.

Leaving the house a minute later to go talk to Marianne, Johnny stepped to the cement stair that ran down the length of Starr Hill. He turned and looked up to the long ridge of Mt. Roberts which dropped just east of town. In its last third of a mil, it turned sharply west, ening in the tree-lined blugg called the Knoll. Growing up, he'd felt their home and neighborhood sat in the protective elbow of the ridge, as if it were a living thing. He felt his eyes tighten, and shook his head. Illusion, he thought. There is no protection, except what you make.

Johnny pondered his interest in Marianne as he strode down on the hill. She was attractive, no doubt about that.

All the years in Angoon since leaving the Marines had been lonely, and he had long been troubled by memories of his experiences in Vietnam. Claymores going off at night. The deep thwap-thwap of the Hueys. The screams after the ambush. Jonny shook his head, trying to stay away from self-pity. Is it too much to want a little damn happiness? He remembered Marianne's laugh back in high school—at first he'd resented her easy life, but in the end her the-river's-full-of-salmon disposition had won him over.

And there was their connection to what had happened to her. One spring day his senior year he'd come up to the top of the Knoll, and Marianne was standing a few feet back from the sheer cliff.

Although it was not a cold day, Marianne had been shivering and startled when she first noticed him. But with the recognition she came to him in tears, falling into his arms, burying her face in his shoulder. He held her until the weeping subsided.

Marianne never spoke a word as he helped her down the mountain. It was the last time he saw her—she'd never returned to school, and her whole family had moved a short time later. It was Mike who told him a couple months later she'd been raped. Apparently she never knew who had attacked her.

Johnny was sure it was Vince. The son-of-a-bitch had all but told him so with hatred in his eyes as he was led off to prison for killing Johnny's dad. It was only manslaughter, though, which still pissed Johnny off.

What was he going to tell Marianne?

Johnny paused as he thought about this. He was just walking by Mike's old house, where his mom still lived. He should try to not hate Mike. Their good friendship had not survived after Vince had killed Johnny's dad. That had been all on Mike. Johnny sighed. He had to admit, it would be nice to have him for a friend right now.

He remembered Uncle's Words.

Johnny, Grandfather opened the spruce box with the sun in it because he loved his grandson. Did Raven do the right thing in stealing the sun? Was it even stealing? Could Grandfather see that maybe it was not? Did he ever welcome Raven back? If you wish he did, then you can see letting Mike be your friend again.

But he had never been able to overcome Mike's betrayal.

Two blocks later he dropped down the stairs to the basement of the Cathedral. The door opened into a low-ceilinged room crowded with long shelves cluttered with clothes, books, and various knick-knacks. The cashier's area was fronted by a glass counter crammed with rosaries, holy cards, scapulars and other religious oddities, mementoes of his own four years at St. Ann's School. A little natural light entered from a couple windows high in the wall. Marianne stood behind the counter, putting a few things in a bag for an older woman. She looked up and smiled as she saw him, then returned her attention to the woman.

"That'll be five dollars and thirty-two cents, Mrs. Bradley."

"Oh, I was hoping it would be less. I really only want to spend four dollars at the most."

Johnny watched Marianne pause for a moment. Then she said with a smile, "You know what, Mrs. Bradley? You can have these at four dollars."

"Oh, you are such a dear. But are you sure?"

"Oh, yes, I get to be the one who decides."

The woman laughed at that and handed her money over. Marianne walked slowly to the door with the woman and turned to Johnny.

"Hey, Johnny," she greeted him pleasantly. "Just let me finish ringing this up." He watched her take money from her purse and add it to the four dollars the woman had given her.

"Ah, so you can't make up prices on your own."

"Actually, I suppose I could, but the money is intended for the poor. Mrs. Bradley was getting gifts for her grandkids, so I don't mind a dollar here or there to help people like her."

Something about her response reminded him of the way Rock and his mom shared out so much to the whole of the family. Uncle had been like that.

But now to his task. Johnny hadn't been out with a woman in a long time, and resisted the urge to wipe his palms on his pants. "I haven't been here since I was a kid. It's a lot different."

"For a couple years now the shop has been taking donations and reselling them. The money is given to programs that help needy families."

"Ah, good. But that's not why I'm here." Johnny felt sweat running down his back. "Well, you see, I was wondering if you wanted to go out to dinner with me this weekend? Friday or Saturday?"

A smile appeared on her face. "Are you asking me on a date?"

"Well, you know, I mean, maybe?"

Am impish look came to her eyes. "Johnny, yes, I'd like that." She raised her eyebrows and half turned her head. Johnny realized she was flirting with him. Damn, he thought.

Marianne continued, "But I work evenings every other weekend at the hospital and can't go this weekend. What about tomorrow? Thursday's can be nice, not as crowded as the weekends."

Johnny felt a little embarrassed. "Well, there's a problem with that—I am borrowing my mom's car, but I couldn't use it tomorrow."

Marianne came around to the front of the counter and her laugh put him at ease. "Oh, that's not a problem. I have a car and could pick you up." She reached out and touched his arm as she said this.

Johnny raised his eyes to the ceiling and responded in mock surliness, "Yeah, okay, that works. I guess." He sighed dramatically, feeling unexpectedly uplifted.

"And what time would his highness like to be picked up?" They both laughed as Johnny set a time.

Marianne felt a little nervous as she parked next to Johnny's house the next day. He invited her in, where she chatted with Evie for a couple minutes, setting up a time in a couple days for her to come over to Marianne's new apartment.

She thought Johnny looked good in jeans and a nice pullover, and his long hair was cut so it hung now to just below his shoulders.

"Nice haircut, " she said in the car a few minutes later. "So where are we headed?"

"It's called the Gastineau View. Do you remember the old Alaska Coastal Seaport?"

"Oh, yes, Michael's dad worked there."

"Just park somewhere nearby. We can walk—it's a nice evening."

"When she parked, Marianne told Johnny to wait in his seat as she got out. She saw his puzzled look change to a smile as he realized that she was going to open the door for him.

"Thank you so much, the perfect gentlewoman."

The pair headed down Main Street, walking side-by-side. Marianne was just thinking to put her hand in his arm when a passing car backfired. She was pulled roughly down by the arm. Johnny interjected himself between her and the origin of the noise.

"Oh for … just a damn backfire—I wish people would take care of their cars," he said with anger in his voice. He rose and reached to help her up.

Marianne felt her pulse racing. Her arm hurt where Johnny had grabbed her. She fought back panic, her old fear of men briefly surfacing, and pushed against her reactive desire to slap his hand away even as she realized what had happened—Johnny had mistaken the backfire for a gunshot.

Marianne took his hand, stood up and brushed her navy knee-length skirt.

"Marianne, Christ. I'm sorry. I just react sometimes. It's ingrained in me. You've got a cut on your knee."

"It's okay, it's just a scrape. I can get a band aid out of my car." She didn't add that it stung a lot.

They made their way back to her car and Marianne got two band aids.

"I'll clean it a bit at the restaurant and then bandage it."

She had put two and two together and as they started back she asked, "You were in Vietnam?"

"I volunteered, two tours, Marines. Third Marine Amphibious Force."

He spoke with pride. And he had volunteered. Twice.

The small second floor restaurant had ten or twelve tables. Three large pane windows opened to a lovely view looking south over the Gastineau Channel. They were led to a window table. Marianne excused herself and returned a couple minutes later. She smile to reassure him and said, "The surgery was performed and all is well."

As she sat she looked out the window, "It's lovely, Johnny."

He nodded his head, dark eyes soft. "Yes, I like the view. It's even nice when it is raining."

After a moment he added, "I miss the days of the Coastal Grumman Gooses constantly coming and going. It seemed a simpler time."

The waitress brought water and menus. Marianne thought about Johnny as she perused the dinner selections. He carried himself with a confidence she found attractive. He caught her looking at him and smiled. They chatted about the dinner choices, and the waitress took their orders a couple minutes later.

"So, Johnny, what have you been doing these last few years?"

"Oh, you know, when I came back from the war I was angry all the time, sick of the prejudice against Tlingits and after a few too many fights, decided I needed to get away." He looked at her as if surprised at what he'd just shared, and laughed, sounding nervous to Marianne. "I ended up in Angoon, a village down near the south end of Admiralty. I liked it there. I was happy fishing and hunting and doing some carpentry work when it was available." He shrugged. "Doesn't sound like much, but it was okay. What I mean to say is, there's a lot of peace out on the water, bringing in a salmon."

"What brought you back to Juneau?"

He hesitated, finally saying, "Family. Missed 'em."

Marianne sensed she'd moved into uncomfortable territory. Johnny asked, "what about you?"

She teared up. "Oops," she said, embarrassed. "I think being back in Juneau has brought back lot of memories."

This man was part of her past and had helped her through one of the darkest days of her life. Yet, she was unsure what he knew—had Michael ever told him what happened?

"Johnny do you remember that day up at the Knoll? I never got a chance to thank you. You were so kind to me."

What he said surprised her, but she was grateful for his directness. "Marianne, this is hard, but Mike told me about everything that happened to you. You don't have anything to be embarrassed about, tears or anything like that."

She looked at him gratefully. "It was a difficult time for me."

Marianne felt uncomfortable for a few moments, but their salads came and the filled the next few minutes in pleasant conversation until their meals arrived, broiled salmon with broccoli for her, New York steak with boiled potatoes for him. She smelled the butter and light garlic in the fish and smiled with anticipation. Johnny ordered another beer, while Marianne nursed her glass of white wine.

She took a bite, closing her eyes in appreciation—it felt so smooth and the taste of garlic, lemon and salmon filled her mouth. She asked, "You said you like to fish?"

"Oh, yeah, I do. A lot. And nothing beats the taste of salmon if it's cooked right."

"But you ordered a steak."

"Well, I eat salmon all the time, steak not so much. Besides," he laughed, "I can cook salmon better than any restaurant, and I heard the steak here is quite good."

She exclaimed, "If you can prepare salmon better than this, cook for me! This is really good."

He nodded. "The steak is, too."

For a few minutes their conversation meandered from food to fishing and hiking. Marianne relaxed, happy to be with him.

Johnny asked, "So what brought you back to Juneau? What I mean to say is, given everything?"

Marianne finished chewing a bite of salmon as she considered her answer.

"It's not easy to explain. I'm pondering changes in my life and wanted a place away from my family for a while. To think and pray, you know?"

Johnny half shrugged his shoulders. "I don't pray much anymore. What kind of changes?"

"Do you know Sister Kristine Marie? She taught at St. Ann's."

"I remember her, I had her in eighth grade. She turned into kind of a radical."

Marianne furrowed her brow. "She's very courageous. I admire what she's done, especially having been to El Salvador twice in the last five years."

"Yeah, I heard about that. There was an article in the *Empire* Evie sent me. I always wonder, why do people go if they might get killed?"

Marianne wanted to defend Sr. Kris, and she hadn't even told Johnny she was herself thinking of going to El Salvador.

"Sister Kris doesn't go to be killed." She heard her voice rise and slowed down. " She feels called by God to help where she can—in her case it is to help those living in poverty in El Salvador."

Johnny was nodding his head. "That's admirable, really, I mean that. But you can't help people if you're dead."

"Sometimes, Johnny, you don't choose. God chooses you."

She took a breath, trying a different way. "Look, you were willing to put your life on the line in the Marines for your beliefs. You volunteered twice. People who go to El Salvador are doing no differently."

He nodded his head again, and Marianne took that as encouragement.

"One of the people I admired most in the world was Archbishop Oscar Romero. He was killed last March in El Salvador while he was saying mass, murdered by thugs and soldiers following orders from superiors who were trained in the United States. It's obscene what our government is doing there."

"What we are doing there is fighting communist incursions into Central America."

She looked at him levelly for several moments, then shook her head. "Violence. How does killing and torturing help anything? Especially the poor?"

"Sometimes all people understand is the end of a stick."

Again she shook her head. "It seems to me all that does is lead to more violence. And especially against those who have nothing to do with it."

Johnny let out a quick breath, looking down at the table in thought. "I see that, but there's times there's no choice."

"There's always choice, Johnny."

Now he shook his head. "Are you telling me you wouldn't defend yourself if attacked?"

Impulsively she pulled her hair to the side and took her necklace off. A crucifix emerged from beneath her light sweater and she set it on the table.

He looked down and then back up at her. Now animation came into his voice. "You can't be...you wouldn't fight if someone like Vince were in your apartment when you got home tonight?"

Marianne flinched back. Johnny's eyes got large, and he immediately apologized. "Marianne, I'm really sorry, sometimes I just get lost in what I'm saying."

"Who is Vince?"

His face changed so subtly Marianne knew she could never draw the close shades of difference from one moment to the next. But in the course of three or four seconds a kind of horror emerged on his face. She looked around the restaurant for a moment, half-expecting something terrible to happen.

"Marianne."

Her eyes came back to him.

He took a deep breath, shaking his head. "Marianne, like I said the other day, I need to talk to you, but not here. Let's pay and walk outside."

A few minutes later they left the restaurant. A light breeze cooled her skin, and she relaxed a little. They agreed to walk over to the freighter dock and arrived a couple minutes later, sitting down on a bench a few feet from the edge of the dock. The sun was far to the north still high in the sky.

Johnny took a deep breath. "Okay, I'm just going to say it. I know who raped you, and I need to tell you because he's back in town too, and you should know. To be safe. It was Vince…."

She reached out and touched him. He stopped. "Wait," she whispered. "What? How could you know? Why didn't you tell?"

"You'd been gone for months when Mike told me what happened to you, and it wasn't until months after that that I found out about him."

She closed her eyes, feeling dizzy. Vince. A name, the cold touch of a past horror that had shut itself to her except one hazy memory. Marianne shivered as if in an icy room, unable to feel her body. She squeezed her fists to bring herself back. Her voice sounded like someone else's as she asked, "Someone named Vince?"

"Yes, his name's Vince Murdoch. I don't know if you knew him or remember him. He was in our class. Really big guy."

Marianne shook her head. "I don't know him." She thought, but didn't say, it had been a very large man.

As unexpected as a lightning strike, anger flared. With nowhere else to go, Johnny became the conductor of its landing.

"How the hell could you tell me this. What am I supposed to do?"

"Marianne, please."

She stood, unable to stop her arms from shaking, a loss of control which added the fuel of fear to the fire of her anger.

"Marianne."

"I'm going home." Without a further word, she was gone.

SEVEN

Anger caused her to bite off her steps in a quick muted staccato. Marianne hurried away. She was startled when she arrived at the side of her car—she had no memory of the route she'd taken or of even intending to come to the car.

Damn him. But even as she thought it, Marianne recognized none of this was Johnny's fault. It was easy to see that the situation had never given him a chance to act on his knowledge. She caught herself biting a lip and consciously relaxed, not at all interested in starting up that old nervous habit.

With too much energy to just get in her car, Marianne started walking up Main Street. In two blocks she turned onto Calhoun Avenue which ran along a hill about fifty feet above the western part of town. Cars came and went fairly frequently. She walked along its curve and stopped at a place where the view opened up. The warning lights on top of the Federal Building blinked. The power for her emotional response ebbed a bit.

She had not come to Juneau for this. Closing her eyes Marianne asked for peace, but as was frequently the case, God was silent.

Marianne wanted to find out who this Vince Murdoch was and what he looked like. Having long thought whoever it was didn't know her, it was a little unnerving that he was a classmate. Would he recognize her today? Johnny had, although it had taken him a few minutes to place her. She thought of where she lived, and for the first time regretted how secluded the apartment was. Except for the house across from Mrs. Mahoney's, there was no place nearby.

Nearby a stairway came up from Willoughby Avenue and continued up to a pedestrian bridge which crossed over Calhoun close to where she stood. A man came along the bridge. He looked her way. The man was large. Did he slow down briefly when he saw her? He continued walking, coming to the short stairway that would bring him to Calhoun, waiting for two women coming up before he started down.

What am I doing here by myself? Marianne had turned and walked quickly away. She looked back—the man was standing where she had been, looking out across town. He turned and walked toward her. She ran to her car and slid in. Her hands shook so much she had trouble getting the key in the ignition, but finally she got the car started and pulled quickly into the street. In her mirror she saw the man at the corner.

A few minutes later Marianne let herself into her apartment and locked the door behind her. She breathed a sigh of relief, happy to be home. She thought about what Johnny had almost said at the end, about someone being in her apartment. What if someone were here? She felt for her pepper spray in her purse.

A small noise came from her kitchen. It's nothing, she told herself. But she got her pepper spray ready. Damn you, Johnny, she thought.

Halfway opening to the kitchen, Marianne stopped with an uneasy realization. Her rosary lay on the end table next to the chair she liked to pray in. It was in front of a photo of her family. She was almost certain she had placed it, as always, behind the photo. All at once her whole body was hyperalert, and her breath got short. Determined, she held up the pepper spray and bolted into the kitchen. No one was there, and she realized the noise was the fridge coming on. A check of her bedroom, even under the bed. There was no one.

Marianne knew sleep would not come right away, so she made herself some chamomile tea. Sitting in her chair, she took up her rosary. Placed it back—behind the photo. It already felt natural to put it there. But she must have set it down in front of the family portrait.

She was almost sure of it.

The next morning Marianne rose after a fitful sleep, uneasy with half-formed memories of dreams of fleeing something. She put on coffee, quickly showered and took care of her morning routines. Coffee revived her a bit, and she grew excited about work this afternoon. It was a good schedule, three evenings with newborns and their moms, and one evening in ICU. These were skills that would be invaluable in El Salvador. If she were to go.

After doing the dishes Marianne sat to pray. Picking up her rosary reminded her of coming home last night. She must have simply placed the rosary in front of the photo. It's not like she'd been here long enough that her habits were ingrained.

She held up the rosary loosely in her open palms and closed her eyes. As always her thoughts settled on the people of El Salvador. This did not happen through any will of her own. It was more as if the longings of her heart were taken by the hand and led to this inner conviction of wanting to care for them.

After some minutes Marianne placed the crucifix between her thumb and fingers and began the rosary. When she reached the first decade of Mary beads, she pictured people she loved and lifted them to God with each Hail Mary. It didn't take many prayers—one for her dad, mom, brother David, a few other relatives. A couple friends from Salem. For the first time in ages, Michael Flaherty.

And longest and first and last she prayed for her daughter, for her happiness. And that someday her baby might reach out to her.

The thought of Johnny jolted her out of the semi-trance into which the repeated Hail Marys usually pulled her. Holding the rosary, she put her hands in her lap and remembered last night. She owed Johnny an apology. Her actions were certainly understandable enough, but nonetheless she'd treated him rudely.

With a sigh she put her rosary down and went to the phone to call him. Before she got there, there was a knock on her door.

Marianne went to the door and called out, "Who is it?" She felt a little rude but was not going to simply open the door.

"Marianne, it's Johnny Williams. Can I…."

She was unlocking the door and opening it before he finished his sentence.

"Can I come in?" At her nod he walked in, face looking worried, already explaining. "I'd have called if you had a phone. I need to know you're okay," he said with a shrug of his shoulders, "and hoped you wanted to talk more."

Marianne nodded her head. "No, come in. I'm glad you came. I got my phone yesterday and was actually just about to call you. We can talk here in my living room. Do you want some coffee?"

"Thank you, yes."

She quickly brought him a cup, and Johnny sat across from her on a small couch.

He took a sip. "This is better than my mom's. But don't ever tell her I said that."

Marianne laughed. "No, I know all about moms. It's from a business called Starbucks in Seattle. I got a pound as a gift from a friend last year and always buy some when I'm in Seattle." She continued, "Johnny, I want to apologize for my reaction last night. It…."

Shaking his head, he held up a hand. "I don't blame you. Walking home, I felt like such an idiot. But I really did think I needed to tell you. I don't know," he shook his head slightly, "if you have any questions?"

"I just keep asking myself, are you sure?" Marianne asked.

"It's like I said last night, they were taking him out of the courtroom. He looked at me, what I mean to say is, his face was all twisted with rage. He threatened me and our family, then he said he'd, well, that he'd 'had you' were his exact words. He called you 'Flaherty's bitch.' But he was being turned away at that point by the guard, and there was lots of noise in the courtroom, so it wasn't as clear—but that's what I heard."

Marianne looked out the window, her thoughts tumbling like water over a precipice. Vince, Vince, Vince ran through her mind.

"Marianne, I brought a yearbook if you want to see what he looks like. I left it in the car, but I could go get it."

She nodded her head. "Yes, that would be okay."

Johnny was back in less than a minute. She joined him, and he set the book on the coffee table in front of the couch, flipping through the pages for a few seconds, finally coming to one with the faces of a couple dozen graduates from 1964. He tapped a photo.

Marianne leaned in a little closer. The face peered out with narrowed eyes at her. His hair was in a crew cut, his large mouth curving in the slightest smile.

"I don't recognize him at all. You said he is big?"

"He's at least six foot. At least." He grew quiet, and Marianne looked closely over at Johnny. His eyes were locked on the photo, and she saw an involuntary tick in his forehead.

Johnny must have noticed her glance. "We fought once. I came home and he'd attacked Evie. And my dad. My dad died a couple days later." She watched his eyes narrow and heard the air rushing through flaring nostrils. "It was a bad fight."

Marianne waited a few seconds, then placed her hand on his forearm.

"Johnny, I'm so sorry."

He nodded his head slowly, then faster. "Yeah, thanks. But now, what about you? What are you going to do?"

She got up and walked to the window. The last of the snow on the peaks was almost gone.

"I wish I could see him without him knowing. I don't know, I thought the police, about going to the police, but it's been sixteen years. I've got my pepper spray."

Johnny interrupted her. "You should get a gun."

She shook her head emphatically. "I won't do that. I can't live that way."

Johnny stood abruptly, clenching and unclenching his fists. "Marianne, you have to protect yourself."

Last night's conversation again. She nodded her head. "I thought to get a dog."

"A dog," he said, sounding as if he'd just heard and offensive joke. He sat down with a breath. "Get a big one."

"And I'm going to get some bear spray. That shoots farther."

"A gun would stop anyone—no dog, no spray, just a bullet."

"Johnny, please, stop with the gun."

He raised his two hands, palms out. "Okay, okay. A dog is not a bad idea. Bear spray too. You should get two of them, practice with one so you know how to use it quick."

In the end Marianne went to the pound and got a one-year-old dog that was a mix of brown lab and something else, maybe pit bull. The only apparent danger it presented was that it might lick someone to death. She named it Skippy. She did as Johnny suggested and practiced with her bear spray—a couple days later she actually went to the spot she'd been raped and shot it in the depression into which she'd been thrown sixteen years ago. It came out with impressive force and looked like it would travel the forty feet it was advertised at.

"Take that," she said to the spot where she'd been thrown down.

Johnny called a few days later. "Marianne, I found out where Murdoch works. We could go out there, and you could get a look at him."

She hadn't really expected him to do that, but did remember saying that she wanted to see what Vince looked like. "I don't know. Can we do it without being seen?"

"The place closes at 6:00, we could just wait in your car and see him when he comes out." Marianne hesitated. Her anxiety from the week before had lessened. Skippy gave her a secure feeling, and the dog was nice company. She liked her work and the importance of it. Things were going well.

Johnny interrupted her thoughts. "Marianne, you have to see him. You need to know what he looks like, so you'll notice if he's," Johnny paused, and she could almost see him shrug his shoulders. "What I mean to say is, if he finds out who you are, you need to know." He said this last with a force of voice that bothered her. Yet his words made sense, she supposed.

Reluctantly Marianne said, "Okay, we can do it. I could go today if you can."

She picked Johnny up by the Cathedral at 5:40, and less than ten minutes later they were parked down the street from Schulter's Auto and Body Shop.

The motor of her little Toyota clicked as they waited. Marianne thought for a few seconds about Michael—there were several businesses here that hadn't been sixteen years ago, but just on the other side of them lay a small sandy beach that stretched to the water. Michael and she had gone there a few times. It was the first place they had kissed.

Johnny started to tap out a quiet rhythm on his thighs, his head nodding. But his eyes stayed glued to Schulter's main door.

A question occurred to Marianne. "Have you seen him since he got out of prison?"

The drumming stopped. He turned his head halfway and looked out of the corner of his eyes at her. Lips pursed, he shook his head.

"Oh, Johnny. We should leave, this isn't the way…."

"There he is."

He was walking out with someone else, but there was no mistaking which was him—only one of the men was large. His hair was longer than in the yearbook photo. Even from here she could see he was a handsome man—full lips and a nice nose. Vince said something, and the other man laughed, after which the pair parted, Vince walking in their direction.

Marianne shook her head. "I don't really know him."

She glanced over at Johnny and immediately felt tense. His eyes were glued to Vince, and he appeared to have not heard her comment. One of his hands was on the handle as if to open the door.

"Johnny," she said, "Don't do anything."

A half block away Vince arrived at his car, but before getting in, he raised his eyes. They paused at her car and he looked for several seconds right at her. Something changed in his stance. She just had time to hope Vince would get in his car when he stepped slowly away and started in their direction. The manner of his approach reminded Marianne of the way an untrustful dog inches toward another, teeth bared.

"Stay in the car, Johnny, please."

Click. The door opened and Johnny stepped out.

Marianne shook her head and got out as well, sending a quick prayer up to the heavens. Vince walked slowly up, stopping about ten feet from her, but his eyes never left Johnny's face. Johnny started around the car. Without thinking, Marianne placed herself between the pair. Vince looked down at her, his eyes quickly dropping to her breasts and then back up.

"I remember you," he said. "You were one of those stuck-up pretty girls that could do anything they wanted."

Marianne felt a surprising calm coalesce in her. An inner tension she'd been holding in like an intestinal ache disappeared.

"Don't talk to her," Johnny said.

"Johnny," Marianne said, "I'm fine. Just get in the car and let's go." When Johnny continued walking, she turned on him, putting her hand on his chest.

"Get in the car, please," she said.

Vince leered with his voice. "I don't know what the hell you're doing here, but I'm minding my own business. You want to fight again warhoop?"

Johnny moved quickly to get around Marianne. But she took a fast step herself, staying between the pair.

"Vince," she said as she turned back to him. "I don't want any problems. Just go."

"So you know my name," he said slowly. "Bet you didn't in high school. Too bad. I'll go, but you better keep that fucking injun away from me."

Johnny's eyes followed Vince for a few seconds. His hands shook. Marianne said his name, and he wordlessly turned and got back in the car.

In the driver's seat again, she turned to him. "What were you thinking?"

"That bast...that man killed my dad, might've killed Evie too if I hadn't shown up."

Marianne took a deep breath and put her head in her hands for a moment. "Look, I'm sorry for that. You know I am. But you can't just. You don't know him, what he's been through, how he might be different. He hasn't done anything."

"You can't clean the stink off a dead tomcod. He is what he is."

"I don't want to talk about this, Johnny. But what's he supposed to think now?"

Johnny sighed and shook his head. "I guess I did kind of screw that up for you. It would have been okay if he hadn't come over here."

They drove in silence. A few blocks from his house, Johnny said in a semi-humorous tone of voice. "I guess this means we're not going on any more dates."

She turned down Harris and pulled over to the curb. "I'm not sure, Johnny. I think you're a good guy, but we don't know each other well. You've got this edge that comes out sometimes. I...."

"I see that, Marianne." Johnny was opening the door as he spoke. "I'll just get out here. It could be awkward with my mom and all." He shrugged his shoulders. "Maybe...."

Marianne got out of the car. "Let's just walk around the block."

Johnny shook his head. "I'm sorry about what happened with Vince. Now he knows you're in town. That's the first time I saw him since he got taken away, and I kind of half lost it. There's bad blood between us. You are right, he's done nothing. But I know he will."

He shrugged his shoulders and continued, "I am edgy, and I don't see that working for you. You're a nice person, maybe another time, but not now."

Marianne felt a stab of regret, but also a bit of relief. Then she realized what he had said and laughed out loud. He raised his eyes in question.

"You just gave me the old, it's me, not you, line."

He narrowed his eyes, looking perhaps insulted or hurt. "Except this time it's true. So let me be my edgy self and say one more time, you need to get a gun and learn to shoot it. Bear spray might not stop him, but just piss him off more. Marianne, I'm not trying to be rude, but if Vince comes after you, he can't argue with a bullet."

Johnny turned away and headed up Harris toward home.

EIGHT

Marianne opened her door and smiled. "Come on in, Evie, I've got coffee on. If you prefer tea, well, I don't have any. Guess I'm not British enough."

Evie laughed as she followed Marianne across the living room toward her small kitchen/dining area. Skippy came over and licked her hand. She gave him a long scratch behind his ears as she said, "Your place is so snug, I love it. Makes me want to sit and watch a storm outside while I drink hot chocolate and read a book."

Skippy jumped up. Putting his paws on Evie's stomach.

"Skippy get down," Marianne said as she came over and pulled him gently away from Evie. Looking at Evie, she continued, "This dog has so much energy, I think I need to get him in a training class - he just wants to run off everywhere and lick everything to death."

Evie laughed and stopped before passing into the kitchen, admiring three drawings on the wall. "I really like these, did you do them?"

Marianne smiled. "Yes, I did. I seem to have this obsession with drawing Mary and baby Jesus."

"The detail is wonderful, and they are so full of feeling."

"Thanks. My parents say I started drawing the first time I picked up a pencil. I used to get in trouble with Mr. Ferrell in Senior English—he was a nice teacher, but couldn't understand why I doodled. I think he thought I wasn't paying attention."

Marianne poured out two cups of coffee. After asking Evie's preference, she added milk to both, and the pair sat in the living room, Marianne on the couch and Evie in Marianne's "Prayer Chair."

"Oh, this is good," Evie said after a sip.

"I was telling Johnny a couple days ago, it's a company in Seattle called Starbucks."

Evie's smile flattened a bit. "Marianne, I want you to know that Johnny told me about, well, after Vince Murdoch was found guilty in our dad's death, he told me what happened to you back in high school. You disappeared so quickly, I never saw you again. I'm so sorry."

Marianne didn't know quite what to say, surprised by Evie's directness. "It's okay. It happened a long time ago. But thank you."

"I hope you don't mind, he also told me about your date the other night. He was mad at himself when he got home, and I can usually get him to talk. I can be kind of a busybody."

Marianne smiled at that, relaxing a bit. "I don't mind. I always considered you a friend. It's all so strange. Johnny's a nice guy, I know that from high school, but he's kind of got an edge."

Evie nodded her head. "He is a great guy, protected me all the time as kids. He told me about the car backfire and his reaction." Evie sighed deeply. "He's got a lot to deal with, something happened in Vietnam and he won't tell me."

"My brother David was there for a year, and he's the same way, holds it inside. He was a gloomy Gus when he came back in 1969. It was really hard to see him in pain. He's better now."

Evie pulled her hair as if to make a ponytail and then let it drop behind her shoulders.

"Johnny's been having bad dreams every night that wake him up. I wish he'd talk with me about it."

The pair sat in a few moments of contemplative silence. Evie indicated the window. "It's a beautiful day, want to go out to the glacier?"

"You know what, I'd love to walk the airport dike trail. I have some nice memories from there." She thought of Michael as she said this. "And Skippy could use the walk."

Ten minutes later Marianne parked her car next to a chain link fence at the north edge of the airport. Skippy ran ahead as the pair followed the well maintained dirt road around the end of the runway.

Marianne called Skippy's name, and he came bounding back toward them. They stopped, and both looked toward Mendenhall Glacier, four miles to the east.

Marianne sighed. "There can't be a lovelier view in the whole world." The glacier curved down between rugged snow-capped mountains to either side, the whole panorama backed by the multiple craggy peaks of the seven-thousand foot Mendenhall Towers.

Evie said, "No, you are right, it is beautiful. The glacier is called Aak'wtaaksit by our people. It means something like "The glacier beyond the little lake." Auke Lake. There were other names too, but that's what I learned. I don't know if you ever met our Uncle Walter. He carried in him so many stories of our people and taught me and Johnny so much. He taught us both to carve." She shook her head. "I miss him."

"Oh, but what do you call it," Evie continued, "a gloomy Gus? I don't want to be gloomy today. I am happy at the return of a friend and hope we can be even better friends now."

Marianne hardly knew what to say. Friendship had not come easy to her since high school, and Evie's simple declaration filled her with happiness.

She beamed at Evie and said, "Oh, I hope so too. I did meet your uncle once with Michael and Johnny. He looked at me and laughed. Called me Sunlit-Hair River. I think he made it up on the spot, but it was wonderful."

Evie had stopped walking, and Marianne looked a couple feet back toward her.

Evie said, "I am so happy to hear that story. It's not often I get to learn something new about him. He was like a dad to me. 'Evie,' he would say, 'you have hair the color of Raven and must walk tall in his footsteps.' I know he was sad we didn't learn the language, but now I am learning it."

Marianne nodded her head. 'I only met your uncle the one time, but he charmed my socks off."

They walked in silence for a few steps. Marianne said, "Johnny told me you tend bar at the Imperial, but are saving to go back to school."

"Yes, I can start here, but I will have to go to Anchorage to finish up. I want to be a teacher."

As they chatted the road turned south, parallel to and a couple hundred yards away from the runway. A man-made lake lay between the road and the airport. Western Hemlock rose up left of the road, while the high-grassy delta of Mendenhall River lay to their right. Other people walked their dogs, and Marianne called Skippy over and put him on a leash. He looked so sad-eyed, both she and Evie laughed.

"You poor poor pooch, your owner is so mean," Marianne said to Skippy. Then with a small grin at Evie, she let him back off. For the moment he walked at their side.

Evie said, "I love this walk. I always hope a jet will come in right when I'm walking by the end of the runway."

"Michael and I did that once, it was a real kick in the pants."

Evie looked serious again. "Marianne, have you heard what happened to Mike?"

"No, is he okay?"

Evie shook her head. "He's okay, but his wife died in a car accident about a year ago, and he witnessed it. There's people saying he was somehow responsible, but no one knows really."

Marianne felt as if someone had hit her in the side of her head. Her ears rang, and everything turned a yellowish hue. She heard Evie say her name as if from a distance.

"Marianne," she heard again. Looking at Evie, she began to return to herself.

"Evie, I heard nothing about that. It's terrible. Do you know what happened? How's he doing?"

Evie shook her head. "My mom told me and that was all she knew. Are you all right?"

Marianne took a long, slow breath. "Better now, for a few seconds I felt like I might faint."

Evie put her hand on Marianne's arm. "I know you and Mike were close. I'm sorry to give you such news."

"Wow, I can't believe how hard that has hit me. I mean, I haven't seen him in sixteen years."

Evie was nodding her head. "We think that is a long time, but our heart treasures things in a way that time does not affect."

"That's a lovely thought."

"Well," Evie said with a smile, "I really can't take credit for it. Mom said it to me a few years after dad was killed."

Marianne started to nod her head, then looked around. "Where's Skippy?"

They could see a couple hundred yards in either direction, but the dog was nowhere to be seen.

"Skippy. Skiiippy," they both yelled, but he did not come running into sight.

"He's probably further down the road," Marianne said, feeling a little worried. "Let's just keep going. He'll probably show up." But he did not, and when they came to the end of the road fifteen minutes later, Marianne looked across the green flats with a growing sense of unease.

"He's a dog, Marianne. There's really nothing out here that can hurt him."

On the way back they asked several people if they'd seen a tan lab-looking dog, but no one had. They came to where the road turned back toward the runway and parking lot, and Marianne looked around in every direction, calling his name several times. She held back tears.

"I can't believe how fast I've come to love that stupid dog. He's a nice companion and always so happy. I don't want to leave."

"He might have come back this way. We should go back to the car in case he's there. If you want to walk the trail again, I'll do it with you."

Marianne looked at her friend with gratitude. "I do want to walk it again, and it'll be nice to not be alone. Thank you."

Skippy was not at the car, and the pair turned back to the road, walking quickly. They were just approaching the lights that lined up with the runway when Evie shouted, "There he is," pointing. Skippy came running around the corner and toward them, covering the two hundred yards quickly. He raced up to Marianne, who bent down at her knees. She wanted to scold Skippy, but she was so happy she couldn't. "Where have you been?" Marianne fairly sang as the dog licked her hands and face. "Oohh, Skippy, don't ever do that again." Skippy ran circles around them, barking and jumping.

Marianne looked at Evie. The pair said at the same time, "Dog training," and broke out in laughter.

A noise drew their attention. An Alaska Airlines 727 was coming through the Cut, quickly getting larger and larger. Less than a half-mile distant and not three hundred feet high it made the final turn.

Evie screamed out, "Whoo hooooo," and Marianne joined her, raising her hands to the sky as the fuselage roared over them leaving behind the smell of jet fuel. It touched down, smoke rising briefly from its tires, the sound of the reversing engines reaching back to them as the jet almost disappeared in a cloud of dark jet-fuel smoke.

They looked at each other and impulsively, as if reading each other's mind, hugged each other. Walking to the car, Marianne was filled with happiness she hadn't felt in a long time.

NINE

"The body of Christ."

"Amen."

The person in front of her moved left toward the cup of wine, and Marianne stepped up to the Eucharist Minister to receive communion. She had been twenty one when she'd started going to Mass again, turning back to God after two years of drugs and easy sex. It was more than having just been in San Francisco in the mid-60's. Exhausted by her ceaseless searching after the rape for any hint of an enduring self-lovability, Marianne literally stumbled into a pew in St. Ignatius Church at the University of San Francisco one Sunday morning in 1967.

She'd begun attending mass as often as possible, and the daily gesture of her open palms asking for and then cradling the Body of Christ had proven to be the genesis of a slow journey back through the wilderness of despair through hope to a place where the freedom of love again illuminated her life.

"The Blood of Christ."

Marianne said, "Amen," as she took the chalice in her hands and sipped from the wine. A half hour later Marianne climbed the stairs across from the church into Chancery and was greeted with a long embrace from Sr. Kris.

"Oh love, just look at you, as pretty as the first flower of spring. After what, fifteen, sixteen years, and all our letters it is wonderful to see you. I'm sorry it took us so long to get together. My vacation fell just at the wrong time."

Marianne felt herself flush with pleasure. The joy of Sister Kris' presence settled around her.

Sr. Kris replied, "Oh, but why wouldn't I—I feel so close to you. When you asked me if you could write me just before you left Juneau all those years ago, I could never have foreseen the Anam Cara, the deep friends we would become."

Marianne's eyes teared lightly, unaccustomed as she was to such words of affection.

"Ah, there now love and isn't that the beauty of true friends, that we can shimmer with tears of joy? And so, I always like to start with a quiet prayer. But not too long, the Lord is busy," she said, looking at Marianne with a mischievous look in her eye.

She lit a candle and the two closed their eyes. Marianne immediately felt peace flow through her. This didn't happen often, and she let herself sink into its embrace. After a couple of minutes, with a deep breath, Sr. Kris opened her eyes. Marianne followed suit. Sr. Kris looked at her and waited.

Marianne smiled with a sigh. "Well, I guess I get to talk." She felt her eyes tighten a little. "I came here against the wishes of my family. My dad was…."

She stopped speaking for a moment, remembering his exact words. "Marianne, you've never been the same since it happened. When you were a girl you never walked, you ran. All day long you laughed and sang. Why do you want to go back to that hellhole where your life was ruined?"

Marianne looked at Sr, Kris, surprised at the sudden twinkle she felt in her eyes. "Let's just say he doesn't have good memories of Juneau."

Sr. Kris let out a quick laugh. "Oh love, that you can laugh about it all a little. And he probably wasn't listening for an answer. But I have wondered what brought you back after all these years."

Marianne put her elbow on the arm of the chair and set her chin in her hand. She notice the subtle smell of the candle.

"You know," she said, "after I came back to the church when I was twenty one, I kind of hoped for a quick healing. But it wasn't like that."

Sr. Kris shook her head. "No it would not be."

"I've gotten better," Marianne continued, looking out the window at a car going by. "Lots of counseling and prayer, but I felt like I'd kind of flattened out. I'm happy enough," she shrugged her shoulders, "but I don't feel like I'm growing anymore, and I, well, I."

She stopped and looked directly at Sr, Kris. "I want to be joyful again. If it's possible, and I think it is. I got this crazy idea that stopped sounding crazy, that I needed to come back here. We left Juneau so unexpectedly, for me anyway, and I never really had the chance to take stock of what had happened.

"It's more that that, though. I met a woman at a parish meeting who has been to El Salvador and shared her stories working with the poor there. Maybe eight or nine months ago during prayer I started getting this urge, this prompting, to go to El Salvador. It's gotten stronger. Ever since Archbishop Romero was murdered, the calling is always there when I pray."

Marianne shook her head and laughed quietly, taking a sip of her tea. "But there's more, Sr. Kris. I have been thinking on and off for a couple years about becoming a nun. So a part of the reason I came to Juneay is to get away from my family and the routine of my life so I can pray and think clearly about these things."

"Well," Sr, Kris said, "that certainly is a full plate. And a lot to talk about."

Marianne nodded her head, and took a deep breath. "But—don't laugh—there's actually something else I want to talk about today."

She reached down and picked up her thing leather carry case, set it in her lap, took out her drawing of Mary with the infant girl and offered it to Sr. Kris.

Sr. Kris looked at it closely, nodding her head after a few seconds. "That's a girl in Mary's arms."

"I was drawing a couple weeks ago, and it just happened without my awareness. It's my baby."

Sr. Kris blew out a breath as she handed the drawing back. Marianne put it away. Sr. Kris looked at her with the soft eyes of compassion.

"I have a secret I've never told even you, Sr. Kris. No one knows."

Sr. Kris folded her hands in her lap and waited.

Vince left Twentieth Century Market and headed up Seward Street toward home, unable to get Marianne's face out of his mind. Her eyes when she'd stepped from the car yesterday and looked at him. He'd realized at that moment he had never really seen her, and all of his memory of the rape contained nothing of her, rather only the force of his domination and that perfect explosive moment when he'd come. That was the event to which he'd returned a thousand times in prison.

Yesterday he had looked into Marianne's eyes, not ready for how pretty they were. That wasn't all though, there had been something else in her eyes, almost like a force, but that wasn't it either. For a moment he'd been distracted and almost missed Williams coming around the car.

Knowing she was frequently at the church, he made the habit of walking by the Cathedral every time he went downtown or walked back. He was a block below the church when what he hoped for finally happened. Marianne was leaving the building next to the church. She carried what looked to be a thin briefcase. He followed her up past Sixth to Seventh. She took the stairway down into Evergreen Bowl, and he realized she was probably walking home.

He stayed well back of her as she walked down into the park and past a large number of children playing games and then ran to catch up as she rounded the far corner on a road that headed out the other side of the park to Calhoun Avenue. She skirted the graveyard and headed up into the Highlands. He was too cautious and lost her in the maze of tiny streets higher up. But there were not many streets to which she could have gone.

Excitement coursed through him. Damn, but he was close to knowing where she lived and knew that he would find out. He thought of her eyes and face and nice body as she headed back home, feeling the singular pull of lust and domination.

As Vince came back down the street, he impulsively headed into the graveyard. He tromped over the grass until coming to his father's gravestone, set flat into the ground.

"John Murdoch. 1924-1971."

That was it and more than the bastard deserved. Drank himself to death. Too bad he didn't do it quicker.

Vince had come here in the middle of the night a few weeks ago, just after he got back, and pissed on his father's gravestone. He felt like taking a damn sledgehammer to it.

Vince felt deeply the wish for another childhood, and something nudged up against his consciousness in a way that allowed him to be grateful to Roger Schulter for the job and the chance to make a new, different life.

He thought again of Marianne Greene. He wondered what it was he wanted to do. He knew what he felt like doing.

PART II

"Go forth from the land of your kinsfolk and from your father's house..."

Genesis 12:1

TEN

Inis Mor, Ireland
August, 1980

As Michael stood to leave the room for the last time he saw his guitar and teared . It seemed too much energy to play even a few chords. What would happen to it?

He thought again of his mother and sister, far away in Juneau. He had tried with every fiber in his being to assure them in his letter he loved them, it was not their fault. He didn't even have the energy now to take it to the post, but trusted that Mrs. Joyce would follow his written directions and mail it. He'd left his mom's phone number as well. This all made him uneasy, but it was too hard to think about anymore. His decision made, this was his only regret—the pain he knew they would feel.

A burst of wind shook the window of his second floor room. Diagonal rain raced by, the horizon beyond circumscribed under dark gray clouds scudding west over North Sound toward Galway Bay. His eyes dropped to the small writing desk, his journal next to his mom's letter, open to yesterday's entry. It was only one word. He walked over and placed a finger on the wood, as if perhaps the contact would grant him a reprieve.

Maggie.

Mrs. Joyce came up the stairs, crossed the wide landing and stopped by his open door. "Well Michael, I'm headin' in to Cill Rónáin for a bit of shoppin'. Can I get ya somethin'?"

After three weeks at Aoife's Ocean View, he was used to her generosity and apparent determination to make his life better. He hoped she wouldn't feel badly tomorrow.

"No, Mrs. Joyce, but thanks. I'm headed out for a hike up to Dun Aengus."

She looked at him as if he'd just picked his head up off the floor and was holding it in his hands. "Dún Aonghasa," she said in Irish, "are ya havin me on? You be watchin' for those cliffs—ain't but a few weeks now a girl slipped off, and there's no livin' after that."

"I'll be careful. I really don't mind the rain. I grew up in Alaska. It rains a lot."

Mrs. Joyce looked at him a moment, then headed down the stairs shaking her head and muttering.

He flipped the pages of the journal to the inside of the back cover, where lay a photograph of Maggie, taken a year ago and less than three weeks before her death. They'd been walking along a sandy beach on the Oregon coast. Camera ready, Michael called her name, and when she turned snapped the photo. She'd laughed at the moment he took it. It was the one photo that really captured her adventurous spirit.

Spur of the moment he sat down to write one last time. His hand shook, but he kept on to the end.

August 3, 1980

Mrs. Joyce—she wants me to call her Aoife, but I can't see my way to it—tells me that there has been a rare number of sunny days recently. Yesterday shone just so. I walked way down past Bun Gabhla to the shore. Brought my guitar and sat near the low cement boat ramp there. Tried to sing but couldn't. Occasionally someone would come or go and would smile as they went past. I played for an audience of one, my own attempt to find any connection with "Before." The notes drifted off on the wind, disappearing into the cries of the gulls and the ever present shush of the waves washing ashore. Underneath all that, I listened for Maggie. The silence.....

He stopped writing, searching for the right word. Even now, he laughed bitterly, even now he wanted to write beautifully. What did he want to say about the silence? Then he had it.

...reminds me of the time Johnny Williams and I went deep into one of the old gold mine tunnels and turned off our flashlights. There is dark, and then there is the deep dark that comes of penetrating a half mile into and six levels down a mine. It seemed to absorb our very breath, and I don't think we lasted ten seconds before we had to turn our lights back on. The silence is like that, suffocating my song and my story. They are so far from me. And who can live without a story?

After an hour, I put the guitar back in its case and started home. As I came up to the fifteen or twenty houses that make up Bun Gabhla, a woman came out the red door of her home. I'd seen her before. She had a fiddle case in her right hand and pointed to it as she smiled at me. I smiled back, holding up my guitar case. God bless that woman for the gift of one last smile.

Michael set the pen down and put on his heavy coat and ski cap. He paused at the door like one leaving on a trip and turning at the last second for a final glimpse of a loved one. After a long moment, he eased away.

Kathleen stretched like a content cat in the sun, a soft moan of pleasure escaping her. A perfect day so far—a fire in her fireplace, a cup of honey-sweetened black tea, and her secret passion—Jane Austin. She was rereading for the umpteenth time her favorite, *Persuasion*.

Smiling at this thought, she got up to reheat more water and to pee. Washing after, she assessed herself in the mirror. Her medium length red hair hung in an almost untamable rumpus. And her crooked nose. A boy had once told her she'd be hot, but for her nose. It's not that bad, another said. Oh well. She pulled her hair back with both hands, putting it into a ponytail. Her mother hadn't really helped when she'd told her at thirteen, "But honey, don't worry your head about your nose, you have lovely white teeth." Which was true, she supposed, but that didn't help much at thirteen.

Kathleen glanced at the clock as she came out into the large kitchen-dining room. Time had gotten away from her. She needed to leave in ten minutes to go check in on Mrs. O'Donnell, unable to walk much these four years now. If the weather looked to clear out, she had the thought to tromp up to Dún Aonghasa.

She returned to the living room and considered her cello and fiddle, or as she sometimes thought of them, Serious and Laughter. She was a real talent on the cello. But she could fiddle too and loved nothing more than to light up Conneely's Pub in the Oat Quarter on weekend nights with quick-tempoed reels and slower, emotional ballads.

Her mother had asked her just yesterday over tea—what are you doing with your life? What can you do with the cello here?

As she pulled on her boots, she thought about how different the grind of being a professional musician had been from her idea of it—the hours of practice, the aching fingers, the ambition that for many slid into ruthlessness. She'd been elated once: selected for the Dublin Philharmonic, the first time she'd played, bad acoustics and all, in the National Concert Hall, the sheer unexpected elation of twelve-hundred people rising to cheer at the end. But after three years the stress got to her, and joy was gone. These two years back home had been happy, although she often felt lonely. She waited tables in Cill Rónáin, played fiddle and sang weekends at Conneely's, looked in on several frail older women and was immersing herself in a long held passion, Gaelic spirituality and the Irish language.

So there, Mother, she thought as she ran out to her car.

He was miserably damp before he reached Kilmurvy Bay. The wind gusted unpredictably, rain getting up under the bill of his cap. He stopped by the sandy curve of the bay and listened to the pound of the sea farther out. Unexpectedly he was put in mind of Marianne Greene. How strange to think of her now. Probably the sand and the rain.

He remembered walking with her to a sandy beach just off the Million Dollar Golf Course in Juneau. The sky to the south had darkened as a storm came in. A burst of wind swirl-gusted around them and pelted them with a few large raindrops that thickened quickly into a dense cascade. Fleeing to his car, they laughed at being wet, euphoric in their shared joy, confident of their growing affection. In a moment of delicious abandon he hugged her close, and they kissed for the first time. Young and innocent, they missed the storm brewing just over their horizon. Who could have ever seen it, he wondered?

Life has too many damn storms. It can sweep everything away in a moment.

So Marianne, he thought, wherever you are in the wide world, I hope it goes well with you.

The rain thickened so that he could barely see North Sound past the bay. It was a quick walk to the ticket booth. He paid the surprised ticket-taker, who said, "Ya be the first ta be coming through today, lad. What with the rain, ya see."

He trudged up the gradual, winding ascent toward the ancient fort. Beside the trail, slabs of stone rose up from the long cracks that split the limestone which made up the island. They put him in mind of a large grave-yard. He pulled up his collar against the rain and lowered his head. With the deliberation of a climber high on McKinley, he placed one foot in front of the next. His progress slowed to a glacial pace, but he did not waver.

"So, Aileen," Kathleen said as she took off her coat, "how are you this fine rainy day?"

"Oh, Katie dear, this old sack of a body has got a few more days in it yet."

Kathleen sat down next to the older woman, picked up a brush from the nearby end table and began brushing Aileen's thin gray hair, hearing about the doings on the island as she did so.

At one point Aileen sad, "I keep gettin' bad dreams about little Claire, can't hardly sleep so. She di'nna fall off that cliff. I always had the sight, you know that, but the Garda say there's no one saw anyone else go up there."

Aileen, I'm not one to dismiss the sight, you know that, but the Garda say there's no one saw anyone else go up there."

Aileen shook her head. "And what was she doing up there so late? There's something bad here on the island. I can feel it."

Katie sighed. She felt a bit of the unease herself.

Afterwards, she held her hands as Aileen prayed.

"Jaysus, You know my Sean was as good a man as ever there was, and let me be remindin' you he always was a fierce one for his Mass. Keep a place for 'im in your heart and in heaven. And bless our two children Rebekah and Rachel and their husbands who are good to them." Aileen hesitated. "And I'm not rememberin' their names then but bless our four grandchildren. And Jaysus, bless especially the family of little Claire Ferrell. Amen."

She stopped, and Kathleen quietly reminded her friend, "It's five grand-children you have then Aileen."

Aileen fairly hooted as she added, "And Jaysus, was you made me bad at the math, but bless that extra one as well, Amen."

"Amen," Kathleen echoed.

"So, Aileen, let's check your fridge and see what you'll be needing for the next few days."

Kathleen took her arm, and the pair made their way into the small kitchen.

Aileen said, "These bones is as slow as a wet week, lass—it's good of you to be patient. Between you and me and don't tell the cow, I'm thinking the milk has gone sour, so. Can you double-check?"

Kathleen took out the liter milk container, smelled it, made a face and dumped it into the sink. "Yes it is, more's the pity. But I'll get you some this afternoon. Looks like you have plenty of bread. Would you like a slice toasted with your Swiss cheese?"

"Katie dear, you are an angel. But could you try and not burn it this time? It was so hard last week I lost two teeth when I bit in." Kathleen could only smile and shake her head as Aileen sat down in a chair, actually slapping a knee as she laughed.

Fifteen minutes later, a short list of food to buy in her back pocket, Kathleen took her leave. "I'll be back in a few hours—the weather looks to be clearing back of the island, so I'm going for a short hike up to Dún Aonghasa. A chance for some quiet thinking."

"Yes, you do like your sittin' and thinkin'. There's folk as said that about you when you was just a child. And in this rain—you always did have a bit o' the fairy by you. But you be careful, up there all by your lonesome."

The ticket booth was a two-minute car drive away. Timo greeted her as always. "And how are ya, lassie? Oh, no, you'll not be needin' to pay today. Maybe of the mornin'?"

"Why thank you indeed, Timo."

"And am I getting a kiss then?"

"Not until I see my ring."

"Oh and ya are a temptation for an old old man, but what would my sweet Rosie be sayin' to that now?"

"Yes, and I wouldn't want to be the one crossing her."

They both laughed as she started past the ticket booth. But at his voice, she stopped.

"Bein' the weather, surprisin' that someone besides you came by today. That stranger from America came through a few minutes ago. You'll not be alone up there—thought you'd like to know. But," and Timo smiled as he spoke, "he paid, so."

It was as he approached the inner and highest of Dun Aengus' three walls that Michael had his first moment of indecision. Even as his feet kept their plodding pace, a thought pushed it unwelcome way in. It struck with the certainty of the complex geometric proofs he'd so loved at Seattle University, as undeniable as a lightning strike.

Maggie would not want this.

Still he kept moving up to and through the dark entry. The wind eased back as Michael entered the inner sanctum of the ancient fortress. He was blessedly alone. The fifteen foot walls formed the curve of a half-moon, enclosing a space that reminded him of a baseball field. He trudged through short grass to a raised central expanse of exposed limestone which ran right up to the edge of the cliff. At the highest point, Michael could see over the wall to fields and limestone stretching west toward the Atlantic. Wisps of family legend came to mind. Somewhere up that end of the island his two times great-grandfather Conor had once launched his *curraugh* into the ocean swells under which swam life and livelihood—fish. Probably was just a day such as this that Conor's two brothers were lost at sea.

He approached to within a yard of the cliff, sat down and rested his chin on is pulled up knees.

Maggie would not want this.

He knew people suffered incredible loss and discovered happiness of a sort again. Why did this seem impossible for him? Had he really tried enough? Michael again imagined his mom picking up the phone to hear the new fo his death and knew that she would throw her very life off this cliff to preserve his.

But oh, the hurt, the hurt, the hurt. The pain pressed like a giant fist squeezing his breath. Having scarcely eaten the past few days, he was all at once ravenously hungry and the absurdity of it all pushed out a bitter laugh. The body want what it will even if the mind has other ideas.

Mike.

Had Maggie spoken? Michael closed his eyes and saw the kindness of her expressive brown eyes, remembered her body entwined with his, her radiating joy when she learned she was pregnant.

How could it be that all that life is just gone?

Agitated, he stood quickly. The cliff loomed close even as he started to turn away. Dizziness hit him hard, and his last thought was that he was falling the wrong way, toward the cliff edge.

Everyone on the island knew about the stranger living among them. Aoife said that he didn't talk much and kept to himself. He plays guitar beautifully, she added. Kathleen had seen him a few times wandering the back of the island, heading up the lonely walled side tracks that often had no real destination but to a single house, sometimes not even that, just petering out into the question why it ever existed at all. Only yesterday he'd gone by just as she'd come out of her house and she greeted him wordlessly with an indication to her fiddle and a smile. His last name, Flaherty, intrigued her, as that was her name as well.

There were a few as said maybe he'd pushed young Claire off the cliff last month. Gossips all.

As she approached the inner fort, Kathleen noticed that the weather was indeed lightening up. Often she came early in the morning, before the tourists arrived, or on bad weather days like today. She liked to sit a few feet back from the cliff and gaze toward the Cliffs of Moher, memorizing stories from Ireland's myth-misted past. If no one were present, she might get up and practice some complicated ancient dance steps. Even if there were many people present, it was still a beauty to look across the heaving water.

Kathleen picked her way up to the entrance and wondered if she might end up talking with the American. As she came through, a movement startled her. A figure fell. Too near the cliff, her mind screamed.

She ran.

ELEVEN

Three days later Kathleen got up from her couch to answer the phone. It was her mother, who started in without the slightest greeting. "And who comes up to me this morning but Tommy Powell, mad enough to spit a pound a limestone out o' his mouth. And why? He said his wife Colleen be all up into herself, all full a ideas, and she wanting money for a trip to Knock and Mary shrine there, and he is welcome to come with her, but if he won't, she still wants to go. And where did she get these ideas, where? I'll tell you where, from you. He said that…."

"Mam. Mom, stop it. Stop." When she sputtered out, Kathleen continued, "I am not going to talk to you about this."

"You're not denying anything?"

"I'm not meaning to be rude, but it's my business. Leave off for now."

"Well, and it's a sad sad day when a daughter won't talk to her mam. You and your da are ladled from the same pot a stew. I'm only after trying to help you, though. Tom is madder than a hawk in a winter gale, and you got no right to be interfering in his life."

When Kathleen didn't respond her mom rang off with a huff.

That just caps my day, she thought. Her mom was always at her, no matter what she did.

Kathleen took a deep breath, trying to be fair, recognizing the still felt bitterness at her mother's smug "and did I not tell ya?" when Kathleen had returned from her three years in Dublin.

She thought of Colleen's man, Tommy—big as a wall, and frankly, a loud drunk with mean eyes who raced around Inis Mór's roads with too much speed, like no one else mattered. He was, in her opinion the most unpleasant person on the island, and it sat like discordant music in her ear that was riled up. She drummed her fingernails on the kitchen counter. Oh, Colleen, she thought, what have we done?

An expected knock on her front door got Kathleen out of her chair and away from her worry. "Hello Mrs. Folan, come in."

"Ah, Katie, I do remember ya as a wee girl runnin' around in red pigtails, but that's thirty years by now or close to it. Just call me Norah," she said as she entered, taking off her coat and hat.

Kathleen hung them up in her cloak closet just to the right of the front door. Thank you, Norah. Here, sit in the sofa, you'll have a nice view down to the water. Would you like some tea? It's ready to pour."

Norah sat down, pulling her plaid skirt over her knees. She ran her hands through shoulder length hair. "The wind is up, gives the air a bit of a chill, so tea would be wonderful, warm my bones, you know? Still, cool as it is the sun is nice."

"Yes, it's a wonderful blue day today. I'll be right back."

As Kathleen finished pouring the tea, Norah spoke up from the living room. "Sure and I was up here many times when your mam and I were girls. She and Colleen Powell and I used to play games in your mam's bedroom for hours on end when winter storms were up. I always liked the fireplace and the view toward the lighthouse."

Kathleen came back to the living room just then. "Yes, I love to sit here with a fire when it's raining something fierce, looking out over the Atlantic, all snug and warm."

She handed Norah a cup of tea and sat down in a chair across from her. A candle burned on a small table next to her, smelling lightly of lavender. Norah said, "Well, Annie Flynn was just after tellin' me 'bout that nasty business up at Dun Aonghasa t'other day. What a thing, then."

"It had my heart turning over, I'll admit to that." Not wanting to talk any further on it, Kathleen continued, "So, then, it's nice to have you here."

"Well and word been gettin' 'round, ya see, and I was thinkin' I might be wantin' ta talk to ya. So I called and here I am."

"Norah, I've been trained in the practice of holy listening. That can mean a lot of things to people, but mostly it is just accompanying you on your life journey. I like to meet once a month or so, and you can just talk about anything at all—your prayer life, your relationship with Jesus or God, or just how life is going, anything at all. I do want to say that I am not a trained counselor, that is something else, but I will listen. What brought you here today, then?"

"Don't be mistakin' me, but our three boys are all grown now, an' none of them are on Island, and my Robert, he's a good man and never laid a hand on me or yelled a single bit, but he has his friends at the pub and me to cook for 'im and do 'is laundry, and I be wantin' more, ya know?"

Kathleen nodded her head.

"It's just the round and round of it all, ya know? I just...I just be wishin' for somethin' more."

"Hmmm."

And then like a bursting dam, the words rushed out of Norah. "I remember bein' young on this island, and it was fun havin' the scope of it all, and then when I was a bit older, how all the boys was interested in me, and how we would flirt an' all, and then Robert and me walkin' out together—but he wasn't the only one, ya know? Maybe ya wouldn't believe it ta see me now, but used ta turn heads. There were some as said my eyes were prettier than the blue sky. And then how excitin' it was, decidin' to marry Robert, and how we was off to dublin on our honeymoon, half the island there to see us off, ya know? And then there was the boys, god bless 'em … ah," and here her voice slowed, "and what I would have given for a daughter like you, Katie … and there was Mary, my sweet little Mary, and why the Lord be takin' her then? That laid a fierce wound on me…."

Kathleen looked into the other woman's anguished blue eyes, understanding intuitively that Norah was not asking for answers, but simply for a witness to her loss and grief.

Finally Kathleen spoke. "What do you think you would like to do then, Norah?"

"I don't know, I don't know … just somethin' for my tears. Somethin' of that old happiness I used ta know." She laughed a little nervously.

At that moment their eyes were drawn to the door as someone ran up the stairs and banged on it. Norah looked anxiously at Kathleen, who rose as she mouthed an "I'm sorry" to her.

It was Colleen Powell, her hair disheveled, eyes large looking as if she'd just seen a Banshee.

"Katie, I'm so." She had to stop to catch her breath. "I'm so sorry to barge in like this." She saw Norah at that moment. "Oh, Norah. I don't want to interrupt anything.."

Kathleen cut her off. "Of course you're coming in, Norah and I were just finishing up."

Norah nodded her head and said, "You're not interrupting anything, Colleen. You come right in." She looked at Kathleen. "Can I call you?"

"I'll call you this evening."

Norah rose, but hesitated as she looked at Colleen. Kathleen smiled at her as she helped Colleen to the couch.

With an "I'll be right back then" Kathleen accompanied Norah outside. "Norah, you know how sorry I am about your Mary. It's an unfathomable loss, and I don't like letting you go now, but you see as I must. But I will call you tonight. I can meet any time in the mornings the next three days. Think about which would be best for you."

Ninety minutes later she hesitantly saw Colleen to the door. Tommy had lost control when Colleen had again brought up going to the Mary shrine at Knock, screaming at her at the top of his lungs, denting a wall with his fist. Kathleen had tried several times to get her to stay with her, but Colleen decided to return home.

Kathleen tried one more time. "Are you sure you don't want to stay the night? Give him time to cool down?"

"Ah, Katie, it's a fine offer, but I think he'd only be worse. He's such a big man, he scared me. But you know, for all his harsh words, he's never the once laid a hand to me. I'm not wanting him any madder at you than he already is."

Tim's taxi showed up and Kathleen waited until the taxi disappeared around a distant corner. Her heart beat fast. The wind ruffed through her hair. Ah lassie, she thought. The sun is still shining, and it's still a good day for a bike ride. She changed into shorts and put on tennis shoes and a light sweater, smiling a bit as she walked her bike down to the Main Road.

Sighing, Michael sat back into the lounge chair, consciously relaxing his shoulders and neck. The sun warmed him, a light breeze occasionally goose-bumping his arms. He sighed again. For the first time in three days he did not have a headache. His journal lay on the small table, his guitar atop its case on the ground beside him. The sun was just fine.

My God.

He remembered everything and went over it again in his mind—the life-ending intention, the hesitant approach to the cliff. And Maggie's voice in his head. Had he really heard her? In that moment, the already wavering death wish had disappeared, but then he fainted, opening a gash on the side of his head when he fell. He became aware of a voice and opened his eyes briefly, seeing a woman with red hair looking over him.

"There you are now," she said a couple times. She got him away from the rim of the cliff, and they sat a while as the weather cleared and warmed a bit. He was weak, but finally they rose and headed back, him leaning on her awkwardly. At some point she yelled and yelled until a man came and helped them make it back to the ticket booth. A call had been made from the museum right next door, and the woman rode with him in a taxi back to Aiofe's Ocean View and Aoife Joyce's clucking. And now, three days later, here he sat, grateful for the sun.

Still miserable.

Michael opened his eyes, momentarily sun-blinded, then gazed left over the nearby road dropping down a mile or so in a straight line to Kilmurvey Bay. Up a long ascent behind the bay rose the distant walls of Dun Aengus. He noticed a bicyclist down that way, coming up the rise of the road. The person got off the bike and began walking it.

Yes, still miserable, but the tension, the psychic squeezing, the unbearable tightness of his being was gone. He laughed quietly at his thought—it's only misery now. Who can't bear that? He picked up his guitar and began doodling in key of G. After a minute, he closed his eyes and lost himself in the music, his natural feel for melody taking over, moving up to the seventh fret and sliding into a rendition of The Beatle's "Here Comes The Sun."

At the edge of consciousness a movement and subtle noise caught his attention, his eyes briefly blinded again as he opened them. He stood carefully and walked toward the nearby road.

"Hello. My name is Michael Flaherty. It was you up at the fortress, yes?"

"Well, and it was. Kathleen ... um, Flaherty. And it's glad I am to see you looking better."

Kathleen was quite a bit shorter than him, and her red hair pulled back in an unruly ponytail. Michael noticed how strikingly blue her eyes were. She smiled as she took his hand. Unexpectedly, the interior goose-bumps of happiness surged through him.

Here was the person who had most closely seen what had happened, and something in her attitude relaxed him, easing the shame he had felt the last three days.

"Yes, thank you, I am feeling a lot better. This sun helps quite a bit. So I really really want to thank you for your help. Up there." Michael stopped, unsure how to continue.

After a moment's hesitation, Kathleen said, "You sure hit your head pretty hard, and it was bleeding something fierce for a while, you know? It took a bit of work to get it stopped."

"So we have the same last name, Ms. Flaherty...."

"She laughed, her face again lighting up. "Just call me Kathleen."

"And I'm Michael. Listen, I think you got my blood on some of your clothes, and I'd like to replace them if they got ruined."

"That is true enough. Mostly it was my jeans, although my gloves got ruined as well. It's good of you to offer. How about I buy some new ones, and I'll give you the receipt?"

For the first time in eleven months, humor bubbled up like an unexpected sunny morning. "Fair enough, but how do I know you won't buy some diamond-studded pair?"

"And what would I be doing with diamonds on a pair of jeans? There's lots of women have jewels, but happiness is a far coin of spending."

She laughed as she said this, but Michael creased his forehead a moment, confused by the almost serious nature of her comment. "A receipt will do fine."

"I'll stop by with it then, sometime next week." She turned away and started to get back on her bike. Then she stopped, turning back to him. "So, Michael, Mrs. Joyce has the opinion that you play the guitar mighty well, and I'd say she's right. That was lovely to hear altogether. What kind of guitar do you have there?"

Michael looked over at his case, sitting next to his chair. "It's a Taylor. They've been around just a few years, but they make nice guitars. I have a Martin back home, but I like this just as good, maybe better."

"A Martin is a fine guitar, so your Taylor must be as well. And where is back home then?"

Unexpectedly, there was life and pain again. His face tightened up. "Seattle," he said curtly, hearing the tension in his voice.

Just a moment's hesitation, and Kathleen said, "Ah, Seattle, way over on the other coast. I play fiddle Fridays and Saturdays at Conneely's, just up the road a ways. If you want to come and listen tonight I'll be there. And you could bring your guitar, you know? I'll be nothing but honest, from what I heard, it would be fine to play with you. Taylor or Martin or a piece of junk, you play beautifully."

He tried to relax, but wanted the conversation to end. "I might."

She looked at him a moment longer. "I'll be off. And hope I'll be seeing you at Conneely's."

Sitting back down, he chided himself for his rudeness. It was just so difficult. For a moment he'd forgotten all his pain, but when it returned, it was that much more piercing for his few minutes of happiness. He turned and watched her slowly pedaling up the road. A quarter mile beyond her a car came racing around a bend. As it approached her, it sharply slowed to a stop. Kathleen dismounted, putting the bike between her and the car. It appeared that a brief conversation took place. The car sped away from her in his direction, probably going well over sixty as it zoomed by him, two figures briefly visible. Way too fast, he could tell. He looked back to Kathleen, who was watching the car as it disappeared down the road. Even though she was a ways away, something about how she stood there looking at the disappearing car struck him as wrong.

TWELVE

"You better listen good. If I hear you talking with my Colleen, all Ireland won't be big enough to hide from me. Báirseach."

Tommy's words from his car a couple days ago still made Kathleen wince inside, and she felt no better for having slept on it. Trying to make sense of his anger made her feel like she was wading into an incoming tide. Her armpits were damp with worry over what she was about to do—Colleen had asked to talk to her, so they were going to meet in secret at Aoife's in just a couple hours.

She decided to head out early, simply for a ride for a while in the beautiful sun. It would feel grand. Just after she started pedaling, she came to a Na Seacht Teampaill, the Seven Churches, and had a quick change of mind. There were only the remains of two churches here, and the reasons given for the "seven" were numerous. She remembered Patrick Doogan joking in grade school that maybe the monks had had a few too many Guiness when they named it. The class laughed, but the teacher hadn't. Patrick served his detention gladly.

Kathleen liked the quiet of the place with its sense of everything returning to the earth. Once this had been a monastery founded by one of the islands' two great monks, St. Breacan, whose eroded cross stone was propped like a bicycle tire against the low stones surrounding his gravesite. All that determined holiness reduced to this rubble, as if the original wild religion of the untamed Brigit and the Tuath de Danaan returned to the island. She didn't exactly regret the coming of Catholicism to Ireland, but Catholicism was so tame when set beside Brigit and the ancient practices. And so damn masculine. There were old stone temple entrances in Ireland that were clearly open vaginas, and she smiled at the memory once of seeing the startled looks on tourists faces when they realized that.

Nonetheless, Jesus suffering on the cross was deeply imprinted in her inner life, the crucifix a visible sign of what she considered one of the deepest realities of all: *that the divine, by whatever name, suffers with us.*

She sat on a stone near St. Breacan's grave, closing her eyes as a light breeze wafted through the grass carrying with it the subtle smells of wild honeysuckle, wild rose, and the wild sea. A couple conversed quietly nearby. This late autumn sunshine was such a gift. She sighed with peace.

A few minutes later Kathleen sighed differently, hearing a noisier group coming down from above. She reluctantly got up and made her way back toward her bike. She saw a familiar figure coming up the road and greeted him with a smile.

"Well, hello again, Michael. And what a pleasant morning it is, no?"

His smile reached his eyes. "It sure is. I decided to run down this end of the island and back, but it's farther than I thought. That hill is a killer." He took a deep breath. "I'm walking back. I get the feeling that this weather is unusually nice, there'd be snow on the higher mountains in Juneau by now. It must be more than sixty, or," and he hesitated a second, "fourteen or fifteen Celsius."

"I'm not knowing myself, but it feels around fifteen to me." Remembering his reaction to her question yesterday, she said cautiously, "You mentioned Seattle yesterday. You lived in Juneau, then? Up in Alaska?"

"Born and raised. I left Juneau when I graduated from high school. My mom still lives there. It's a small city, but beautiful—I miss it sometimes."

"We both know what it's like to grow up in a small place. But for three years in Dublin, I've lived here all my born days."

Michael changed the subject. "How was it at Coneely's?"

"Busy. The tourism is slowing down, but many still come to hear real Irish music." She laughed. "I sing a bit, play the fiddle a lot, and accompany a good singer on some songs. You really do play well. Do you perform?"

It was his turn to laugh. "I used to be in an Irish folk band!"

Kathleen looked at him again. He was quite a bit taller than her. Over six feet, she guessed. Wavy dark hair framed his bearded face and fell almost to his shoulders, his eyes a pale blue and nice to look at, although his face looked thin.

"Tell me some songs you know." He seemed hesitant as he replied, "*Red is the Rose* is a favorite ballad, and *Wild Mountain Thyme*, although I think that's Scottish. We didn't like the ending to that one so I wrote a different verse for the end."

"*Red is the Rose* is Irish. The other is a bit of both Irish and Scottish. More Scottish, I suppose. And lovely, aren't they? So, how do you end the song?"

He hesitated, cleared his throat and sang a few words in a voice that cracked a bit. He stopped, looking surprised. Then he started again, his voice clearing after the first phrase, "And the seasons with their comin', we'll put new seeds down there yearly, and the bloomin' will not end, with our passin' from this mountain."

"Ah, and that's right enough, indeed, Michael. A better ending, I agree. You've a bit of a poet in you. And you sing well, a nice Irish tenor."

Kathleen realized to her surprise that at some point they had begun walking along the quiet road. She was happy to be with him. Remembering her reason for going to Aoife's, Kathleen wondered if she wanted Michael to know she was headed to the same place he was.

"So, maybe I'll take you up on that offer and come by Conneely's tonight?"

She smiled. "That would be wonderful. I know both the songs you mentioned if you think maybe you'd like to sing."

Like yesterday she saw his face darken and wondered at it. She'd learned the rumor he lost a wife and some told as there'd been kids. Someone even said he was fleeing the law, but she gave that no mind. But she did wonder. What had happened up at Dún Aonghasa was puzzling, he'd been so near the cliff face. Something seemed amiss, and his swift change of mood reinforced this.

He sighed and put a smile on his face. "I haven't sung in quite a while. I do play, but I hurt my left hand, can't do everything I used to." He held up his hand for her to inspect. A long scar ran from the web between his thumb and index finger across his palm. His fingers were long, the fingernails neatly trimmed. "I can't play for as long and don't have the reach I once had."

People told her she had good instincts, and she followed them now, asking no further questions. They walked in silence for a few moments.

He said, "Let's see what I can remember," and he began singing. He stopped, shook his head with a huge smile as if at some secret and continued. "Oh, the summertime is comin', and the leaves are sweetly bloomin', and the wild mountain thyme, grows around the bloomin' heather…." When he started on the refrain, Kathleen joined him in harmony. "Will ye go, lassie go. And we'll all go together, to pull wild mountain thyme, all around the bloomin' heather…."

Kathleen and he smiled at the same time. Their voices blended beautifully, and she thought it would be fine indeed to sing with him.

Just then Kathleen noticed an approaching truck slow down and pull over in a wide spot fifty yards away. Conlon Conneely got out as they approached. "Katie, can we talk for the minute?"

"Well, and sure. Conlon, this is Michael Flaherty. Michael, this is Conlon Conneely. He owns Conneely's Pub with his brother Patrick. Are you needing something then?"

"Nice to meet you, Michael." Conlon hesitated. "Maybe we could talk alone a minute?"

Kathleen turned to Michael. "If you don't want to wait, I hope I'll see you tonight."

"I'll probably just go on then, but I'm planning on being there."

Kathleen smiled. "Wonderful. I look forward to seeing you." She watched his back for a couple moments before turning to Conlon.

"I'm glad I found you, Katie. When you weren't home, I hoped you'd be on Main Road, not wandering off on some side track. Listen, my da was just after telling me about Timmy and how he's fuming about something to do with you. What's going on?"

Kathleen looked at her friend, unsure how much to share Very little, she thought, thinking of Colleen's trust in her.

"Just something that happened. Don't you worry your head about it, okay? It'll be fine."

"I know Tommy's really gone over the cliff 'bout something. You know how he can get when he drinks. Da says he'll be at our pub tonight." Conlon paused. "Just watch out for him, okay?"

"I'm sure I will, then. Thanks, Conlon. See you this evening."

"All right, see you then." He looked like e wanted say more, but he finally turned and got into his truck.

As Conlon drove off, Kathleen checked her watch. Twenty minutes yet. She walked over to the stone wall, low at this point, and sat down on it.

Maybe she needed to meet with Tommy. Get this all out. She had done nothing wrong with Colleen, of that she was certain. Tommy was a hothead, but she couldn't imagine he posed any real threat to her. Why then, she asked herself as she got up, am I so nervous?

Fifteen minutes later, she leaned on her bike at the wall to the left of Aoife's bright green door. She entered the B and B, headed across the large vestibule and knocked on the door opposite. Aoife answered, smiling at Kathleen.

"Katie, and it's nice to be seeing ya. Come in, then."

The pair went into Aoife's living room and sat on her sofa. Aoife continued, "I have some news for ya. It's about Colleen. She rang a few minutes ago, saying that she couldn't be coming today. And that's a sour-milk face ya have then."

Kathleen sighed, "Ah, Aoife, I just…..Did Colleen say anything else, give any reason?"

"Ah, me, Katie, she surely did not. She sounded a bit tense, though. Is there some trouble? Conlon came by earlier looking for ya and looked upset when I said ya was meeting up here later with Colleen, if he wanted come back. What be troubling ya, then?"

"Aoife, you have been such a friend to me." She hesitated. "It's just…. Colleen and I been visiting, you know how some of the women come to me?"

Aoife nodded her head. "And it's a fine thing."

"Colleen has my support to do some things that have Tommy all up into himself, and he seems terrible mad at Colleen and me as well. I know Tommy isn't the nicest man on the island, but it's all out of proportion. He practically threatened me yesterday. No, he did threaten me."

"Ah, my sweet Katie, I be wanting to tell you some things, so. Let me pour some tea—the water's already hot."

Kathleen felt relieved to have the chance to share a little of her burden. She liked Aoife's small set of rooms in one corner of the B and B—this living room, her small kitchen, and a separate bedroom. The bedroom had a small fireplace. She went to the living room window, looking southwest across the rolling stone walls and limestone-and-grass checkered landscape. It was a beauty that rooted all her born days.

Aoife returned, gave a cup to Kathleen and sat across from her.

"So then, Katie, Tommy's a mean one and that's the truth. Always has been. I couldn't be happy for Colleen when she married 'im, but there's no accounting for being young and in love, I guess. I don't know all what you done and don't need to know unless you be wantin' to talk, but it makes sense that he be reacting all out of proportion. There's something you might not know that could be a part of it all. When they were young, your mam and Tommy were sweet on each other as it happened. Until he lost his temper once at something or other and threw her off the dock in Cill Rónáin, right into the Atlantic! She never did let him back in her life, though he begged her for forgiveness. I think it was him as wanted to marry her. Smart, your mam was."

Kathleen was dumbfounded. Her mom had never mentioned walking out with Tommy, but then, now that she thought on hit, why would she? Maybe that was why her mom had been practically hysterical on the phone yesterday. "I never knew that about Mom. But you really think Tommy'd hold that against me? I mean, why?"

"T'aint no logic to that man. He always had his way when he was young, his mam making endless excuses for his bullying. Ain't no one ever really said 'no' to him before your mam, and you see him, he acts like he owns this whole island. And now Colleen's standing up to him in some way, and you got your spoon in the stew? Oh, Katie, I can see how your mam comes right into whatever is going on. He's a bad one, and he remember. I wish i could tell ya to pay him no attention, but I think, love, it would be good ta watch yourself these next few days."

Aoife thought a moment. "But Colleen, now. If you want to try again to meet her, we can have it here and t'aint no one need to know."

October 18, 1980
I can't believe I am writing this—for a good while, I was happy today.
Actually, I still feel happy.

Michael put his pen down on the desk. It ad felt good to run again, but it was even better waling back with kathleen. She was easy to talk to and could sing like an angel. He'd noticed that she was coming up from some old ruins of a monastery when he ran into her, and wondered if she, as he, liked her quiet moments. It was only a feeling, but he sensed there was real depth to her. She radiated such positive energy. He still could hardly believe that after all these months he had sung. How had she done that?

For the first time since Maggie died, he'd felt physical interest in a woman. Like a boy entering a narrow, dark cave, he let his attention probe Maggie's death. It still hurt like hell, but something was changed. He was not afraid of the pain and he knew all at once that he would be able to come out the other side and be happy again. Not yet, not yet, but it would happen.

Evenings were always the worst, his fear growing like an approaching storm each night as it grew dark. He'd slept with the light on every day since the accident.

The accident. He always tried to avoid thinking about that, usually without success. The heart could be a hole of recrimination even when the head knew better. Did I have any choice? Who wouldn't have done what I did? No one, not a single friend, not even her parents, had held anything against him.

But my God, I killed Maggie.

Well, at least tonight he wouldn't have to face the dark right off. He was nervous, thinking about the two songs he'd sung with Kathleen—it sounded as if she wanted to sing them with him at the pub.

Maggie had loved them both, and he feared he might choke up if he attempted to sing either. Why hadn't he chosen some easy songs like *Nancy Whiskey*, or *Gather Up The Pots*?

Just then there was a knock on his door. Surprised, he got up to answer it. Kathleen stood there, looking a bit sheepish.

"Michael, I was here visiting Aoife, and I asked which room was yours. Do you mind?"

"No, not at all. Come in!"

Michael went to the room's one chair and moved some clothes from it to the bed. He felt a bit awkward as the room was somewhat untidy.

"Oh, you don't have to do that, I'm not staying. The reason I came up was I just wanted to say, to invite you again to come tonight. I think you'd have a good time…." Her voice trailed off and Michael was surprised to see she looked a little embarrassed. Had she come merely to invite him again? Or was there something more? He liked that thought. He liked that she was here.

Kathleen looked around the room. Her eyes paused at Maggie's photo on his bed stand, taken at Lincoln Park in southwest Seattle. Impulsively he said, "That's my wife, Maggie. She died just over a year ago in a car accident."

"Oh, Michael, I didn't mean to pry. And I am so sorry. She was lovely."

"I suppose people know—I see them looking and wondering. My first day here I was still in so much shock, and after a couple Guiness, I let slip to a waiter that I had a wife who died. I'm not sure all of what I said, but I think word got around."

A sadness came over him as he looked at the photo of him and Maggie. He took a deep breath and glanced back at Kathleen. But she was looking unexpectedly out his window. He turned and saw the same car that had stopped by her yesterday parking in Aoife's small lot. A man got out. A very large man.

THIRTEEN

Kathleen looked at Michael. "It's Tommy Powell."

"He's huge," he said and looked away from Tommy back to her.

Kathleen took a deep breath. "There's some as say he's two meters tall. I'm going down. He probably is looking for me." And then, after a moment, "Would you come down, just kind of be there?"

He had already turned to follow her. Kathleen put out her hand and quietly asked Michael to wait by the door. Tommy was standing a few feet from his car. She wondered what Tommy was waiting for as she stopped some distance from him. Tommy swaggered up to within a few feet of her like Balor with his evil eye. His graying hair was cut short, his dark eyes narrowed in a mean way. Kathleen felt intimidated by his sheet bulk. Although carrying a bit of a "Guiness-paunch" his arms and shoulders were thickly muscled. A sheen of sweat dampened his forehead.

"Well, Kathleen Flaherty, my Colleen was just after tellin' me you'd be here. I come by to give you a friendly reminder-like. You always was one to be pokin' your finger in other people's cake, but I'm tellin' you now, you need to give off with my wife."

Kathleen pushed through her anxiety. "Tommy, listen, can we just talk?"

Tommy looked her over, letting his eyes settle on her breasts for too long, then down lower. He made a dismissive sound as he brought his eyes back to hers. "You remind me a lot of your mum, you know that? And about as bossy, as well. You want to talk? Talk, then." As he said this, he moved a step closer.

Taking a breath, Kathleen said, "Look, Tommy, I don't understand what has happened…."

"What *happened*," he said, spitting out the word, "is that my Colleen comes to me and says she wants this and she wants that, and if I don't like it, she wants it anyway. Where came these ideas, then? From you. I don't need you interferin' in our lives. Stay the hell out."

As Tommy spoke, Kathleen thought of Colleen and at his last words felt her anger getting the best of her. She took a deep breath to calm herself—yelling at Tommy would help no one, most of all Colleen.

She said in an even voice, "Tommy, I am not trying to interfere in your lives. I simply listen to people, and Colleen has some dreams, some…."

He again stepped closer, into her personal space. It took all her will, but she did not give ground although she felt like she was disappearing in his shadow. This time Tommy's voice was raised and strained as he said, "Then that's for her to tell me, not some wet behind the ears, failed cello player. We is doin' just fine. If she got some fancy-dancy-so-called goddamn dreams, she can bring them up to me." On the word "me" he poked her hard between her breasts and she backed up a step, shocked at his aggression.

A movement to her left drew her eyes, and Tommy looked over at Aoife, who had walked up.

"Tommy, you need to be backin' off a bit here," the older woman said, stepping up alongside Kathleen. She saw that Michael had come up to her right.

"Sir, I don't all know what's going on here, but where I come from, we don't intimidate people like what I'm seeing right now." Michael's voice was flat, definitive.

Tommy turned his gaze to Michael. Michael started to reply, but Kathleen addressed him first. "Michael, it's alright." She was desperately afraid everything might spiral out of control.

Sarcasm punching his words like a boxer's jab, Tommy turned his focus full on Michael, "You that American been wanderin' the island like some lost puppy? Well, you ain't in America now, and I don't need no words comin' from no damn Yankee-*nina*. Unless you'd like to do somethin', I be thinkin' you ought to shut your gob."

Kathleen felt Michael tighten at the words and turned to look him in the eye. She hoped he hadn't understood the insult Tommy had thrown at him. She saw his anger as he stepped away from her. But, to her surprise, he put his arms out to his side, opening his palms as he said, "I mean no offense, and I don't want to step in where I'm not wanted. It's just you're like twice the size of Kathleen here, and I can read body language as good as the next guy—hell, wouldn't you step in if you saw someone being bullied by someone else twice as big?"

Tommy hesitated at these words, tight anger evident in the set of his haw and his eyes. He took a couple breaths, then turned to Kathleen. "You heard what I said, then. Give off." When he was back in the car, he unrolled the window, eyes boring into Kathleen. Never taking his eyes off her as he backed out, Tommy sped off down the Main Road.

The reining trio was quiet for a few moments, as if dazed after the passing of a winter storm.

"That is not a nice man," Michael said, turning to Kathleen with a half-smile. After a moment, in a cathartic release of tension, she burst out laughing.

"Are you alright?" Michael asked.

Kathleen let out a breath. "I am now. Michael, thank you for coming out. You too, Aoife."

Aoife spoke up. "I've known Tommy all his born days and ain't never seen him that mad. Michael, you don't want to be fighting that man—he's a hard one and mean as well."

Michael looked at the pair. "I'm certain I don't want to fight him either." He thought a moment, then added, "Is there any police on this island, maybe you ought to call them? He seemed…."

Michael stopped at their quick laugh. "There's no Garda on the island," Kathleen said, "Not enough real crime to need one."

"Remember the great robbery of '76?" Aoife asked. She looked at Michael. "When the police arrived at Conneely's, Conlon told them, 'It was Patrick Doogan as did it—you'll probably find him in Cill Rónáin, drinking at some other pub with my money.' And that's exactly where he was, already drunk half the money away! I think Conlon even thought of not calling the Garda at all, being as they have to come all the way from Galway, and Patrick wasn't going anywhere. Surely ain't no strangers livin' on this island."

"I'm a stranger, I suppose," Michael said with a smile.

"And as to that, Michael," Kathleen immediately replied, "come to Conneely's Friday night, sing a bit, get to know some people better."

Friday at last arrived. Michael decided to walk to Conneely's, carrying his guitar. That had been a last second impulse, and now he was not sure he agreed with his own decision. But there is nothing for it, he thought. Besides, it's not like I can't play.

The front door opened to a large room sixty feet or more in length, and half as wide. Conlon Conneely stood behind the bar, pulling a beer and talking to a waitress. The wall behind him, some kind of medium dark wood, was lined to either side with dozens of whisky bottles. Several baseball caps hanging from wooden dowels in the middle along with the pennants of what Michael assumed to be Football clubs. The rest of the room, with its darker wood, was filled with tables of various sizes and chairs, a lot of people and conversation, some cigarette smoke. A couple men smoke pipes at one table, a dog laying at the feet of one of them. The ceiling was low, but painted white, which gave the room a slightly airier feeling than many pubs Michael had been in.

What really grabbed his attention was the music coming from the fa corner, as Kathleen and a man on a guitar raced through the reel. The man sat on a stool, eyes closed as he quickly strummed. Kathleen stood, swaying a bit, her head down as her fingers flew over the strings. Maggie would have loved this, he thought. And she'd have had me up dancing, right next to the table. Or been dancing herself.

In spite of his own not inconsiderable facility on the guitar, Michael knew he was in the presence of a true musician. Kathleen was amazing. As the pair increased the tempo, the crowd whooped and stomped their approval. All at once Michael felt out of place. He thought to leave, but at that moment Kathleen raised her eyes, found his as if she had known he was there and smiled even as she played. Well, he thought, there are worse things than being stuck here looking at her.

He went to the bar, squeezed in between two occupied stools and caught Conlon's eye. "Michael, isn't it?" the bartender asked with a raised eyebrow and voice.

Michael leaned in to get past the noise of the crowd, which swelled as the pair brought the reel to an end. "Yes, thanks for remembering, Conlon. Can I get a Guinness?"

"You can! Katie told me you might be coming. And looks like you be thinking of playing with her. Must be good, then?"

Michael felt unsure of an answer. As Conlon built the Guiness, he said, "I'm not as good as Kathleen is on that fiddle, but I can play a bit, yes."

Conlon turned his head from the pull tab. "That's no shame—there might be no woman or man in all Ireland who is er equal when she gets er reel going. And she said you might be singing. You're surely welcome to, but you'll get yourself thrown out if you're not good!" he said with a large smile. "Ah, and here is er highness as we speak."

Michael turned to Kathleen as she approached. She looked up into his eyes with a smile as she said, "I'm glad you've come, Michael, you and your guitar—that surely means you've come by to play then? Listen, I have a small bit of time, let's sit here a minute." She turned toward Conlon, who was setting Michael's Guinness in front of him, and said in mock anger, "Barkeep, I have thirst. Get me a Harps. Now." Conlon laughed as he turned to draw er beer. She slid into a stool next to Michael, pulling her hair back from her eyes. Slightly flushed, her blue eyes shone with feral energy. God help me, Michael thought, I haven't seen such beautiful eyes since the day I met Maggie. Like a slow dawn, Michael realized that for the first time in eleven months he was thinking of her without grief. With a start he saw that Kathleen had said something.

"What? I'm sorry, I didn't hear…."

Kathleen chuckled, reaching out to touch his hand as she said, "And no wonder, then, you looking to a be million light years off."

"Sorry, I was just thinking, remembering something."

"I wanted to know what you'd like to play? I'd love to sing *Wild Mountain Thyme* with you, I mean, we both know it, and we sounded good, don't you think? Even if we can't practice, I know the crowd would like it."

Michael hesitated just a moment. He was unsure he would be up to the task—he hadn't performed in a year, and the scar tissue on his left hand sometimes tightened painfully and unpredictably. But then, for the first time since Maggie's death, he had sung the other day. With this woman in front of him. He said, "I'm having second thoughts about this, Kathleen."

She pursed her lips, a small furrow appearing on her forehead. Michael laughed inside as he found himself not wanting to disappoint her. "Listen, why don't I start by playing *Red is the Rose* on guitar. Then maybe I can sing with you later." But he felt his nerves increase.

"You said it, so it is!" she responded, and with another smile stood up and headed to the bathroom. She turned a few feet away and said over her shoulder, "If you haven't eaten, order the Fish and Chips. They're over the moon, I promise."

A half hour later, as Kathleen and her guitar player—Paddy Curran, Kathleen had introduced him—brought another song to an end, she stepped up to the mike, and spoke with a natural showman's voice, "And now I'd like to ask a newcomer up to play for us. He's come all the way from America to play, so welcome Seattle's own Michael Flaherty." She finished with a slight flourish at his name, without overstating it.

His stomach tightened with nerves as he made his way amid the scattering applause to the musician's corner. He'd had no real chance to warm up and was afraid the scar tissue might interfere with his playing. Keep it simple, he thought. You don't need to take it up to the seventh fret. He took out his Taylor and briefly tuned it with Paddy's, who gave him a look of encouragement as he stepped aside. For the first time since Maggie had been killed, MIchael looked out to an expectant crowd. And was shocked to see at a nearby table three men glaring at him, one of them Tommy. What the hell, he thought. REsisting the urge to ask them right through the mic what their problem was, Michael took a deep breath and, using an old trick, looked around and found a few other faces looking more positive.

"I'm going to play an old love song. The melody crosses cultures. It's found in folk music all over the world, but here it's all Irish." And without naming the song, he started in, fingerpicking the chords with the melody always highlighted, adding some simple alternating bass notes with his thumb. The crowd recognized it immediately, and he felt them settling back to listen. He stumbled a bit at the end of the verse, but kept on. In a way that remained mysterious to him, he felt the people responding to his playing. With eyes closed, he let the haunting beauty of the song carry him, beginning to syncopate the melody line against the background mixture of chords, parts of the melody coming in now a half beat after the bass notes. And then, a moment of absolute magic. Kathleen joined him with her fiddle, weaving in complex harmonies to his playing. Mostly she played a third above the melody, but she laid in an occasional dissonant note which would flow hauntingly in to the next harmonious line. Genius, he thought. Michael turned, and her smile was like a full moon on a wide expanse—he almost forgot to play! She sensed it, and turned away, but not without a wink at him. As they came to the refrain for the last time, she whispered into the mic, "Sing it, all." And they did, with all the harmonies of a people long schooled in song, their voices rising and falling like a breeze over gentle hills.

Red is the rose, that in yonder garden grows,
And fair is the lily of the valley,
Clear is the water that flows from the Boyne,
But my love is fairer than any.

As they neared the end, their eyes met and they nodded, playing the refrain one more time as the crowd sang. Michael plucked the last chord as Kathleen drew out her final note. A moment of silence and then the crowd cheered enthusiastically. Kathleen leaned over to him and said, "You won't be a stranger long now."

It was a blur after that. People called out songs, and discovered that Michael knew and played many of them, with Kathleen and sometimes Patrick accompanying. *Gather Up The Pots* was followed by *Mari's Wedding* by *Those Long Winter Nights* by *Morning Glory* until Michael lost track.

Upon request, Kathleen sang in an old style, unaccompanied. It was complex as she often inflected notes with quick higher and lower notes. To Michael it possessed a haunting, mysterious quality. When she finished, she immediately started a second song in the same style. The room was quiet as she stood before them, eyes closed, holding the mic with her left hand as she slightly swayed. It felt to him like a sacred moment for everyone present.

She brought the song to an end, opened her eyes, and seemed to take an instant to come back to the room. The crowd did not applaud, but there were several compliments quietly spoken aloud—that's our Katie, there you are now, Katie, and on long "ah, lassie," at the end.

Kathleen smiled. "So, one last song, and Michael and I will be singing. You'll recognize the song, but you should know Michael here rewrote the last verse, so be listening."

Unrehearsed, Michael started in, Kathleen layering a simple harmony over the top. In a quiet relaxed voice, Michael started.

> *Oh, the summertime is comin'*
> *and the leaves are sweetly bloomin'*
> *and the wild mountain thyme…*

At the refrain, she sang the melody with him, but the second time it came, she went into harmony. Their voices swayed and soared like two gliders marking long, synchronized arcs across a wide sky. As he came to the start of the third verse, Michael glanced at her. She nodded, and looked with her eyes to her fiddle. He didn't sing as she played over the top of his guitar. Then they sang the rewritten verse, which she remembered perfectly from his singing three days ago. He could tell the crowd like it. To his surprise, Kathleen let him sing the final refrain alone.

Will ye go lassie go
And we'll all go together
To pull wild mountain thyme
All around the bloomin' heather
Will ye go lassie go.

As he plucked a last quick arpeggio on the D chord, he looked at Kathleen, and was surprised to see tears in her eyes.

Fifteen minutes later, after all the congratulations, he, Paddy and Kathleen sat at a table. The crowd had thinned, and it was quieter in the pub. Conlon brought them three Guinness. Paddy took a huge gulp, and banged the pint glass down assertively. "Ahhh, that's a fine drop there, now." He looked at Michael. "You've got a singin' voice on ya, lad, and you and our Katie together is really somethin' to give ears to. I hope ya won't be the stranger her after tonight."

Michael smiled. Such a compliment coming from another musician felt good. But he had a question for Kathleen. "Tell me about that wonderful singing you did—everyone listened so intently. It was beautiful."

Kathleen said, "It's an old kind of singing, call Sean-nós. It pulls us back to long-ago times, old love songs, the sad harshness of life that we still love for it's simply being so, a few hero songs. Beautiful lullabies. Some small part of it is religious."

"It isn't everywhere you hear it, mostly here in the west," Paddy interjected. He sighed. "Be a sad day to see Sean-nós disappear, but with the likes a Katie here, maybe it never will. I bet she can sing thirty, thirty-five songs off by heart."

Shaking his head, Michael said, "I don't see that happening, it's so beautiful."

Michael listened to the pair for nearly a half hour as they spoke of music, language, and the revival of Irish. Kathleen asked, "Will we be having another Guinness, then?"

"Oh, I've been too long away from my bed as it is," said Paddy. "*Some of us have to get up early to work.*" And with a wink at Michael and a nod at them both, Paddy was off.

"What about you, then?"

Michal wasn't sure he felt like another Guinness, but he definitely warmed to the idea of spending time alone with Kathleen. At is assent, she headed to head bar to order a couple pints. Michael breathed in relief, closing his eyes and relaxing a minute before looking around. Couples sat at a few tables, and a group of men surrounded a large table at the other end of the pub. The pipe smokers were still at heir table, dog asleep. They had been an enthusiastic crowd, and Michael realized how much he missed performing. Then, as his eyes moved, there was that glare again coming from a pair of men sitting at a table two dozen feet away. Michael gave a perplexed looked at them, but they continued to glare. At that moment, Kathleen returned.

She saw his face, "What's wrong?"

"There's been men glaring at me, like they hate my guts. Same pair as stared at me when I went up earlier to sing. Tommy was sitting with them before, but he's gone—don't look."

It was too late. Kathleen turned back and asked, "You mean the pair near the bar, one in a red shirt?"

"Yeah, that's them."

"That's Bobby and Seamus Cooley, a couple of brothers who work on the ferry. You don't know them, do you?"

Michael shrugged. "Never seen them before, that I know. Oh shit, here they come."

The pair approached the table like forest predators. "So, Katie, you seem to mighty taken with this one, here." It was Seamus who spoke.

"He's a friend. And a good singer—I enjoyed our time tonight. Did you?"

"Oh, he can sing fine enough, but that's not all I hear he can do. He was arrested, did you know that?"

Michael tensed at Seamus' lie.

"I hear he was arrested," said Bobby, "for killing his wife."

Another damn lie Michael thought, even as he was out of the chair, unaware he had risen, his fist smashing into Seamus' chin an instant later. As Seamus fell away, Bobby swung at Michael. Michael heard a huge roar as he blocked Bobby's punch, and turned to see Tommy racing across the bar.

FOURTEEN

A couple days later, Michael looked up from his desk at the downpour outside the window. A gust of wind sent the rain rattling against the glass, momentarily obscuring his view. He felt as bleak as the blurred barren landscape that emerged as the windowed clesared somewhat. Some small flame of hope had been extinguished. Her name was Kathleen.

Everyone called her Katie. Perhaps, he mused, he'd continued to call her Kathleen to subtly distance her, to keep him from opening the path into his heart. Michael laughed, but it was not a pleasant sound. He knew well the risks of love.

Love? He couldn't love Katie.

He faced an undeniable truth: he wished she'd called or come by.

His journal was open to a blank page, the date inscribed in the upper right corner—August 28, 1980. No thoughts came. Crossing the room, Michael picked up his guitar, sat back down at the desk, strumming a few chords. Put the guitar back. All at once, the need to leave became clear. He was a stranger on Inis Mór, and most unwelcome by the biggest man on the island. He genuinely laughed—he had so few possessions here that he could pack and be out the door in twenty minutes.

He heard quiet footsteps, and a knock on the door. It was Aoife.

"Katie just rang, wantin' ta be certain ya was still here. She's comin' over and surely not ta see me."

"Honestly, Aoife, I feel like a total outsider here. Maybe it's time for me to go."

She interrupted him. "I got two things ta say to ya. I spent my child-hood days up north of Sligo, but I met and married my Sean all the way back in 1926 and he brought me here to his home. I been on this island for fifty-four years and there's still some as treat me like sour milk. But I hear ya made quite the impression the other night, before the fightin.'" She laughed. "Well and the fightin' made an impression as well. So, there's those who will make ya welcome, and those who never will, more's the pity. You ask me, I wouldn't be worrying your head about those others."

Both looked out the window as a car pulled into the lot, and Kathleen got out, hurrying across to the front door.

Aoife spoke again. "And second," hitting the word with emphasis, "I saw how she looks at ya. If ya can't give that look back, you need to get off this island."

Aoife's voice hit like a hammer strike. He wanted to protest, but she had turned and left the room.

Kathleen appeared in his open door, taking off her ski cap. He took her coat and put it over the back of his desk chair. She smelled of damp hair and something fresh. They looked a moment at each other, then she smiled slightly.

"Michael, what is it then you can't do? You play guitar, sing wonderfully, write poetry, and evidently you can fight quite well. What...."

Michael interrupted her flow of words. "I, well, I took boxing lessons while in college."

"Boxing lessons?" She queried, looking at him as if he'd just grown a second head.

Michael genuinely laughed. "It's a bit complicated—my dad was a boxer in high school and taught me when I was a kid. Something about always being able to defend myself. He died when I was in high school, and I did it partly to remember him. I used to head from Seattle U down to this ratty gym. It gave me confidence and a sense of what my body could do. I sparred three times a week with young up-and-comers and got pretty good. I have, I was told, excellent eye-hand coordination."

"Well, evidently you had a good...coach?"

He smiled. "Trainer, actually."

"I'm sorry about your father."

"It's okay, a long while past now," he responded, shrugging his shoulder. And then added, "He died on a rescue mission in a plane crash."

"Ohh, Michael."

When he said nothing, she continued, "You might be glad to hear that the Garda was not called. As Conlon said, 'Just a bit of an Inis Mór dustup.' Thank God Conlon and a couple other men got to Tommy before he got to you. But you didn't make yourself any friends. They don't take kindly to getting beat up. Two against one and you unscratched. Brigit help us. Be ever so careful of Tommy."

"But that's not why I really came." Kathleen took a deep breath. "I'll just say what I'm thinking. I like you. And unless I'm dumber than a pile of Inis Mór stone, you feel something toward me. But there's a secret clinging to you like a ghost on a foggy day and that makes me nervous. I'm inviting you to dinner tonight at my house. This weather is fierce altogether, so I could pick you up on my way home from work about 6:15."

He didn't hesitate. "I'll come. And I'll tell you my story, as best as I can."

By the time Kathleen arrived, the sun was pushing through long holes in the clouds. The wet Main Road gleamed like a river in the light, and Michael paused a moment as he got out of Kathleen's car, breathing deeply from moist air shot through with the fresh ocean breezes. The spare landscape which had looked so forlorn to him earlier shone now with a simple, clean beauty. It heartened him, and he believed in that moment that he could let his story out to Kathleen.

"Come on in," Kathleen said as she unlocked her bright red front door.

Michael looked around her home as he gave Kathleen his coat. He liked the feel of her living room, with a fireplace and a couple of comfortable chairs, plus a couch facing a large window with a spectacular view of the west end of the island as it dropped a mile or so to the Atlantic beyond. Her violin and cello stood in beautiful stands to the right of the window. He walked over to it, noticing the lighthouse in the distance. He heard Kathleen reenter the room and come stand next to him.

"The living room is an addition my grandfather put in fifty years ago. I love to sit here on rainy days, a fire in the fireplace, and read, or play my cello."

"It's lovely, Kathleen, a bit of paradise."

She blessed him with a radiant smile, and he blushed a bit. "What's for dinner?"

"I thought you'd like a nice salmon, Flaherty style, marinated with vinegar, spices, honey, and Paddy's Whiskey. I'm also cooking up a side dish of Colcannon—I'll have that in the oven right off, and the salmon will take no time at all to bake. And now, the most important question of all—would you like a Harps, a Guiness, or some red wine?"

"A Guiness."

Again she smiled at him. "You knew the right answer from the other night."

"And if I'd said Harps?"

She laughed. "That would surely have been just as right." A moment's hesitation. "I, however, actually have no red wine, so thank Mary and her Holy Son you didn't want any of that." They both chuckled.

They chatted easily while she took out the potato dish and baked the salmon, the house filling with their rich smells. Michael told her of Juneau and she interspersed with tales of the island, all the way through dinner. She spoke fondly but also with regret of her time playing in Dublin Philharmonic. An hour later, the kitchen cleaned, they headed to the living room with two cups of tea, sitting on her couch.

"So, you're good on the cello?"

"No sense denying the truth of it. I am. I still play every day, but as I said, at least right now I don't long for the life of a professional musician. I do miss the...well, there were times at the Dublin that I miss. It was the togetherness of all of us become as one. It was just indescribable. As if it were the music that played us, not the other way 'round."

"Would you play a little?"

She stood to get the instrument, picking up a bow as well. She sat for a moment in the chair next to the fireplace with it between her legs, working her fingers a bit on the neck, and then, closing her eyes, began to play. The room immediately filled with a deep and rich tone. At first she played a few small scales. She opened her eyes, looking for a moment with Michael. "This is a famous Neapolitan song called 'O Sole Mio.' It's probably overdone these days, but it really is a haunting melody. It's one of my favorites, about a man who feels like the sun when he sees his love."

Kathleen was right, it was beautiful. He closed his eyes and rested his being on the melodic wave that filled the room, slowly becoming unaware of all but the music, rising and falling with its ascending and descending tones. He would later remember these two minutes, before he wept, as having been like being gently rocked by a light wind.

But poised on the crest of the emotive force of music, between one moment and the next Maggie was suddenly before him, her dark hair back in a short ponytail, deep brown eyes looking at him as she had when she told him they were pregnant. She let out one of her infectious laughs, and Michael fell into the abyss of her presence even as his mind knew she was gone forever.

"Dance, let's dance, honey," he heard her say, just as she would at almost any moment music was present. He had danced with her in their living room, restaurants, city streets, parks, along beaches—she never cared what others thought, and he'd learned to love her for it. He put his face in his hands and trembled with the pressure of his long withheld grief. He tumbled in its rocky current and wept. Some sound must have escaped him, for suddenly the music stopped, and he felt another presence come and sit next to him.

"Michael." So quietly he barely heard it. And again, "Michael."

When Michael started to speak, Kathleen immediately recognized the words' importance. She put her hand on his arm and listened with all of her considerable empathy.

"You see, we took two cars that night—I was afraid I might want to leave early. Just visiting some friends in Olympia, a birthday. It is so damn... why did it have to be two cars? I was just tired and really didn't want to go in the first place. Thought I might leave early. But I didn't leave early, and she was right behind me when we left. We got on I-5 in Olympia, heading north toward Seattle. It was late, after midnight, and not a lot of traffic. A few exits up...." Michael stopped a moment, taking a couple of more deep breaths. "I was tired, not like falling asleep, but I wasn't one hundred percent alert. A car, a drunk driver, came roaring onto the freeway, the wrong way. I...." He moved his arms in a gesture of resignation. "I just reacted, swerving out of his way. And *then* I remembered, too late. Always too late. Maggie. When I looked in the mirror, he had already hit her. She must have had time to turn away a bit, and her car smashed through the gaurdrail, off to the side of the freeway, rolling into the wide median between the north/south lanes." He closed his eyes. "Rolling and rolling."

"The car landed upright, but it wasn't a torn up mess. I ran, thinking she would be dead, but she was not, she moving and groaning. I don't think she was really conscious. Her window was partly smashed in, and I pulled away the rest of the glass." He looked at the scar tissue on his hand, and held it up to her.

Kathleen nodded her head. This is terrible, she thought.

"I couldn't get the damn door open. Oh, God." He put his head back in his hands.

"Then the engine caught on fire."

"Oh my God, Michael." She sat stunned as the horror of it slowly opened to her. How does he bear it?

But Michael was not done.

"I couldn't get her out. I couldn't get the door open. When I reached through the window and pulled, one of her legs was crushed under metal. My hands were all bloody and kept slipping. And then she looked at me."

He stopped talking. Kathleen heard the clock above her mantle ticking. Finally, he spoke again, quietly now.

"I couldn't get her out. I couldn't....do it. The flames...." Michael could not go on. His hands began to shake, and Kathleen reached out and took his right hand in her. She leaned in, bringing her mouth close to his ear, and whispered, "Michael, you are here, right now. Be here. There you are, now. There you are." She felt him move slightly in her direction, his forehead touching hers.

He finished in scarcely more than a whisper. "Her car was in this wide median...oh, I already said that. I looked around. There was a large stone, right at my feet. It was so dark, I would never have seen it, but it was *right there*. I picked it up as the flames rose higher, and she began to scream. I ran as close as I could and heaved the stone into her skull." He stopped a moment, and then the words lurched out between ragged breaths, "She stopped screaming."

Kathleen would never know for sure how long she sat with her hand in his as he wept. She moved closer to him, but made no move to take him in her arms. She wanted to, but as she watched his interior anguish flood up and out, she knew that her embrace was his to ask for, not hers to force. When he stopped, his breathing still ragged, he looked at her, and she was reminded of a photo she had seen once of a starving child, eyes full of despair and an inability to understand the emptiness of her stomach.

"I have good eye-hand coordination, you see."

It was a moment before she realized he had tried to make a bit of a joke. She pulled back, offered him a fragile smile. He closed his eyes, shaking his head back and forth as if in denial.

Kathleen had trouble grasping the totality of his story—it was one horror piled onto the next. That he was still alive showed the strength of his inner reserves, even though at times he seemed incredibly fragile.

"There was some talk about putting me on trial for murder. That was squelched pretty fast, but in the interim, it came out that Maggie likely died from a skull fracture—my stone."

"Michael." But Kathleen had no more words. They sat in silence. She heard the refrigerator come on, again the ticking of the clock. The fridge went off. At some point he put his other hand over hers, lifting it a bit from his lap, then raising her hand to his lips. "Thank you," he said, "Singing with you the other evening was like coming back to life. But beautiful music is a double-edged sword, as you saw. I know what you want to say—that it wasn't my fault. And I know as well that you are right. But sometimes, maybe a lot of the time, knowing something in your head is like trying to sew up a deep cut with a piece of hair. It just doesn't help."

Kathleen roused to that. "That's right enough, indeed, Michael. But isn't it a place to start—that there was nothing else you would ever have done? Could ever do? Life simply comes at us as it does, and we have to believe that we can allow ourselves to feel the pain and come through it and be happy again. We...hope."

Michael seemed to ponder her words a few moments.

"Kathleen, you're the first person I've told the story to. That I've wanted to tell."

"My *maimeo,* my grandmother, used to say I have a gift. She told me I would be an *Anam Cara* to everyone I met—that I have the gift of really listening, and that people could sense it. She was the first to encourage me with my cello because I could *hear* the music. It might sound trite, but she said the music is the true voice of the universe."

He took another deep breath. "That makes sense—even when I came tonight, I somehow hoped to be able to share what happened with you."

They sat in companionable silence. She became more aware of her hand in his. As if the thought had occurred to him at the same time, he looked down at their hands and gave a squeeze, just before releasing hers. Thinking he might like a little alone time after his emotional release, she offered to make more tea, and he said yes. She busied herself in the kitchen, pondering their relationship. They had met just three weeks ago, and she was powerfully if a bit hesitantly drawn to him. But now that she knew the extent of his interior anguish and damage, her hesitation remained. How needy would he be if they developed a relationship? The problem was, she was so damn attracted to him—physically yes, but emotionally as well. She had seen his generous courage a few days ago as he stood up for her to Tommy.

Michael was funny, and although she was not certain of his religiosity, Kathleen sensed a deep spirituality in him that was open and searching. When they sang together, it was like each became an extension of the other. And there was something else, something elusive that she could not put her finger on, that drew her to him. But of course, she thought, it's Bog Irish nonsense that you just add things up or make a list to explain attraction to another.

Michael was standing by the window when she returned with the tea. Kathleen thought for no the first time how striking his eyes were, and how she wanted to kiss him, but she pushed the thought away. She leaned his direction just a bit more. No, she thought and pulled fractionally away. Regretfully.

Looking back out the window, he said quietly, "I never could have imagined my life would end up like this. I had a job I loved, a wife who took my breath away, we were going to have a family, children, and in one moment, it was all gone. Honestly, Kathleen, there are some nights where I feel so tight, like a thick rubber band wound and wound tighter and tighter. Until it feels like I will snap, literally, my aorta or something, will actually snap. And I am so alone. Maybe," and he turned his head to her with a slight smile on his lips, "I shouldn't be telling you this. Singing the other night, it was the first time that Maggie was not on my mind, that I was happy. I hated the way the night ended—I don't mean the fight, but that at the end of it all, I was alone again in my room." He turned back to her. "And that I didn't know what you thought. I was so relieved you asked me here this evening."

Their faces were less than two feet apart. And your eyes are so lovely, Michael, thought, and gave over to the longing of her own loneliness. He caressed her cheek briefly with his right hand, and leaned down to her. Their lips met, their mouths opening a fraction. He put his hand on the nape of her neck. She raised up on her toes.

Michael broke off the kiss, stepping back as he did so. For Kathleen, it was like taking a mis-step off a stair. Emotions threatened to overwhelm her—regret, anger at herself, disappointment, anger at Michael, and the return of her own loneliness. She was unsure what he saw in her face.

"I can't...I can't do this, Kathleen. Jesus Christ, I'm sorry. I'm just, I don't know. I just can't. I'm sorry."

Kathleen knew she needed to say something, but was rendered mute before the raw power of her complex emotional overload.

He looked at her as if pleading, and then walked quickly to the door, opening and closing it behind him without a word. Silence replaced his presence.

FIFTEEN

Tommy got off the ferry in a sour mood. That bitch Fiona was all full of herself, thinking that her job as deck supervisor made her better than him, ordering him around as if he were some schoolkid. She doesn't even have the strength to do half the shit that I have to do. He could throw her into the water without even raising a sweat—everything was fucking backwards from what was his rightfully.

And now he had to go home to his whining wife, wanting to go to Knock and do this and do that because of Katie-bitch-Flaherty. Colleen was worthless, all sad-dogged just to put a meal on the table. Shit, she wasn't even good for anything in bed anymore. It was easier to rip apart the jaws of a Blue Shark than to get her to spread her legs.

He turned left out of Cill Rónáin, and was cut off by a car coming out one of the side lanes—old Mrs. Derrane, Fiona's mother. Fuck it, there was Derranes all over like rabbits. He thought to get on his horn, but she probably wouldn't hear a damn thing anyway. In frustration he smashed his palm onto the steering wheel. Tommy felt that life had trickled by without him getting anything he wanted. Oh, he'd gotten into Colleen's pants, but that wore off real fast. Just about everyone he knew pretended to live by some code that was good. They said the word "ought" like it was some goddamn treasure.

The only "ought" he wanted anymore was his own. He was done with living by everyone else's rules.

He had that small, old house away in a part of Connemara where electricity hadn't found its way yet. Not even Colleen knew about that—he got it from some sexless biddy back before he even got married. He got up there once, sometimes twice a year, making repairs, chasing out rats. It was practically a ruin, but it was a roof and walls. No one knew. Maybe he'd just move out there when he got his pension.

People thought he was big and mean. Well, he thought as he pulled into his house, that's what I'm going to be. Take what I want, and if someone don't like it, they can try me. My life, the way I want it. And I know where I want to start—with the biggest bitch of all, Katie-goddamn Flaherty.

An hour later, Colleen stumbled out her front door into the evening clouds and drizzle, chased by Tommy's laughter. As was more and more frequently the case, he had spent the hour since coming home from work on the ferry ridiculing her—the way she looked, the way she dressed. Her cooking. What she wanted to watch on television. All her married life she'd told herself, at least he doesn't hit me. And that was still true, although she was becoming afraid of him. There was new viciousness in his verbal attacks. She felt like she was walking in a minefield—anything could set him off, and something inevitably did. Last night it was her hair. This afternoon it was that she improperly poured his Guinness. Too much foam.

He came to the porch another Guinness in hand. "You thinking about running off? Go on out into the world? You'll never do it. And if you do, I'll come and get you. This island isn't big enough for you to hide. Not even all Ireland." And he turned his back on her, returning inside.

Colleen considered his words, and courage of a sort coalesced in her—she would never be happy around him. In the past, fear had always driven her back. She had no job, no money, no family. Nothing. But, tonight, she thought: I'd rather die than live like this any longer. I'll go somewhere, anywhere. Wait tables. Clean rooms. Anything. Not sure if she'd really follow through, she turned her back to him and her miserable life and started walking. After a few hundred meters, she came to a Y—she could go to the right into Cill Rónáin, or left on Pump Road, that led to Kilmurvey Bay and eventually to Bun Gabhla and Katie's home.

Michael hurried up the road from Kathleen's house. It was a long trek home, but he needed to be alone. Dammit, he thought. Dammit.

After a couple minutes, he slowed, and then stopped, sitting atop the low stone wall to his right. He could still see Kathleen's house. Home. It felt like a home.

He'd been too long without a home. He remembered a time he walked by a woman near his home in north Seattle who was wearing the same perfume Maggie had worn. His legs nearly gave way. He retracted his steps to his house and fell shaking to the floor just inside his front door, no longer at home inside his own walls. That was the day he decided he needed to leave, to get away from the constant reminder of Maggie—everywhere he turned were memories of her that dug at him like a needle in a wound.

And now, out of the blue, he had been happy. Michael looked again at Kathleen's home. Smoke began to rise from its chimney in the dimming evening light. He thought about their short history—she running up to him at Dun Aengus, introducing herself to him a couple days later, inviting him to sing at Conneely's, and coming to him after the brief fight at the pub. Their singing together. Her presence to him an hour ago when he told his story for the first time.

Dammit. Michael was all at once filled with the determination to reclaim his life. He would not walk away from living again. Stepping off the wall, he shivered in a sudden breeze, aware for the first time that his coat was back at Kathleen's. A sign, he laughed. Had to go back anyway.

As he neared her home, dark clouds were gathering in the distance beyond the lighthouse. The ocean heaved with whitecaps visible even from this distance. Sure glad I won't be walking home, he thought. Unless Kathleen tells me to take a hike!

Michael walked up the front steps and knocked quietly on her red door. A sound from inside, and the door opened. Her eyes were lightly red-rimmed. He looked at her and shook his head briefly.

"Kathleen, may I come back in? I don't want to leave things like they are."

She hesitated a moment and then invited him in with a brief smile. "You forgot your coat."

"I know—I noticed right after I turned around. Thought I might use it as an excuse for coming back, but that would be a lie."

She released a trembling laugh. "I was about to throw out the tea, and I thought out throw out your cup as well. It's good then that I didn't."

They sat down, and she immediately raised her cup to her lips. She started to stand as she exclaimed, "Oh, it's gotten cool, I can reheat…."

Michael shook his head. "No, no, I don't need tea. I just want to talk."

Colleen shivered in the cold wind, the first raindrops hitting her in the face. In moments her hair was soaked, and she began to cry. Don't let yourself go to bits, she chided herself. You've got to make it to Katie's. She wondered if her husband worried for her, and in a moment of clarity understood that he did not. He would be angry about dinner, nothing more. How far to Katie's house? Soaked now to the bone, she gathered her reserves of strength and started walking again. Never, never, never, she started quietly saying to herself, stepping to the beat of the words. Never going back.

Kathleen sat, lowered her eyes a moment, and then raised them to his, running her hands through her wavy hair, pulling it behind her ears. Waited.

"Kathleen, I'm sorry. It's just all so sudden—three weeks ago—you know this—I was up at Dun Aengus in a really bad space. And then you show up like a saving angel who turns out to be a woman I like a lot."

"Michael," she said quietly.

He shook his head slightly, then finished, "When I am with you, I'm happy. I mean, like I said, singing with you was incredible, but tonight, too, eating and visiting, laughing. Feeling the warmth of this place."

After a few moments, Kathleen said, "I should have known better, Michael. I do know better. I don't mean I am not interested in you. I am. But you're still too much in your grief. It's too soon."

Kathleen stood and went to the fireplace, warming her hands a moment and then turned her back to the fire. "I surely don't know what all it is that attracts two people one to another. Some of my friends say I like to fix things," she shrugged her shoulders, "fix people, that I make them my special project. I did have a boyfriend like that once. For two years, I thought that wanting to fix him was love. That was some part of the reason I left Dublin and came back here. That time I saw you outside at Aoife's and introduced myself to you, I could feel how fragile you were and had no intention of getting into that again. But then we sang together on the road, and when Conlon drove up, I noticed how perceptive you were that I needed to talk to him alone. And how you came out and defused Tommy in the parking lot. Holy mother Mary, wasn't that something?"

Michael started to speak, but she put up her hand, walking to the window, looking west to the intermittent sparkle of Eeragh Lighthouse. He could see her face reflected in the glass. There was a gust of wind and a smattering of first raindrops hit the window, blurring the reflection. Then the rain thickened, and he lost her face. She shivered. Without turning she continued, "I've been lonely these three years, you see? I have a busy life that keeps it at bay most of the time—waiting tables, playing at Conneely's, playing my cello here, listening to the sorrows of some of the women on the island."

Kathleen turned and faced him. "Time just got away on me, I'm thirty-four years old, living on an island you can spit across in a good wind, with a few hundred other people I have known since I was jumping around in pigtails. There's some as say I failed, you know? The local girl who made the big time and then came running back less than three years later. I try not to care too much about that, but it can sting sometimes."

She hesitated a moment, shrugging her shoulders again. "This feels so fast, but I won't hide my feelings. I want us to have the time to see where it leads." She took a deep breath, nodded her head briefly as if to say, there, then, and came and sat back down.

He started to speak, but she added one more thought, raising her hands and dropping them to the couch as she spoke, "Brigit help me, but here it is. I want you to stay a while, not leave the island."

She has so much damn courage, Michael thought. He was overrun with emotion, the complexity of which was bewildering. He recognized that some of it wasn't necessary—but what was the use of trying to deny that he felt guilty? As if he were betraying Maggie? He knew what Maggie would say, what she would want—for him to be happy. He'd want the same for her. He sensed briefly something else, something deeper, but it flitted away like a bird in the corner of his eye.

Kathleen pulled up both her legs.

A strong gust of wind hit the front of the house, rain smashing against the window. Michael started, and then laughed. "I'm going to need a boat to get home in this weather, and even then it'd be iffy."

Kathleen sat up straighter, a look of wonder appearing on her face. "Ohhh," she quietly said. He looked at her, wondering what was happening.

She reached without reservation and lightly touched his cheek with three fingers of her left hand. He did not pull away. "Sometimes when the weather's fierce altogether, like tonight," she said quietly, "I bundle up and walk down to the Atlantic, listen to the ocean heaving in and back out. Endlessly. It reminds me of eternity. If you hadn't come back, I'd probably do it now. Down there sometimes I feel the presence of my family. Including my great-great-great grandfather and his brother, who lost their lives fishing. They left of an afternoon, a storm came up. Like this one. Worse, I'm sure. Their *curraugh* was never found." She paused a moment, then continued. "You said you had ancestors who came from here. Michael, do you know, then, did you have a great-great-great grandfather named Conlon?"

It took a moment to register. When it did, goosebumps ran along his arms. "Yes. He left Inis Mor when his brother died—they were all brothers?"

"Yes."

"Then we're like, thirtieth cousins or something!" They both laughed. Then Kathleen looked serious. She chose her words carefully, looking to Michael like a child concentrating hard on a new task. "Michael, I don't know what you believe, your religion and everything, but I think that is a part of what attracts us to each other. I am not saying you were destined to come here, I am not meaning that—it would have been a good thing for you and Maggie to have lived your lives together. But I think wounds and grief can last across generations. Somehow you and I being together, we're like a point of coalescence for all that hurt from the past."

He looked at her and was aware that she was gazing carefully at him, gauging his reaction. "I'm Catholic. Wouldn't I be, then? I mean, Conlon married an Italian woman. I got Catholic all over me. But...." He stopped. "But that's not your point, no. I guess, I mean. I don't know what to think."

Kathleen continued, "When I listen to the women who come to me, there are times I intuit deeply that they are carrying pain from the lives of people long dead—grandmothers, great-uncles. Fathers and mothers.

Carrying their joys as well, but the joys are not the reason they come to me. I would not be surprised if our ancestors were in the rafters of this very room, looking down on us. I know if I can get these women telling stories...I am a part of this island, you know? I've heard all the stories, too. When I get them to share the pain of their ancestors, and the happiness, and we laugh together at the absurdness of living on this island, they leave somehow freed."

Michael nodded. "And you and I, we, well hells bells, Kathleen, I have no idea how to finish that. That we are." He stopped, thought a moment. "That we are bringing back together what was torn apart one hundred years ago?"

"Exactly, like knitting something back together again. Well, actually, less than exactly, it's a bit of a mystery really. I think we are bound more deeply than just the last three weeks. We share an old pain and grief that draws us one to the other. But," and she smiled at him, "that doesn't diminish my feelings for you."

Michael's thoughts went unfinished. There was a sound, and he quickly realized it was someone running up Kathleen's steps. Someone pounded on her door, followed by a woman's voice, "Katie, are you there?" She hurried to the door, and Colleen, soaked, nearly fell into the living room. She looked startled to see Michael.

Before he had time to say anything, Kathleen spoke. "Oh, Colleen, come in here now out of this weather. Michael, there are blankets in my room, on the end of my bed. Get me a couple of them. My robe is in there, too, bring it. And some towels from the bathroom." He moved quickly, as he heard Kathleen speaking again, "Colleen, you're a mess. My God, you're shivering. Let's get you out of your wet clothes."

Michael stepped through the kitchen into her bedroom. The bed was neatly made, and some knitting lay on top of a pillow. He found the blankets and robe in a small closet and brought them back to the living room, think-ing to get more wood for the fire when he was done. Kathleen was helping Colleen out of her clothes—Michael turned quickly away, as Kathleen said to him, "Thanks, one more thing, can you bring in some wood from the back porch—I want to get the fire going."

Again, he went into the kitchen. He put the already heated teapot back on the stove—tea to warm Colleen up. He went quickly through to the back door and returned with a load of wood, entering the living room just as Colleen said, "Oh, Katie, I'm sorry then to be such an old bother, but Tommy is just getting worse and worse, and I can't be with him anymore. He's gotten so mean. I don't know what to do. I'm afraid I'm bringing something bad down upon you, but I, I have nowhere else to go."

Kathleen gave her a big hug. "There you are now. There you are." But as Kathleen looked over Colleen's shoulder at Michael, she looked afraid.

SIXTEEN

As they had arranged the night before, Michael arrived at Kathleen's home just before noon. She ushered him quietly into her living room. Colleen sat on the couch. She had shoulder length hair, brown, with a touch of grey. Her blue eyes looked at him with caution. A nice looking woman, he thought. She stood up as they were introduced.

"Kathleen tells me you have met Tommy."

Michael laughed lightly. "Yeah, well, not under the best circumstances, but then I gather there may not be such a thing."

Colleen did not laugh. "She also tells me that you won't tell anyone I'm here."

He looked over at Kathleen, raising his eyebrows quizzically.

"Colleen wants to leave Tommy, leave the whole island. I'm going to help her do that." She looked at him appraisingly, "But, where's my manners? I promised you a lunch. Let's go into the kitchen."

The kitchen, as she called it, was actually a large room that took up much of the back end of the house. There was plenty of space for a wood table with four chairs, which sat next to a south facing window that looked out over a yard, the back stone wall of which opened up to the rise back to the northwest, toward Dún Aonghasa. Another window faced west toward Eeragh. Both were bordered by bright flowered curtains. There was a door in the back wall that let out to a small covered storage area and patio. On the left were two doors, to the bathroom and Kathleen's bedroom.

"It smells really good," Michael said.

"It's my mom's version of Irish Farm House Soup—lots of root vegetables and plenty of beef. Cabbage and potatoes. Our whole history in a bowl!" She laughed. "And some thick bread for dipping. Would you like a salad?" she asked, looking at Colleen and Michael. Both indicated yes.

Kathleen hummed to herself as she prepared the salads. Michael suddenly felt uncomfortable in the silence and the way Colleen stared out the window. He knew he had intruded on a conversation, and some complex dynamic of the island. Regretfully, he decided to leave as quick as possible after lunch.

"We're ready, then." Kathleen brought over the salads and the soup in two trips, while Colleen rose and laid the table with bowls and spoons. Michael declined the offer of a Guiness, asking for water instead. They chatted for a few minutes, when all at once Colleen put down her spoon and sighed deeply. "Ah, Katie, I'm so all wound up, I can't find the heart then for food or conversation. I hope you'll excuse me, I'm just to take a quick walk in your back yard." She looked at Michael apologetically, rose, and went out the back door.

They looked at each other. Kathleen got up and walked to the door.

"See what I mean? I like to fix things—that's what my mother and friends say. They don't always mean it in a good way. But how can I turn my back on her? I never could. They call it fixing. It's just compassion."

Michael looked at her—the way her medium length, wavy hair lay on her shoulders, how beautiful her eyes were when so full of concern, her manicured, long fingers, the warmth that emanated from her, and could not deny it—he was falling a little bit in love. His struggles last night seemed far away.

"Michael, she needs to get away from this island, and I mean to help her. I'd like to get her off the island without Tommy knowing—but he works at the ferry, and a lot of his friends do, too. I'm trying to think of someone who's got a boat to take us across. But it's got to be someone I can trust completely." She sighed deeply. "That's not so easy."

A slow smile crossed his face. "I think I can help you there."

She looked at him quizzically. He told her his idea.

"Ah, Michael, you are a wonder then. You can fly a plane? When in the name of Brigit did you have the time to learn to do that?"

A few minutes later, the pair went out to Colleen, and explained their plan.

Kathleen's phone rang early the next afternoon. She was quickly to the phone.

"Hello."

"Hey, it's me," Michael responded. She heard a sigh. "This is going to take an extra day at least. I need a flight check before I can use the plane. There's a group here called the Galway Flying Club. You can't really rent a plane, but I joined them. They have a brand new Cessena 152 that I am familiar with." He chuckled. "I learned to fly in one. But even if I get checked out today, I can't use it until the day after tomorrow. Also, I know you wanted to come, but it only seats two."

Kathleen felt disappointed. "Oh, that's okay, Michael. The most important thing is Colleen."

His next words brought a smile to her face. "Yeah, but it's kind of a bummer—I looked forward to, you know, hanging out with you on the way back."

"I did, too, Michael."

"I'll call you tomorrow about this time, but I'd say plan on seeing me Thursday."

"Okay." She added, "Michael, I could take the ferry over and meet you somewhere, maybe Galway. Depending, I guess on the timing of everything, we could spend the day together and come back in the evening."

"I can't think of anything I'd like more."

He called back the next day as promised. Before she had a chance to say anything beyond her name, Michael started in. "Guess who passed his flight check and can get the plane tomorrow morning about nine? I'll arrive at the airport in Kil Ronin by 9:30."

"Michael, that's wonderful. How long will it take to get to Tralee?"

"It's Farrenfoe airport, between Tralee and Killarney. It's less than eighty miles—we'll land before 10:30. I'll see her on the bus out to Dingle— there's one at 11:15, and then fly back—I should easily be back to Galway before 1:00."

"Let's meet about 1:30 then. You can find Salmon Weir Bridge—it crosses the Corrib River to the Cathedral. We can meet at the main doors to the Cathedral."

"That sounds great, but the timing could be a bit tight."

"Well, I'll be there at 1:30. If it's raining, I'll be inside."

Kathleen heard Colleen, who had been in her back yard, come in the back door.

"Alright, I'll see you tomorrow."

"Bye."

When Colleen heard the news, she smiled. "Well, and that's nice. I'm...I don't know if I can do this."

Kathleen took her hand and led her into the living room where they both sat on the couch. "Colleen, this is totally your choice."

Colleen sighed, then went to the window. "When I was a child, I used to love to come up to this end of the island, throw rocks into the ocean. Norah, your mom, me, we did everything together. Everything. People used to call us the Triplets. Tommy was handsome and was so attentive. Maybe I thought...."

She shook her head, turning back to Kathleen. "This island held everything we could want—cliffs, the ocean, fields to wander in, even the occasional tree to climb—lots of places for imagination and away from parents! I will never be that child again, but I'd surely like to wake up feeling a little of that wonder about life. It'll never happen here, with Tommy. Why do I have to leave everything I know to have any hope to be happy?" She teared up and turned back to the window.

Kathleen waited a moment, then went and put her arm around Colleen's shoulders. They looked together to the Atlantic. Though the ocean was too far to really see well, she thought of the waves incessantly coming in and out arriving and leaving. Arriving and leaving. Kathleen left Colleen to her thoughts and started to cut vegetables for a soup. She jumped at the loud pounding at her door. A voice yelled, "Katie, you got my Colleen in there? Colleen, I know you're there."

Colleen looked at Kathleen, who put her fingers over her lips and signaled for her to go into her bedroom. She looked around for sign of Colleen's presence, quickly putting her coffee cup in the sink.

"Kathleen, open up this damn door before I come through it."

"Wait a second, and stop yelling, I'll be right there." As she crossed the living room, she saw nothing that indicated Colleen's presence. She opened the door, and Tommy charged past her into the living room.

"Tommy, I have not invited you in…"

"I know she's here. COLLEEN. Where the hell is she, where are you hiding her?"

Kathleen moved into the opening between the living room and the kitchen. "Tommy, what are you talking about? Colleen isn't here, I haven't seen her since you told her she couldn't see me anymore."

Tommy looked down at her. "She's hiding in your bedroom, isn't she?"

"She is not here. I want you to leave."

"You get out of my way, or I'll move you."

Kathleen swallowed, but refused to move. Her heart turned over rapidly, and she felt bile and panic rising. Tommy reached out with both hands, grabbed her by the shoulders and physically forced her into the kitchen. He gave her a little push and turned to the bedroom. She went to the drawer and took out a knife just before he came back out. She left it on the counter as he turned back to him.

He stomped to the back door and looked outside a moment. He glared at her when he came back. "She's probably long up the hill now. Well, she can't run forever, can she?"

Making a decision, she left the knife behind her on the counter but did not move away from it. "Tommy, you need to leave. You are not welcome here."

To her relief, after staring at her for a few moments he turned without a word and walked out, slamming the door.

Kathleen went shakily to the window and watched Tommy pull away in his car.

"Colleen?" she said as she sat down at her table. Her hands started to shake. She startled as the back door opened. Colleen came in, her eyes huge. "Oh. Oh, and if he'd of stepped out, he'd of seen me. I went outside instead of to your bedroom. I wanted to be able to run. Oh Katie….." She looked to cry, but held it in. "And what then have I brought down around you?"

"Don't you be worrying your head about that. He knows nothing." Colleen came to her, and they hugged.

"Tomorrow, Colleen, we'll take the back roads to the airport, get you on the plane, and he'll be none the wiser. No one will ever know."

Michael turned the Cessena out of the dogled, lining up the runway. In the distance he could see the town of Kil Ronin. He pushed in the throttle a bit, chuckling at the plane's simplicity. The throttle was just a knob one pulled out, pushed in. He adjusted the trim, and lowered the flaps halfway. The trip over had been short, but he experienced the freedom of flight, the feeling of liberation from gravity, and the sense that one could go anywhere, literally any place at all. Just point the nose, and see what was beyond the horizon. He thought of his father, plying his way up and down the waterways of Southeast Alaska, loving his job as no other person he'd ever met. His father's voice came into his head, talking of flying in that dangerous land. "Son, there's always more than one way to get there. Don't be afraid to take the longer route."

It was a cloudy day, but no rain and minimal wind. He adjusted the flaps to full, pulled back even more in the throttle, and eased the craft onto the runway. One small bounce—not bad, but disappointing all the same. He was able to slow enough to make the left turn into the drop off area before he ran by it, and he saw Kathleen and Colleen get out of the car. He pulled near them, set the brakes, and got out to help Colleen in. He put her suitcase in the small storage area behind the two narrow seats, and she got in the plane. He stepped back and looked at Kathleen. She said to him, "Wow, that is a small plane."

"Yeah, but it's a good one. No worries, we'll be fine." She stepped closer and spoke more quietly. "This is a fine thing, then, that you're doing, Michael. She'll be gone, and no one the wiser. Thank you."

Michael leaned in. She did not pull away, and he reached out to touch her hair. "I'll see you later today, promise. I'm glad."

"Yes, I have a ferry to catch."

Bobby Cooley, still smarting from when Michael had beaten him and his brother in a fight last week, watched the plane take off, rise out over Killeany Bay and turn right, heading southeast across South Sound. He ducked down in his car as Kathleen drove right by him a few moments later, and watched as she headed toward Kil Ronin, a couple miles distant. Tommy had asked him and some others to be on the lookout for his wife, but it still had been a bit of a lick to the pair driving by on the back roads. He went to a nearby phone booth, and called the ferry office, asking for Tommy. Their conversation was brief, and he liked their plan. Tommy was going to suddenly "get sick." Then, just as he was about to hang up, their plans changed—Tommy had just seen Katie come into the ferry office, buying a ticket. She was going to be off island. No one would be at her home.

"I've never flown in a plane this small," Colleen said over the sound of the engine.

"Don't worry, it's reliable—Cessena has been making these for a long time."

She looked at him. "This is...beyond thanks. It's hard to even know then why you'd do this for me. Other than, that is, that you like our Katie."

Michael smiled at the coy look in her eyes, transforming her face.

Our Katie. He had known that feeling of place once, growing up in Juneau. A thought struck him. "You're giving up a lot, leaving the island."

She sighed. "I am at that. I have nothing but hope. And the generosity of Katie."

He looked at her quizzically. "Tommy is working today—we stopped off at home on the way to the airport. I got a few clothes, a couple heirlooms from my family. I don't have much money. Katie gave me over two thousand pounds. That gives me three or four months to find a job and get established. I'll pay her back." She looked at him fiercely.

"Yes, I believe you will," he said. He smiled as he thought of Kathleen.

They passed the long green finger of Loop Head with its natural stone bridge and turned south and a little west toward the mainland. Crossing over, he was struck by the beauty of the green land below him, walled off into smart little sections. Then it was time to contact Farranforre Tower and begin his approach to the airport. Fifteen minutes later, Michael and Colleen were walking toward the bus stops. Then she stopped and touched his arm. "Michael, I need you to tell something to Katie. I am not going to Dingle, as I told her. I've somewhere else in mind, but I came here in case Tommy tries to follow me anyway." She took a deep breath. "Let her know I hope to see her again someday, and I am…." She stopped, suddenly unable to go on.

Michael nodded. "I know. You are grateful. I'll tell her."

She looked at him. "If you love Katie, be ever so kind to her."

She hugged him, and he kissed her lightly on the cheek. "That is from her. God bless you."

Back in Galway he approached the Salmon Weir Bridge, the freedom of flight still in his hands. He looked across the river to the Cathedral. The church was a massive basilica, with a huge green dome. He crossed the old stone bridge on the narrow sidewalk on the left, looking around for Kathleen. She'd said she might be inside, but it wasn't raining. He looked at his watch—1:50.

Then she was there. She walked quickly up. "I hope you haven't waited long—I wasn't sure which set of doors were the main doors—it looks like most people enter here, but this is the apse entrance, so I was around the corner at the main entrance. Did everything go well?"

"Yes, and she told me to thank you again. Also, she didn't go to Dingle." He explained what she'd done.

Kathleen shook her head. Michael continued, "Smart, I guess. She also told me about the money."

She gave him a half-smile. "She has the courage now, but needed the money to actually leave."

"She said she'd pay you back. But I don't think that matters to you."

She blessed him with a smile, put her arm in his, and asked, "Where to, then?"

He looked at her. "What?" You're the Irish woman here, show me something interesting. I want my money's worth!"

And she did. First the pair went in the Cathedral. It was massive inside, with a long, barrel-ceilinged central nave. He liked the Rose Window and the mosaic of JFK. They sat in a pew for a few minutes, and he knelt and prayed for Colleen, later lighting a candle for her just before leaving. The sky turned partly cloudy and they walked along the tree-lined river in a warm, dappled light. Kathleen suggested a small pub, and the Fish and Chips and Guinness were delicious. More than anything, Michael liked the feel of her arm in his. They caught a five o'clock bus to the last ferry of the evening.

Halfway into the forty minute boat ride, the sun slipped below some distant clouds. Their undersides glowed pink. The outdoor seats were narrow, and their shoulders touched. His left arm lay on the armrest between them. Kathleen pulled on a ski cap and rested her head on his shoulder, reaching across with her left hand, laying it on his arm.

He looked at the pink sky, remembering bits of his life—the way his father died trying to rescue some people in a winter storm, how his mom struggled so much after his death, his short time with Marianne Greene and the abrupt end to their relationship, and most of all, the years with Maggie. He caught the scent of Kathleen's hair. As if she felt it, she lifted and pulled her head back, looking him in the eyes. A bit of her red hair peeked out of the front of the ski cap. He reached over and pushed it away from her eyes, remembering the way she'd laughed at some dumb comment he'd made earlier. She smiled and lay her head against his shoulder again. It was exactly four weeks since he'd hiked up to Dun Aengus and its cliffs. Not enough time to love her, he thought as he closed his eyes. But what more can life offer? He thought again of Colleen, whose flight had changed today into a journey toward something new, flying on the fragile wings of hope. Oh, God bless you, Colleen, he thought again and moved his right hand over to take Kathleen's. This is enough, he thought, and gave himself totally to the feel of her head on his shoulder, the way her fingers caressed his hand. The warmth of her nearness. She dropped him off at Aoife's with a promise to see him tomorrow after work. He went to his room, sitting in his chair as the dusk turned dark. When she'd let him off, he'd leaned and kissed her lightly on the lips. As he pulled back from the kiss he saw a shift in her eyes, and it had shaken him. He had seen that look before—the way Maggie looked at him in their best moments. He touched his lips now.

He heard Aoife hurrying up the steps and knew with an unexplainable certainty that something was terribly wrong.

"Michael, its Katie. She's asking for you, but almost incoherent."

He raced down to the phone. "Kathleen, what's wrong."

"He's...Michael. My...my..." and then she started to cry.

"Kathleen?"

All she said was, "Please come, Michael. Please, now." And then started crying again.

SEVENTEEN

He hung up, and looked across to Aoife.

"What's happened? Is she okay?"

Michael felt panic threatening and took a deep breath. "I don't know, but it sounds bad—she could hardly talk. I need to…."

"Take my car," she said, turning and picking the keys up off an end table.

Michael grabbed them with a thanks and raced outside to the small Toyota. He yanked the door open and was slammed by the memory of running up to Maggie's car after her accident. Hit with a terrible immediacy, as if the experience were happening right now. He stood panting, right hand atop the open door left on the roof of the car, head drooping between his shoulders, his wife raised her dazed and confused eyes to his blood pouring from a wound on her head. For a moment he was no longer in Ireland but standing in the median of I-5 an hour south of Seattle, hand sliced open and bleeding, unable to get Maggie unstuck as the car caught fire. He reached to her again, and the fire got too hot. Backing away, the heel of his right foot hit a large stone. Looking down, he shrieked, "NO." Picking up the stone, running toward the car….

"Michael. MICHAEL," a voice yelled at him. Confused, he turned. A thought came to mind. Aoife.

"Michael, you can't go to bits now. You need to get to Katie."

It was as if the focus of his eyes went from something too close to see to something still near at hand, but farther away. Kathleen. Without a word, he got in the car and sped off. He raced west, going into the curve past Kilmurvey Bay a little too fast. His thoughts raced even faster, flitting from Kathleen to Maggie and back and back and back again. And then his last words to Marianne Greene flashed into his consciousness. The guilt and grief of final good-byes dimmed his vision, and fear for Kathleen shot through him and pressed his foot harder on the gas pedal. The road veered sharply left. He slid into the stone wall so hard he was violently slammed into the door. He jammed on the brakes and screeched to a stop.

"Fuck. Dammit!"

He started the car up again, driving fast, but not out of control. Less than three minutes later he pulled up in front of Kathleen's house, leaping from the car, running up the steps, knocking but not waiting she entered her living room.

Kathleen was kneeling on the floor, sitting back on her heels. She looked at him and dropped something, raising her hands to her face, covering her eyes. A sob escaped Kathleen as he crossed to her.

"Mag...Kathleen," he said, finally coming fully into the present moment. He looked again and at last saw the source of her suffering. Her cello lay on the floor, smashed into a hundred pieces. Her fiddle too was destroyed. A rage arose in him, at Tommy, but he could feel more behind it—at Maggie's death, at the stone he killed her with, all the way back to the guilt of turning his back on Marianne and further back to his father's choice to fly into impossible weather to try to save lives.

"I'll kill that…."

Kathleen looked at him and rose, taking a half-step away. Michael could not read her look, and his anger was cut off. For a moment, neither spoke into the silence.

"Kathleen."

He took one step, and she came to him. She nestled her head in his shoulder, and he buried his face in her hair. The deepest compassion he had ever experienced overwhelmed him like a flood of cool water, but the fire of anger was there, just to the side, hot coals waiting only a breath for ignition.

Finally she pulled gently away and sat back down on the floor. He sat next to her. She reached out and picked up three or four pieces as if to put the cello back together—but there was no fixit that could ever undo the damage.

"My grandfather played this fiddle all his life, got it from his grandfather and gave it to me when I was just eleven, right before he died. This cello." She shook her head and continued, her voice shaking. "Ah, Michael, it was a beautiful instrument, I could never have...the people of this island raised over, over twenty-thousand pounds for me." Kathleen looked at him, her eyes rimmed with tears. She dropped the slivers of wood back to the floor. He picked a couple of pieces up. What had once been capable of such beautiful music, what had been the gift of her whole community and the instrument of her soul, was reduced to mere wood. This he thought, is the full ugliness of Tommy's action. He was almost overwhelmed with the depth of the harm and felt the anger that had destroyed the cello.

"Michael, you scared me a minute there."

She was looking at him intently. "I mean, for a moment, you looked like."

She hesitated, opening the space into which his anger flared. "You really scared me."

He physically jerked, as if struck. Pushed the anger down. His voice still sounded harsh to him. "What do you mean? I looked like who? How can you compare me with that vile man?"

"I don't mean...."

He stood, his voice hard-edged in tension. "The whole way over here I was desperate for you, even smashed Aoife's car up a bit going around a corner." And his voice rose, "all I could think was the worst, and you...damn it."

He walked to the large window, already regretting his words, intent on making them right. At that instant, there was noise, and a woman rushed in. She took in the room for a few moments, then went to Kathleen. "Katie, Aoife called me, and I came right off. This is a terrible thing, Your cello. Sit down, here my love." Then, in a more practical tone she asked Kathleen, "Have you called the Garda in Galway?"

Michael turned just as Kathleed looked away from him to her. "Oh, no, I haven't thought about that. I suppose I should."

"Ah, Katie, and you had better. Do you have any idea then who could do such a thing as this?" She looked at Michael with distrust in her eyes.

"I don't know for sure, but probably Tommy."

"Do you want me to call for you?"

"Oh, please, yes, do."

The other woman went into the kitchen just as the phone rang. Kathleen said loudly, "Could you go ahead and get that, Maureen?" Then Kathleen turned to Michael and continued, nodding her head, "You must know I didn't, I don't think of...." She looked down at the waste on the floor. "It does no good." She spoke slowly, as if considering her words carefully, but Michael could see her hands still shook a little and her voice wavered. She took a breath, shook her head and looked up at him. "This is one of the worst things ever in my life, Michael. You only made it worse with hateful threats toward Tommy. I get it, but."

Her words petered out. Michael thought of the last bit of air leaving a balloon.

He felt caught in a tightening vise between a tidal wave of anger and his longing to hold her, comfort her. He was about to go to her when the woman, Maureen, came into the living room. "I suppose then that you're Aoife's renter—she says you need to come right off. It's an emergency call from America, and they're calling back in twenty minutes."

Michael looked back to Kathleen, shaking his head, no. Kathleen sat down on the couch, again putting her face in her hands. They stayed like that. Michael actually felt the ten feet between them seem to lengthen as each second went by. Maureen, who had returned to the kitchen yelled out, "Katie, I have the Garda. The line is ringing."

Kathleen stood. "You need to go," she said and waited. Ashamed and regretting his earlier response, his re-experience of Maggie's death still in his consciousness like the afterburn of a flash, worried about what the phone call meant, Michael froze. The moment turned into a second moment, and a third. Finally, Kathleen turned away to the other room.

He was desolate the whole drive back, worried about the call and the thought of leaving Kathleen like that. Michael knew his emotions had totally gotten the better of him, but as he calmed down, he recognized that it had been an overwhelming combination of past grief and present concern that had almost drowned him in its power. He desperately wanted to talk to Kathleen, but that had to wait. As he sped away from Kilmurvey Bay, anxiety rose like bile in his mouth.

Michael put down the phone, and said to Aoife, disbelief in his voice, "My mother's had a heart attack. I have to go home."

"Ah, Michael, and I am so sorry then. Has she, is she…."

"She's in the hospital and not expected to die."

"Ah, well there's that then. But it will take so long to get to her, and I am sorry for that. Do you want help with the airline?"

"If I could just get a number to British Airways or whomever."

Later, they sat together, Aoife having some brewed tea.

"Aoife, I have to go on the first boat, and it's so bad for Kathleen. And I mucked it up." He recounted what had happened, promising incidentally to pay for her car repairs.

"And you needing to leave so early in the morning. Listen to me. You have to believe that if you stayed the two of you could talk it out. I see how Katie looks at you—I know what that look is and have never seen it in her face before. Actually," she said as the thought occurred to her, "you should go to her now, even if you have to stay up all night."

He felt relief, as if her words gave him permission. "It's not as if I'll sleep. If I promise not to wreck your car again…."

Aoife laughed, "Go on ahead and wreck it—I'll make you buy me a Mercedes. Of course you can use the car."

He drove more slowly this time, thinking about what to say. At the end of the day, he really didn't care about Kathleen's words—he knew her well enough. And he had to admit, he had been damn angry. If he'd frightened her, that was on him.

When he knocked on the door, it was Maureen who answered.

"Michael," she said when they were sitting on the couch, "it is Michael, no?" He nodded his head. "She's taken a powerful sleeping pill and is finally out. You shouldn't wake her."

He sighed and looked down. "I'm going to get some paper and a pen and leave her a note. Can you give it to her?"

"Ah, yes, lad, that I will."

"What time is the Garda coming?"

"They said they'd be here by ten in the morning."

He wrote slowly, carefully, thinking about each sentence, sealing the letter in an envelope, giving it to Maureen.

Kathleen woke and glanced over at her clock—6:34. Memory came flooding in—her cello and fiddle. She lay, staring up, feeling as blank as the ceiling above her. When she had gotten home last evening, filled with the lovely afternoon and Michael—oh. Oh. Michael. A second wave of emotion washed over her—disappointment and sadness at what had happened between them. And concern, for whatever had occasioned the phone call from Juneau.

What a relief, when he'd come through the door. Seeing the instruments laying in slivers across her living room floor had left her numb with disbelief. Such an action was beyond any limit of behavior she had ever experienced, and next to the death of her dad four years ago, was the worst thing to ever befall her.

She heard a rooster crow from one of the broods that wandered the island and belonged to no one. She yawned as she went to the bathroom and brushed her teeth. Maureen was sleeping on the living room couch under one of her large shawls. Kathleen smiled in gratitude. Looking out the large window, she decided to walk down to the ocean, leaving five minutes later, closing the door quietly so as to not awaken Maureen.

The wind was pushing in lightly from the west and woke her all the way up. She quickly left the whitewashed homes behind, pausing occasionally to let the feel of the air collect her attention. In twenty minutes she reached the shore by crossing over the loose stone and small patches of scrub grass, looking across the short distance to the flat Brannock Islands. The incessant sound of the Atlantic soothed. The tide was in, water surging over the small cement breakwater built decades ago. Eeragh Lighthouse lifted from the farther of the two small islands, beyond which lay the ocean. Kathleen sat down among the stones, pulled up her knees and closed her eyes.

She felt their presence immediately, like pockets of subtle light among dimmer shadows and thought about what she knew of them—her family made real in stories she could recite by heart, all the way back to her great-great grandfather Tomas. With his brother Sean he'd put the currach near here, been caught in a storm and never returned. Her great-great grandmother Mauve walked the high cliffs of the island every day after their disappearance—some said she was mad as can be, but at this moment Kathleen felt she understood Mauve. The loss of her instruments and the uncertainty about Michael and his phone call brought an aching to her heart such as she had never experienced. She thought for some odd reason of a magazine article about how geese mate for life, and that when one died, the other would stay nearby, exhibiting all the human signs of grief. A wave shushed over the seawall. Kathleen watched for several minutes as wave after wave gurgled over and disappeared back into the ocean. She was pulled into a depth of restless questions that seemed to drop into an unfathomable deep devoid of all light.

She felt the moment her ancestral loves reached out and touched her and sat for a few minutes wrapped in their love and the peace that came with it.

She still didn't know what Michael's phone call had been about. The first thing she would do when she returned was head up to Aoife's and find out.

Then, as if her ancient loves warned her, Kathleen turned. A couple hundred feet away, Tommy stood, still as a statue, his eyes intent on her. She realized in an instant that he was closer than she was to the nearby "T" in the road she needed to reach to get home, nearly a mile distant. He started slowly toward her as Kathleen stood and edged sideways toward the smaller crossroad nearby, dropping down and picking up two large stones just before stepping onto the road. If she needed to, she would throw the stones at him and run. He stopped about forty feet from her.

"Where is Colleen?"

"I don't know."

He took a couple more steps. "Here's what I know—that fucking American flew her off the island. But he's not here now. This is just you and me. Where did he take her?"

"She'll not return to you, Tommy. I don't know where she went. You are blocking my way. I'd like to go home."

He said with a quiet intensity that frightened her, "Where did he fly her, goddamn it?"

Kathleen wondered if she could get around him, outrun him. She was slim and had always been a swift runner as a child. She was not sure she could outpace him in a dead sprint. But he was big and a bit overweight. If she could get away with a small lead, she might be able to stay far enough in front of him until he tired. It was her best chance, to throw the two rocks and try to sprint past him.

Just then two young boys and a girl came walking into sight at the "T" and she didn't hesitate. When Tommy turned their direction, she dropped the stones and ran as fast as she ever had, past him even as he turned back to her. He gave chase, but then the sound of his pursuit stopped. Turning onto the main road, she looked back. Tommy was standing and staring at her. She slowed her pace, but kept running. He moved then to her dismay, she realized she was running by his parked car. Panicked, she sprinted again. A short time later came the sound of his car starting. It would be impossible to reach the relative safety of the houses still far up the hill in front of her, so she raced to the waist-high stone wall on the right, crossed over and angled up and away from the road. She was fifty yards away when she heard the car stop, and the engine turn off. Tommy got out, but to her relief he did not pursue her. As she stood panting, he yelled.

"You surely can't hide from me on this island. I won't stop until you tell me where my Colleen is. Eventually, you will tell me." Then he got in his car and left.

Shaken, Kathleen continued across the grass-clotted, deeply cracked pavement toward home. The Garda was coming in a few hours, and she was relieved. For now she wanted to see Michael something fierce and have him hold her.

At 7:20 Michael called Kathleen, but no one answered. He hugged Aoife good-bye. When the taxi let him off at the ticket office, he hoped to see her waiting for him. He stayed on the dock until the last moment, eyes scanning the road for any sign of her. She did not come. At last he boarded the boat back to the mainland, trying to block his pain, ignore his frustration. He wanted to hope, but it was small comfort.

Maureen was not there when Kathleen got home, but a note explained that she would be back in a couple hours to see if Katie would like her there when the Garda came. She smiled in relief as she absently picked up the envelope underneath Maureen's note—she would indeed like Maureen to be there. Thinking to have Aoife there as well, she went and dialed her up, but no one answered. A glance at the clock, and Kathleen laughed at her absurdity—it was just 8:25, and she was going up to Aoife's anyway, to see Michael. She could ask Aoife then. She returned and picked up the envelope, seeing immediately that it was a note from Michael. She quickly scanned it.

Kathleen,

I came by just after midnight to see you, to talk, but you were asleep, and it seemed best not to wake you. I'm sorry for my reaction tonight, and I really want to see you before I go. I'm leaving on the 8:30 ferry. I have to go to Juneau. My mom is okay, but she had a heart attack. Can you meet me at the ferry terminal? I'll be checked in before 7:30, so we'll have some time together before I leave.

M

Kathleen looked again—she would miss the departure time by a few minutes, but it was not unheard of for the ferry to be late. Grabbing her purse, she ran out to the car and raced toward Cill Rónáin. It was 8:35 as she sped down the turns that led to the front street of the town. The boat was gone. She parked and walked up to the dock. The ferry was visible in the distance. Knowing it was fruitless, she waved and watched until she could see the boat no more. "Safe home, Michael, safe home," she whispered, lonely.

Tommy was standing by her car, but in her sadness she walked right up to him. "Get out of the way, Tommy, unless you're going to threaten me right here," she said, indicating several people on the street nearby.

"I just started two weeks of vacation. If I get you alone, the first thing I'll do is…."

Anger rose up. "I'm seeing the Garda in an hour, Tommy. Care to finish that sentence?" She knew she was being reckless but could hardly stop herself.

His eyes looked flat as he said in an emotionless voice, "The Garda will leave. What then?" She watched him walk away.

"Ah, then, Katie, you are a fool of a girl," she said to herself. Not ready to head home and face the Garda, she crossed the street and walked down onto the sand and gravel brach. The bay was roughed up by the freshening west wind, and she sat on a stone near the water, thinking. Slowly, an idea came. She didn't smile because the idea would be dangerous, but if the Garda did not help, she would not simply wait for Tommy. She would act first.

PART III

"Go forth from the land of your kinsfolk and from your father's house to a land I will show you."

Genesis 12:1

EIGHTEEN

Juneau, September 1980

Vince found it ridiculously easy to follow Marianne because she spent so much time in the Church. She sat on the left, a couple rows back from the front. Two or three times he'd carefully taken the narrow stairs up into the choir loft, his heart racing at this tiny invasion into her life.

She was stupid clueless. Today he'd been lucky. He'd seen her come out of the 5 & 10 store and cross Front Street to Casler's Menswear. He wondered what she'd buy in a guy's shop. Now she trudged up Franklin to Fourth. Damn. She was a looker. Can't believe she don't have a man. With no idea where this would lead him, he had no plans to just forget about her. He liked his job well enough but following Marianne brought excitement into his life.

He was disappointed when she ran up the stairs into the building next to the church. Impulsively he decided to go on into the church anyway, sitting up front on the right side, his eyes drawn ever back to the nearby statue of Mary gazing at the baby Jesus in her arms.

A half hour later Vince was back home. He liked having a day off in the middle of the week, although he sometimes wished he didn't have to work Saturdays. It was nice to have the apartment to himself for a few hours. He felt edgy. Last night, now that he had been good. For the second time he'd gotten into a fight. Although, it hadn't been much of a fight, so to speak of. He'd clocked Bobby twice from behind, and Bobby hadn't gotten up.

Oddly, he'd refrained from kicking Bobby a couple times.

It felt good. That asshole probably didn't even remember him from sixteen years ago. Before he'd accidentally killed the Williams' dad, he'd bragged to his friend Bobby about how he was going to beat the old man up—but then Bobby had snitched on him at the trial. Well, Bobby boy, he thought you got what you deserved. Revenge is best served as a cocked fist.

Pellets of hard rain splattered against the living room window in a massive gust of wind. Vince went over to it and looked left toward Starr Hill a couple blocks distant and just out of sight behind some trees. Johnny fucking Williams lived up there. And his sister, whatever her name is. Eve, Eden, whatever.

Johnny. Now Johnny was no Bobby. Johnny was dangerous. He'd been as mean as a bad dog as a kid and had been in the Army, Special Forces, he'd heard. He'd been vicious in their fight sixteen years ago. Well, Vince is dangerous too, he thought to himself. And I want Johnny to see me coming.

Another gust hit the window, and the view disappeared as the dense rain blurred the pane.

"Hi, Marianne," Sr. Kris said, "get that wet coat off. What a soggy drencher—Winter isn't far away now. Would you like some tea or coffee?"

"Thanks, Kris, a cup of coffee would be nice. Just black is fine."

Sister Kris headed back to the Rectory kitchen. Marianne pulled her hair back, fingers running along the damp hairline. A candle burned on an end table between her chair and Sr. Kris', filling the room with a pleasant, waxy scent. She half-closed her eyes, glad to be out of the storm and into a quiet, calm space. So, Marianne thought, El Salvador and becoming a nun.

Sr. Kris returned with the coffee. The pair sat in silent prayer for a minute. Finally, Sister Kris took a breath and the pair opened their eyes.

After a couple moments, Marianne said, "I'd like to talk more about El Salvador. And maybe a bit about becoming a nun. It's hard for me sometimes to keep the two separate. I could go to El Salvador, I mean, my nursing skills would be so helpful, whether or not I'm a nun or sister. I have written the Maryknoll Missionaries in California, expressing my interest."

Sr. Kris nodded her head. "I think they'd consent to you living with them for a while to see what convent life is like. It's a serious decision, as I'm sure you're aware. I like being a sister, I am happy. I have close friends, and every day my life is filled with prayer and purpose. It isn't always easy, and I sometimes get lonely. I miss my community in Victoria a great deal. And sometimes I do feel the loss of not having a husband and family. But no life is easy. Grief and struggles seem to always be waiting behind the next turn. No one escapes this. You know this as well as anyone. I am grateful every day for my life and vocation and would choose it again."

Marianne smiled, liking that Kris, while sensitive and compassionate, did not avoid difficult topics, got right to the point. Her thoughts flitted quickly over her struggles in her early twenties.

"Honestly, I feel peace about El Salvador when I am praying, but the idea of going down there feel absurd sometimes because I jump in anxiety at every little thing." She stopped, furrowing her eyebrows as she sipped on her coffee. "I know that sounds contradictory—when I am praying I feel peace, but later it seems ridiculous."

Sr. Kris nodded her head. "I understand that well. It's not all that unusual. Partly this comes from your past, but prayer is often like that—we walk slowly until our choice clears. It means you need to continue to pray, and if the call is genuine, you will find the peace that surpasses all fear, as St. Paul said." Sr. Kris smiled. "Somewhere in one of his Letter, I'm not exactly sure which."

Marianne laughed, pulling her hair back.

"But that peace, even joy," Sr. Kris continued, "will move more into the whole of your life. This is how you learn to trust your decisions.

"As to the risk in El Salvador, how could I say anything that you haven't already thought of? The danger of being killed is real. If they'll murder someone like Archbishop Romero, they'll kill anybody. Still, if you continue to feel this peace in prayer," here she paused, pursing her lips, "I have never thought it healthy to flat out desire martyrdom, as some of our early saints did. But he needs of the poor are real there, overwhelmingly desperate, and so your call might authentically be to go there. You are right about how helpful you could be as a nurse. But have no illusions about the risk."

Marianne nodded. "What you say makes a lot of sense. I've never thought God has a specific plan for people or for me. I do think we are all called to use our talents in his service. Yet, when I gaze at Jesus on the Cross, it is as if God looks right into my soul and is asking me to be his presence as a nurse to the poor in El Salvador. It's an odd feeling, I mean, that it is so specific."

"Then keep praying, and listen. Nothing is more important than a listening heart."

Silence again inhabited the space of the room. Sister Kris waited.

Marianne said "I'm not as sure about being a nun. I guess I am concerned about what we just started talking about last month—that I am afraid of intimacy with men since I was raped. Except for Michael, I have never had a healthy relationship with a man. It's not as if no one is interested, lots of men are and I've gone on dates, but I'm never happy after a short while. Of course," and here she frowned, "some of them were troglodytes, acting as if having sex with them ten minutes after we met was some kind of gift." Her laugh was brittle.

Sister Kris thought a moment. "I've known women who became nuns because they feared men, and in some cases it led to a deep unhappiness. I would encourage you to take you time, just as if you were thinking of marrying someone. Pray about it, think about it, write about it in your journal. It's a life decision that deserves your total presence."

After a little more silence, they chatted about their sadness over Archbishop Romero's assassination, and then about the new young Pope John Paul II, who was emerging as more conservative than either of them would prefer. At Marianne's request, they ended their time with fifteen minutes of silent prayer. They set a date to meet in a month. Marianne pulled on her coat and cap, took a deep breath and stepped out into the stinging rain. She kept her head down, eyes focused right in front of her as she made her way back to her car.

Earlier in the day Johnny had woken when the wind shook his bedroom window. Coming home had complicated his life. The war dreams had returned—not flashbacks exactly, but close enough to what he'd done in 'Nam that his guilt took on a renewed immediacy. Most nights he watched the minutes tick off the clock: 1:13 AM, 2:28 AM, 4:01 AM. He feared sleep, but it always came eventually. Last night was the same, and eventually he drifted off into his dream-hell. Again, he pressed the trigger of his M60. Again, he heard the screams of children as the shells ripped their bodies.

This morning he'd stayed within himself. Some days, like a raft on a river, he seemed to drift, occasionally even uncertain if he still had his arms or his legs It was a strange sensation in which some small part of his mind knew the arms and legs had to be there, yet it still seemed he was without them.

Thinking to himself, got all my body parts, so it's a good day. He rose and walked over to the window. Happy fucking anniversary.

Johnny looked into the steeply rising back yard where their father had been murdered by Vince sixteen years ago today. He was sure it was Vince who had brought about the return of his nightmares. Truth was, hard as this was to admit, Vince probably actually hadn't intended to kill that day—beating people up seemed to be his style. Mike had been right about that. Made no difference.

Rising up from the grass of their yard like a whale's back was a protrusion of slate, the hard, immovable solidity upon which his father had fallen and fractured his skull after a punch by Vince. As his father lay dying, Evie, who'd been picking blueberries with their dad, attacked Vince from behind. Vince had flung her aside as easily as if he were swatting at a fly. She could have run then, but didn't. She leapt up and came at him again. Vince hit her hard two or three times just as he, Johnny, having arrived home with his mom, came around the corner.

Taking it all in in less than a moment. His father unmoving in the middle of the yard. Vince standing over his moaning sister. Hatred overpowered him. Little of what followed was clear to him. The police arrived, to find Johnny on the ground bleeding from serious cuts on his face, hurting from two broken ribs, dazed by what would be diagnosed as a serious concussion. Vince tried to flee, hampered by an arm that Johnny had broken, his mouth bleeding where two teeth had been knocked out.

Their father had died a few hours later from an internal brain hemorrhage. He'd been a security guard for the Alaska Steamship Company. It came out during the trial that Vince was exacting revenge on Robert, who had testified against him after Vince attempted robbery at the company's freighter dock.

He was found guilty on the lesser charge of manslaughter. Vince had turned toward them with hatred in his face as he was led out of the courtroom the final time. He'd mouthed something—Johnny always believed it was, "You're dead," just before he'd casually thrown off the words about having raped Marianne.

He heard his sister in the hall before she knocked. As always, Evie entered with two cups of coffee. She handed him one and looked out the window. Neither spoke for a few moments.

"God, Johnny, that was an awful day, the worst of my life. I wanted to kill him—if I'd had a gun, I would have. I'd of emptied it in him."

"World'd be a better place."

She looked at him and he felt the contradiction between the love in her eyes and his inner chaos.

"Still every night, isn't it?" she asked.

He didn't pretend to not understand. "Pretty much—it's a relief mom's bedroom is so far away. She doesn't hear, doesn't know."

"Johnny," she whispered, "what can I do? Can't you go see someone?"

He shook his head. "I won't say counseling didn't help, but I've lived with this a long time. I won't lie to you, It's worse since I came back to Juneau."

"I've read about new medicines."

He cut her off. "Yeah, I know about some new drugs. I won't be taking any of those. They blunt your clarity, some of them even take away your self-protection instinct. I won't risk that while Vince is around." He seemed on the verge of saying more, then stopped.

"What?" she asked.

"It's taken a long time to say this. Marianne Greene has actually got me thinking. I've never seen a Vietnamese person as more than the enemy. What the hell was the value of war? Oh, hell, I sound like one of those damn protestors. It's not that. What I mean to say is, sometimes I think of all the killing all that fear and hatred was released in me, and I think I'll never live a regular life again."

"Johnny, don't say that. Please. There are thousands, tens of thousands of mothers who grieve that their sons are dead. Life always has value.'

She set her coffee down, put her hands on his shoulders and looked at him. It was like looking into the eyes of their long dead father, deep brown pools of determination below a high forehead. Love leapt between them and he hugged her.

"All right, Johnny. But please, please, *please*, if it's ever too much, come to me. I'll help you make it through the night. I will be there."

Unusually for Juneau, a jolt of thunder made them jump. You won't be there, he thought. I won't let that happen.

NINETEEN

After closing the front door hard on his way out, Johnny walked down Starr Hill and headed along Basin Road as it curved up and around the Knoll and into Last Chance Basin, the narrow valley behind Juneau. The rain from yesterday had stopped, but the road was still wet in the damp air. The forest dripped, painting the leaves of Devil's Club with a sheen of moisture. Clouds draped the steep side of Mt. Juneau down to a few hundred feet, its massive cliffs invisible behind their curtain. The trees seemed alive with movement as thick fog flowed sinuously up through them. Feeling the tension in his shoulders and neck, Johnny finally slowed at the end of First Bridge. Except for the rush of Gold Creek, it was quiet, all animals hidden in their lairs. Including all the people, he thought, noting that there was no one else back here with him.

Evie had tried twice yesterday to talk to him. He shook his head. He knew she loved him, but Evie wanted more than he could give. She would never understand if he shared completely what had happened that day in "Nam."

Today was one of the times he could not feel much. He knew he loved Evie and his mom, his cousin Rock, Aunt Chicken, a couple friends. But he did not feel it. The moments of his days seemed to emerge from a deep obscurity, scenes appearing like a photo album of someone else's life as the pages randomly turned. The past and present interwoven too tightly. The horror of what he'd done in Vietnam, his father's death and his hatred for Vince squeezed into immediacy.

He was homeless in a world of normalcy—he doubted any longer that such a thing as "normal" really existed.

Not far from Second Bridge, his sister stepped down from the forest on the right. She had taken the Shortcut, an old switchback above their home, and dropped down a deer trail from the top of the ridge to meet him here.

He glared and shook his head. "Just go home, Evie. I don't want to talk to you. Jesus, can't you get that?"

Evie nodded her head slightly. "I get it, Johnny. But I couldn't just let you go." She gazed at him a moment as she pulled her ponytail forward, tucking it under her green Halibut Jacket. "I feel like you are changing right before my eyes. Don't think Mom hasn't noticed. Yelling at us like you did—what is that? What is it? You left in a huff and she asked me to see if I could find you, and I figured you were headed to the Stump."

He smiled a bit, his tension easing. "No one else would know that but you. I always liked that Uncle would take the both of us to the Stump to teach us. Christ, the things we can do—call grouse, find where the ripe blueberries are, when."

Evie laughed, her voice softening. "How many people our age can build a salmon trap?"

"For all the that does us."

She responded, sounding wistful. "You used to carve so beautifully, Johnny. I was envious."

Uncle Walter had lived as a child in their ancestral village down past the mouth of the great Taku and was a boy of seven when most of the village moved to Juneau in the late 1800's. He'd died when Johnny was a year out of high school and thinking of joining the Marines. After he died, when Johnny needed to think, he would walk to the Stump and talk with Uncle. People might laugh, but he believed Uncle was present to him there.

As if she could read his mind, Evie said, "You aren't the only one who goes to the Stump. He would not be happy that you are cutting us, me, out of your struggles."

He said flatly, "There are things not even Uncle knew about, Evie. Just go home."

He put a hard edge in his eyes.

She said mockingly, "You can't scare me."

Johnny felt a surge of reckless anger. "You wanna know then? You wanna know what the hell I did? I set a booby trap, Evie. I set a goddamn booby trap and a bunch of runts come along and got blown the fuck up." He punctuated the last few words hard, each coming out like a rifle shot. "That's what I did, I blew up a group of children. You think Uncle has an answer for that?"

Evie stared at him, her eyes getting large. But she did not waver. "You used to protect me, Johnny. I remember in first grade, crying and crying because I had been called a dirty Tlingit so many times that I would come home and take a shower and put on clean clothes and still feel dirty. You were just eight yourself, and you held my hand and swore no one would hurt me. And I know you hated that you couldn't make that true, but you were always always there. You never let me down."

Then Johnny saw something he hadn't seen since the day Vince killed their father. Evie cried. She wiped roughly at her cheeks with two fists and dropped them to her side.

"I know your heart, Johnny. I know it, and it is good. You would never deliberately kill children, you would protect them. You walked little Albie Johnson home to his mother when he fell and skinned his knees bad. Nobody else helped him. You did. I remember you singing to that dying grouse we came across up past The Cross, trying to comfort it as it died. If the war did that to you, then it could do it anybody. So go on to your Stump, but remember that, Johnny. Remember who you are."

Evie looked at Johnny a moment longer, then turned back to the trees and headed up the deer trail. Before she disappeared into the forest, she wiped again at her tears.

He did remember helping Albie. How, Uncle, have I become so much less?

Johnny stopped for a moment on Second Bridge to watch the creek rush by underneath. The clouds thinned, and he watched them for a couple minutes slowly rise like a curtain. Light flooded the narrow valley. The high stony ridges of Mt. Roberts, rounded like giant shoulders, appeared as if from nothing. He'd shot his first deer on its flank when he was nine. Slowly his memories began to seem like *his* memories again. He felt momentarily like an empty basket that was filling up with the contents of his life.

Will I ever be able to share with Evie, or anybody, the worst of it?

Johnny.

It was as if Uncle stood next to him, so clearly did he hear his name. He turned and headed the rest of the way across the bridge. A hundred feet further and he took a small track that angled to the right a few feet then left it and headed between two massive boulders to the nearby creek. The Stump was just that, a stump half in and half out of a calm eddy. He sat down on a large boulder nearby. The sound of the rushing water soothed his racing mind, and Johnny allowed himself to relax his accustomed alertness, thoughts drifting like the earlier fog. He remembered Uncle and their last conversation in St. Ann's Hospital.

You are too angry, Johnny. Too ready to fight. Fighting, that should be rare. Words are better. Once you choose to fight things fall out of control. You think you have taken care of what is right in front of you, but somewhere else that you don't see the violence pops back up.

Uncle, how can you say this to me? You know how I defended Evie, and so many other kids. Should I have just let the bullies walk all over us?

No. But now, Johnny? I love you more than my life and tried to guide you along the right trails of being a Tlingit. But you are too ready with your fists. You must be careful or everything will turn into a fistfight. Raven always used his wits to outthink Grandfather. Tell me, be honest. How is it that you could lose such a friend as Mike?

His inner conversation was interrupted by an intuitive sense of change, as if a deer was noiselessly passing by. He opened his eyes. From the side, something. He looked more closely and his mind erupted in a cacophony of off-key voices. Less than a hundred feet away, up Basin Road, Vince stood still as a mountain. Johnny was off the boulder and moving up toward him before he'd even thought to do so. Vince stepped off Basin onto the smaller track. The two stopped when they were about thirty feet apart, Vince slightly uphill from Johnny.

"Nice teeth," Johnny said, referring to the replacements for the ones he had knocked out seventeen years ago.

Ignoring the comment, Vince said, "Warhoop, I just saw your sister."

Johnny felt rage and panic rise like bear claws in his throat.

Don't worry, I left her alone. I saw you talking to her, and when she came back up the trail, I hid. She walked by without a clue. I was behind a tree, could'a hit her ten times outta ten with a rock, she was so close. Some Injun she makes—I thought you people were supposed to be like...."

"If you threaten my sister, I'll break you right now."

Vince shrugged. "I heard you were good at killing Asians. You think you can break me, you're welcome to try." He stopped for a second, as if thinking. "But hell, I ain't interested in your squaw-sister. I ain't even really interested in fighting you, 'less you want it."

He began to speak more slowly. "It's that blonde I got my eye on. You know the one? I saw you with her. Marianne. Mmm. She's fine. I had her once, you know? Right back there, other side of the bridge. My first. She whimpered like a runt dog. What d'you think of that?"

Johnny said nothing. He started forward, but just then a figure raced by Vince and up to Johnny, pushing him back. He stumbled a bit, then found himself looking into the eyes of his sister. She turned back to Vince and said, "This dumb squaw knew you were there, you, you....I followed you back here." Then she turned on Johnny, breathing hard. He had never seen her look so fierce. "You have to walk away from this, Johnny. Think. Think for Christ's sake. If you hurt him, what then? What then, Johnny?"

Vince spoke up. "Hey, bitch, what if I don't let him walk away?"

Johnny watched his sister turn to Vince.

She said, "Then you'll have to fight me, too."

Vince laughed. Johnny was proud of Evie in that moment but afraid for her as well. He said quietly, "Evie, get the hell out of here. You'll just be in my way." She turned back to him, and at that moment Vince sprinted toward the pair. Johnny pushed his sister aside, bracing himself too late as Vince ran into him. Johnny was touch but outweighed by a lot and grunted as he hit the ground hard, his head banging onto the packed dirt. Dazed, he tried to roll. Vince hit him twice in the jaw. Johnny tasted blood. He tried again to roll, his body sluggish to respond. Something happened, and Johnny realized that Evie had attacked from the side, hitting Vince in the shoulder with a large tree branch. He leapt off Johnny, reaching for her. She was quicker and backed away. Then she screamed and came at him, swinging the branch. Vince blocked it, grabbed her arm and pulled her body into his. He picked her up and threw her through the air. She hit the ground, rolled and lay still.

Johnny rose unsteadily. Vince laughed as he walked toward him. Johnny watched through dazed eyes as again a figure flashed by him, hitting Vince from the side, knocking him off his feet. Evie? He thought in confusion. How could she do that?

It was not Evie. A tall, slender man leaned down and put his baseball cap back on as Vince rose to his feet and backed off a few steps.

The bearded stranger said, "You better think twice about fighting. It'll be two against one." He turned as Evie came up beside him. The man nodded his head and added, "Not two, three. And Evie here looks like she means to knock your brains out with that branch."

Johnny felt as if the earth were wobbling under him.

Wait. Evie? How did this guy know her name? He watched as his sister looked at the guy and smiled. Johnny took a breath, walking to stand on the other side of Evie. He wiped blood from his chin.

Vince eyed the trio warily. "Listen, buddy, I don't know who you are, but this ain't got nothing to do with you."

The stranger replied immediately, "I'm not the type to stand by and watch another get beaten up." At that he shifted his feet, turning partially sideways to Vince, looking ready to fight. But he kept his hands down.

Johnny bristled at what this new guy said. If Evie hadn't got in his way, it'd be different right now. Vince raised his hands and backed a couple more steps away, saying, "How about I fight you one at a time, right now?" He waited a few seconds. "No? Chicken-shits. You, baseball cap man," he continued, "you better hope I don't run into you alone. I'll put you in the damn hospital for a month."

The stranger said nothing. At that Vince turned and walked quickly away, back toward Juneau. No one moved until he was across Second Bridge. Then the man walked up to Basin Road and said without turning around, "I see nothing's changed with you. Still leading with your fists." He turned right, away from Juneau, toward Perseverance Trail and the high ridges that lay beyond.

Johnny, his head pounding and still feeling hazy, turned to Evie. "Was that....?"

She shrugged, wincing as she did so, grabbing at her shoulder. "You could have thanked him."

"Wouldn't'a been necessary if you hadn't shown up, got in my way. Vince rushed me and because of you, I didn't have time to get ready."

Evie sighed deeply as she rubbed her shoulder. "What are you going to do when you beat him up, Johnny? What then? What are you going to do when the cops come? And what if you can't beat him? You may not have noticed, but we're the ones hurting. Even if I got in your way."

"Did you hear him? Did you? He said he's the one who raped Marianne. And threatened her, too. And I don't believe that crap about him not being interested in you. What the hell do you want me to do?"

Evie looked deflated. "I did hear him, I did." She shook her head. "I don't know, Johnny. I don't know what the answer is."

"You were plenty willing to fight."

"I know. I know, I know, but somehow, we've got to find another way." She sighed again. "Let's not you and me fight."

Then he saw the wound and went to her. She had a cut that was oozing blood into her hair, a slight trickle of it running behind her left ear. She looked at him, saw the blood on his chin, and said, "Johnny, I am sorry I got in your way. And yes, it does hurt. I hurt all over. What are we going to tell Mom?"

He thought a moment. "You fell coming down the ridge, and I tumbled coming to your rescue."

"Why can't I come to your rescue?"

They both laughed, breaking the tension. "Well, you're the one with the cut on your noggin." Johnny continued, "Evie, well, I'm glad you're on my side. Why didn't you hit Vince on the head with that damn branch?"

"I was trying to, but I missed."

They laughed again.

Johnny said, "So that was Mike. Didn't recognize him with that beard. Guess I'm glad he came along. Looks like he's going back to Perseverance Trail." Johnny looked up the road, momentarily wishing to follow. He thought of how it had all ended between them years ago, the wish disappearing like a whale diving deep to where little light shines.

TWENTY

Michael took the stairs down two at a time. His mom called to him, "Don't run, Mikie." He smiled at the childhood refrain, kissing her on the cheek on his way to the kitchen. She smiled in return, asking for a glass of water. His mom was home now, after a minor heart event, as she liked to call it. Dr. Gibson had put her on a heart-healthy diet and moderate exercise regimen. She was thin, but her color had returned.

"Thank you, Mike," she said as he gave her the water.

"I'm thinking of heading down to the church for a while and then tromp on up to Cross on Roberts. You want to come?" he asked, jokingly.

"Ah, Mike, maybe someday I'll take you up on that. Seems I haven't exercised enough. Dr. Gibson has a pretty detailed exercise plan for me. Awfully optimistic, I'd say—he's got me walking three miles each day by April. Is he expecting me to walk through the winter?'

"Mom, they keep Basin plowed up to Second Bridge all the way through winter. I bet it's close to a couple miles anyway, up and back. Ready made for you. Just wear your winter clothes. I can help you get some good boots."

"Oh, Lord, I need a cigarette," she said, smiling as she did so.

Michael just looked at her. She laughed, then, waving him out the door with her hand.

It's not funny, he thought as he opened the door to leave. "Love you, Mom."

Within two days of arriving in Juneau, Michael thought it might have been better to have come here rather than remaining in Inis Mór. He'd had the idea before fleeing Seattle that he needed to be away from his mother and sister. And maybe that was right. But now, walking the narrow streets of his childhood he felt his sense of who he was solidifying and grew more peace as he considered the bewilderment that was Maggie's death and his part in it. What had felt false up until recently he now recognized most of the time as true. He had ended the suffering of the one he loved the most when all hope of saving her was lost. And if he didn't always feel the peace, he was learning to accept that as well.

But it was the long ridges between the mountain peaks that worked their healing power on him. He had climbed Mt. Juneau a couple days ago and then headed east along its rising four-mile ridge to the peak of Mt Olds, right to the edge of the Juneau Ice Field. It had been a cold, clear day, and the massif of Devil's Paw out at the Canadian border was dusted with snow on its upper reaches, appearing impossibly close. It was like looking at Antartica. He could see the beginnings of the huge Taku Glacier. Bundled up, he sat for a long time on a flat stone near the peak, and let the utter bounty and size of it all work its mercy, feeling his smallness, his insignificance in comparison to the vast panorama that opened up before him. The sheer grace of beauty softened a hardness that had sat for months like a stone in his gut, and joy bubbled up as he beheld the ice, the snow, the glaciers, the raw mountain peaks, the pale blue sky. Michael filled his lungs with the cold, crisp air that smelled of clean snow and promised winter.

He felt somehow enlarged even in his diminishment and smiled, remembering Father Reichert from Seattle University. The old Jesuit talked of paradox in such a way that many students felt compelled to write the word in capital letters in their notes. Enlarged in diminishment—PARADOX. He'd raised his eyes to the sky at the thought, breathed again and relaxed. Kathleen, as was frequently the case, slipped into his thoughts.

Michael wanted to call her every day but settled for every second once. Their conversations left him dissatisfied. They avoided what had happened that last night in Inis Mór. He longed to talk about it but not over the phone. And she was evasive when he brought up Tommy, saying merely that she was okay, staying at Aoife's, and was going to work something out. It had only been nine days, but he felt a distance opening up between them, and he was unable to tell if that was simply their enforced separation or something more.

Michael thought all this in the two block walk from his mom's home to the Cathedral. He sprang lightly up the steps and entered the vestibule quietly. In the church itself, he noted absently that there were two women in the front, a younger one on the left and an older one on the right, with an older man sitting a couple rows behind her. He walked quietly up the aisle, genuflected briefly, and sat down a few rows behind the younger woman.

As a child, Michael had loved the details of the old church—the dark stained-glass windows, the statues and Stations of the Cross, even the intricacies of the wooden beams supporting the roof. In the intervening years the old windows had been replaced by ones that allowed in more light, but beyond that little had changed. The sanctuary even smelled the same, a mixture of wood, wax, incense, candles burning, and aging carpet. He looked down at the rounded top of the pew against which he kneeled, seeing where his friend David had in Sixth grade carved his initials, DB, into the grain of the wood. He'd wanted to do it too but chickened out. Now he wished he had.

Michael sat back into his pew and raised the kneeler up with his right floor. He always liked the quiet of the church. After yesterday's violent incident in the back Basin, he was drawn to this quiet memory-saturated space to acknowledge his need to pray.

It had been a disturbing scene to chance upon. He'd needed a moment to recognize Vince, but he knew Johnny and Evie right off. Neither Johnny nor Vince appeared to know who he was, although Evie had. Vince had been an asshole back then and was still one now, evidently. He shook his head and closed his eyes. He pictured Johnny in his mind and prayed for him. Lord, let Johnny know Your peace. He prayed for Evie as well. She'd possessed a fearlessness yesterday that he admired, but the anger in her eyes had taken him a back. He wondered again precisely what brought the fight about. Did people just get caught in a rut that kept bringing them forever back to the same old streets of hatred? Not that he couldn't understand Johnny and Evie. Jesus, Vince had killed their dad.

His thoughts darkened a moment as he remembered the end of his friendship with Johnny. He regretted it but knew he would do nothing differently if given the chance.

He did the hardest thing—he prayed for Vince. He imagined Vince's face before him and asked God's blessings on him. Michael always strove to pray from deepest part of his being and recognized that when it came to Vince, he was not able to do this. He did the best he could.

A subtle noise. Or a shadow. Something caught his attention, and he opened his eyes. A woman stood in the aisle a few feet away, looking at him intensely. For a couple seconds he saw simply a beautiful face, then everything flowed into a person and a name flooded with memories.

"Marianne?"

Without a word she entered his pew and sat right next to him. "Michael." She smiled. "Michael Flaherty, of all the gin joints, in all the towns, in all the world, you walk into mine."

He looked at her and laughed, a little too loud. Out of the corner of his eye, he saw the older woman turn their direction. But how could he not laugh now that Marianne quoted from *Casablanca*? Their movie. He remembered how hard Marianne had hit him in the shoulder when he coyly suggested that

Ingrid Bergman might be prettier than her. Which he hadn't really believed. She hit him so hard she hurt her hand and blamed him for that as well. But she'd been laughing the whole time.

He said, "Well, if I remember correctly, I was the one born here." He turned his lips up a bit. "The real question is, what are you doing here?"

She laughed quietly, turning her head back to the front of the church. Michael saw her eyes tear up. His protective instinct surged, and he was aware how close she was sitting to him. He remembered the time when she had been crying after her grandmother's death and how salty and warm her lips and breath had been. And later that evening, how soft her breasts.

She turned back to him. "I'm sorry, it's just so unexpected, you see? I'm not sure why. I just need to cry." She reached for his hand and squeezed it tightly as more tears flowed down her cheeks.

"Michael, how perfectly wonderful," she said, and that was all.

He looked at her as she silently let the tears fall, feeling again his guilt for having turned away in her moment of deepest need. Her face was a little thinner than he remembered, but she was, well, still lovely. Blond hair, shorter than it had been, flowed lightly over her shoulders and a few inches down her back. One of her front teeth still sat slightly crooked—he'd thought back then how that tiny imperfection made her sexier. But it was Marianne's eyes and long lashes that drew his attention the most, especially when she turned her head and glanced upon him. Light blue and beautiful.

The smell of her hair wafted to him, and he closed his eyes as more memories surfaced. For sixteen years the bitterness and guilt of the ending had darkened all his memories of her, of them. Now the sweetness of their year together filled him like the music of the morning birds. His eyes watered a bit as well. He thought of the song "O Sole Mio."

Vince had been frustrated yesterday when Mr. Baseball Cap had shown up and defended that asshole Johnny. He couldn't believe it when the same guy walked through the intersection a half block ahead of him and turned down Harris and could only laugh when the jerk went into the church. Vince waited a couple minutes and entered, tiptoeing carefully up the balcony stairs, wincing at the squeaks they made. He stopped near the top and peeked over the edge of the balcony stairs, wincing at the squeaks they made. He stopped near the top and peeked over the edge of the balcony into the church. Marianne was there as well. This did not surprise him. He watched as she rose, started back, and stopped by the man. She said something and sat down by him.

Well, look at those two love-birds, Vince thought. It took a minute, but then he knew who it was—Mike fuckin Flaherty. The perfect couple. To think I managed to break them up! He ducked as they stood, and a few moments later heard them leave the church.

Vince waited and then walked down the stairs. At the church's outer doors he saw the pair on the sidewalk below and stepped back. He strode a few steps back to the stained glass window opposite the main doors into where the pews were. It was actually three windows, set closely side by side, but clearly once scene. Writing in the left lower corner identified it as the Wedding of Cana. Screw weddings. His parents had hated each other, far as he could tell.

His mom. Vince experienced something unusual for him—gratitude. As a kid he'd never liked his mom. But she'd been nice to him since his release from prison. At first he hadn't trusted her, but he'd been home for weeks now. She always asked how his day was, and recently Vince found himself actually talking a bit about his job, the stuff he liked and didn't like. He no longer cringed when she hugged him or touched his shoulder walking by.

Vince went back to the church door. They were gone. He stepped cautiously out of the church, looking up and down 5th. A woman with a young boy in hand went by pushing a stroller. He walked quickly away from the church, passing Stroller-Woman just before the corner. About to cross, he stopped for a car that was coming down the hill.

He heard the woman shriek something, and the little boy raced by him into the street. Without thinking he ran after the kid, picked him up and leaped—a second too late. The breaking car caught him in the knee, spinning him in the air. Vince landed hard on his back, cradling the boy. Fuck, fuck, fuck.

He stood up and set the boy on his feet, who began crying loudly. Dammit but his knee hurt. Crying incoherently the woman, still pushing the stroller, ran up and grabbed her son, asking him over and over, "Are you hurt, Benjie? Do you hurt anywhere?"

Vince limped to the sidewalk. The driver got apologetically out of the car. Shitdamn it hurt. But he could walk. Maybe not broken. Now Vince just wanted to get away. No. No. No ambulance. I'm okay. I'm fine. Don't worry, don't worry. And the car was gone.

The boy's mother stood a few feet away. She said in a quavering voice, "Sir, oh God, thank you, thank you, thank you—you saved my boy's life." Vince heard her words from a distance, but then he looked at her, saw the fear and gratitude there and was pulled out of the pain.

She said again, "You saved his life. I can never thank you enough."

Vince nodded his head saying, "It's good, I'm okay, just glad the boy is okay."

Fifteen minutes later Vince sat on the couch of his mom's living room, leg resting on the coffee table, ice on his knee. He'd begged off from the mother as quickly as he could, unable to get the look of gratitude and words of thanks out of his mind. They left him bewildered, so far were they out of his experience. He felt like a pinball banging randomly around, pulled always toward some dark hole of "game over," but propelled anew back into the realm of play. Every time he tried to think back to her words, his whole life's experience rose up in defiance. What she said, it's bullshit. She doesn't give a flying fuck about you. She's just another bitch.

A picture kept emerging again and again in his imagination—it would not let go. He sat on the couch for a long time, unable to deny it: the look on her face as she thanked him. It did not lie. He knew the word for it. He felt it toward his mom. Gratitude.

He'd done something good. Even though his knee hurt, Vince couldn't sit still. He got up and limped out of the apartment.

TWENTY ONE

Inis Mór, September, 1980

Michael's tired voice spoke in her earpiece. "Kathleen, it's pretty late, I need to get to bed."

She heard him yawn and felt her usual uncertainty when saying good-bye to him. Where one might typically say "I love you" there was only good-bye.

She replied, "Okay. It's good to hear your voice."

He yawned again. "Yes, it is, Kathleen. Talk to you in a couple days?"

"Michael, I'll be off island for a while—call me in four days, okay? Sorry, it's a last minute thing," she lied. "I'm going to Galway to help my Aunt Claire, who fell and broke her arm."

"Oh, bummer." He hesitated, as if wondering why he couldn't call her there. But Katie didn't offer, so he said, "Well, I'll talk to you in four days then."

"Bye, Michael." Kathleen hung up the phone. She liked to take his calls at home, rather than at Aoife's, where she'd been staying, so she came down to her place those mornings. She sighed, looking west toward Eeragh Lighthouse and the Atlantic. It seemed like every time she and Michael talked, the distance between them lengthened. His mom was out of the hospital and doing well, which was clearly a great relief to him. But he never spoke of returning to Inis Mór, and she was not going to ask about that. She heard energy in his voice when he talked about being home in Juneau. The very way he said the word "home" left her feeling like an outsider. There was nothing to draw him back here anymore, unless it were her. He had returned to his real life. That's the way it felt. He arrived on Inis Mór like a whirlwind, and in the wink of an eye, blew away. They hadn't even really kissed. The singing together, the wonderful afternoon in Galway, the trip back on the ferry when they had held hands, their deep conversations, all that had drawn her to him—it was only two weeks ago he had left, but it seemed like a lifetime.

Still, he continued to call every other day, and she could feel his anxiety for her when he asked about Tommy. She chastised herself a bit for her life, but he would only worry if he knew what she was thinking about doing. She wanted to have time to carry out her plan and see it all the way through before she talked to him again. Four days seemed like enough for this.

She thought her plan a good one, but it depended on her ability to convince both Conlon and Tommy. To her relief, Tommy did not seem to be following her, and she considered doing nothing because there was a bit of a risk involved. But as always when thinking of Tommy and what he'd done, she felt her temper rising, and she was simply sick of the whole thing. He needed to be held accountable, and frankly Kathleen did not trust that Tommy was going to leave her alone. She was tired of worrying her head about him and decided to act.

She noticed the weather clearing out to the west. It looked to be a cool but dry day into tomorrow. Well, there's no moment like this one. She went to her phone and dialed Conlon's number.

When he answered, she explained what she would like to do.

There was doubt in his voice. "Are you sure about this, Katie? It sounds a little, I don't know, do you think it's a good idea?

"I'd rather be going on a picnic, but I've given this a lot of thought."

"All right, then."

It had been hard to wait all day, but finally it was evening. She picked up her phone, and dialed.

"Yeah."

"Tommy, this is Katie."

There was a pause. "What, then?"

"I've been thinking I want to meet."

He waited, so she continued, "I want to meet at Dún Aonghasa at 7:15 tomorrow morning."

He was quiet a moment longer, then asked, "Why the hell up there?"

"I want to be alone. There's things I want to say."

"You're gonna meet alone with me at Dún Aonghasa?"

She heard his skepticism and replied in an even voice, "Why not, now that I know I can outrun you? I'm safe there. And I want to be absolutely sure we're alone. There'll be none but us that time of day."

He laughed. "Yeah, you're fast like a deer. But it's a small island."

"That's why I want to meet. I'm tired of this. Just so you understand, I've let Aoife know where I'll be and why."

"You gonna be telling me where Colleen is?"

"I'll tell you everything I know. On my grandmother's grave."

Kathleen left just before 6:30 the next morning and headed cross country through the gaps in the stone walls, occasionally climbing right over them. Arriving at the west-side curve of Dún Aonghasa, she walked carefully to where the massive stone wall edged up to the cliff's rim. She stopped and looked east far across the water to the Cliffs of Moher. Somewhere out there Colleen was making a new life for herself. She sent a prayer to Brigit for her. Kathleen approached a ledge between the end of the wall and the long drop to the ocean made her way carefully across it, and scrambled up and into the inner sanctum of the ancient fortress. Staying away from the cliff face, she crossed to the raised stone platform in the middle of the enclosed space and headed to the entrance on the opposite side. It was early and the attraction would not open for two hours. As Kathleen approached the entrance, she veered slightly to her left, up to the wall. Hands and feet finding niches between the stones, she climbed to a ledge eight or nine feet up and peered over the top. She saw Tommy in the distance making his way up the path toward the ancient fortress. Between him and her two smaller outer walls rose, with a large area of tumbled stones to her left, looking like a graveyard of giant tombstones after an earthquake. A thousand years ago, any attackers would have had to stumble through these to reach even the shortest, outer wall.

Lots of hiding places.

Tommy stopped as he saw her looking down on him from above. When he came through the entrance, she picked up a couple stones.

"Jesus, you and stones. You threatening me again?"

"They'll hurt, and I'll run."

Tommy looked at her for a moment, then put his hands out. He said, "Nothing's changed. You know where my Colleen is, and I want to know." As he talked, he took a couple steps toward the wall.

Kathleen raised a stone, and said, "Just stay back. I promised to tell you everything. I really don't know where she is." He frowned as she continued, "Michael flew her to Tralee. Where she went after that, I have no idea." Against her will, she felt her temper raising. "But even if I did, you'd not learn from me. You went and destroyed my cello and fiddle. I wouldn't tell you now if you hung me over that cliff."

"You deserved it, Katie Flaherty," he said in a mocking voice. "You been thinking you're something special since you was young. But you're nothing. Worse than nothing. All those people gave money for that instrument, and later you come whining back here like a hurt puppy. Pathetic. You never deserved the thing in the first place. That's what people are saying, you know? How do you show your face?"

Kathleen felt hurt and responded impulsively, "You think that makes it okay to destroy my instruments? That's sick." She heard her voice rise at the end. Watch your temper, lass.

Tommy laughed. "I punched a hole right into your cello with my fist. Then I stomped on it with my boots. Smashed the fiddle over my knee. Listen up, lassie—you need to tell me where my Colleen is, or it'll get worse for you."

Bile rose in Kathleen's throat as he described destroying her instruments. Tears filled her eyes.

A voice spoke, "That's it, Katie. I think I've heard enough.

Tommy turned in confusion. Conlon walked through the entrance. It took a couple seconds before Kathleen could see that Tommy realized what had just happened. He looked up at her, hatred in his face.

He turned back to Conlon, shaking his head, saying, "I been friends with your da all my life. I held you when you couldn't even hold your head up."

"Doesn't make what you did right, Tommy."

Suddenly Tommy charged Conlon, slugging him low on his cheek. Conlon fell like a stone off a cliff. Tommy turned and ran to the wall, leaping and grabbing the ledge where Kathleen stood. He pulled himself up. She threw a stone, missing him, and took off running along the ledge. Tommy leaped back to the ground and ran across the grass inside the curve of the wall, cutting her off from an ancient stair that would have been her way down. She stopped.

Furious, she yelled down at him, "What the hell, Tommy?"

Conlon groaned as he sat up. Watching Tommy carefully, Kathleen retraced her steps on the ledge and climbed down to Conlon. She bent over and was helping him stand as Tommy came up. He stopped a few feet away, panting.

She stood, afraid and unsure what to do.

Conlon rubbed his jaw and said, "Goddamn Tommy. Funny way to treat someone you held as a baby."

"Oh, eff off. I suppose then you're going to be seeing the Garda."

"You've been going on Kathleen too hard. Breaking her instruments? What's that for? That cello was a gift from this whole island to her. You can count on one hand the people that didn't give. Hell, I've seen you at my pub on Fridays listening to her play and sing. She's a light for all our people. It's Colleen that left. Nobody forced her. Except you."

Kathleen could see Tommy tense his muscles, start to make fists. Then he turned quickly away, tromped across the space to the far side and stepped down onto and across the same ledge Kathleen had used fifteen minutes earlier.

She said, "You okay? Conlon, I'm sorry, I didn't mean for this to happen. I never imagined he'd attack you."

"I got a nice little headache for it. But it's better now, this way. Hopefully he'll back off, knowing we're going to the Garda. Let's head back and give them a call."

Kathleen took his arm and the pair started back. When they arrived at the road twenty minutes later, Aoife was waiting for them. She blurted out, "Conlon, what happened?'

He explained.

Aoife said quickly, "I'm surely sorry for that. But I got news, I got a phone call this morning. You'll never guess what."

When she explained, Kathleen thought, she's right, I never would have guessed. This might change everything.

Three evenings later Tommy walked into Conneely's pub. It was unusually busy for a Wednesday. He'd been brought there by his old friend Sean, Conlon's father. Conlon and Kathleen sat at a table at the far end of the room, and the pair went over and sat down.

Conlon said, "Guiness?"

At Tommy's nod, Conlon looked to the barkeep and held up two fingers. When he was done, Tommy said, "Look, Conlon, I'm full sorry for what I done. Wasn't any call to cold hit you like that." He took a deep breath and looked at Kathleen. "You've pushed me mighty far. Sean has been trying to show me I'm wrong, but I don't see it. I haven't hurt you, nothing like that. Maybe I was wrong about the instruments, but you got a secret...."

He stopped as a large group of people came into the pub, Aoife among them, which was surprising. Then more came in. The tables quickly filled, as more and more entered. Within a couple minutes, people were standing along the walls. Aoife came forward.

She said, "Tommy, Kathleen came to me with a request. Everyone here knows what you done, breaking up her instruments like that, threatening her. You probably notice the Garda hasn't been called on you, though it's been three days since you clocked Conlon. Things been getting out of control."

As she spoke, people continued to trickle in.

"For the last couple days, I've been meeting with lots of people, trying to find some way out of this mess you've made for yourself. We come up with a plan, and need to know Katie here is all behind it."

Kathleen stood up, looking directly at him. "Tommy, you brought this on yourself. I did nothing that Colleen didn't ask. You might ask yourself why someone would leave everything she knows to get away from her husband."

"I don't have to listen to this," he spat at her, standing. The crowd murmured.

"Yes, you do, Tommy Joyce. You got to listen to this. You been in the wrong with Katie this whole time. It's me what's been wronged, and I should not have involved her. But you will hear this."

Tommy's eyes widened as Colleen stepped out of the crowd.

She continued, "I've been dying inside these ten years, but I should never have left the island, let you chase me away. Last couple a weeks, I got myself a job down in Sneem. Was making friends. Then I realized I didn't want to give up my only home. And hear me good, this isn't any of it Katie's fault. This is all on you."

Tommy stood with his mouth agape. Then he sat back down.

Colleen went on. "You need to hear this, Tom…." She choked for a second, lowering her eyes, then forced herself to continue, her voice trembling. "I'm back here to live, it's my home. I'll not be moving back with you. Ever. I'd divorce you if I could, mores the pity. You need to figure out how you will live on this island without being a bully." As she said this last, she raised her eyes to his.

He looked to the left and the right. Everyone's eyes were on him.

Aoife, standing next to Colleen, spoke again. "Tommy, I've known you since your da's fisherman's cap was new. I babysat you. You always were one for fightin', but also always been good in your own way, and you got friends here. You're a part of us. There's many here tonight know what all you done, but no one will be callin the Garda. We want you to be able to stay. Isn't that so?" she asked, and many, though not all, murmured assent.

"But, Tommy, you got to stop bullying Katie, or anyone else. And you got to leave Colleen alone." She shook her head. "And you gotta help pay for what you broke. End of the day, we're here to help you be a part of us. We won't be calling the Garda, unless you do something more."

Someone spoke up. "Tommy, that's serious business busting Katie's cello, and you should be payin' somethin' back. I can't argue with what Colleen is doing. But I remember when my big shed burned, and how you was there to help me rebuild it. Won't be forgetting that."

Someone else spoke. "I was stuck back on Sea Road, and you stopped and helped me fix my flat."

A third person: "Your boat was the first one in the water when the Flynn boys was missing."

Another voice, more critical. "All that's good, Tommy, but you got stop drivin' so fast. There's kids what play in the roads."

A couple more people spoke up in a similar vein. Sean, his old friend, put his hand on Tommy's arm. "You gotta listen to this, man. Maybe you don't be seein' it, but these people are carin' for ya."

Tommy stood up, eyeing everyone. He walked up to Colleen, looked at her, and then pushed his way through the crowd, leaving without a word.

Conlon looked at Kathleen. "What do you think?"

She furrowed her brow. "He didn't fall sobbing to his knees, promising undying gratitude to the people of the island. But I don't know, maybe it's a start. At least he didn't run out screaming his revenge on everyone."

Sean opined in his gravelly voice, "I known him all his born days. Can't say for sure, but I'm thinkin' he'll leave you alone. Not as sure about Colleen— we'll have to watch him there. It's good she's stayin' at Aoife's."

Conlon interrupted. "It's getting really busy at the bar. You mind if I go help?" he asked Kathleen, an apologetic look on his face.

"Not one bit. You've done so much for me, thank you."

When he was gone, Sean asked, "What about you, Katie, you gonna be movin' home?"

She nodded her head. "I think I'll be giving it a couple more days at Aoife's, then move back. You've been his friend a long time, Sean. I hope you're right about leaving me alone. I hope he leaves Colleen alone as well."

"I sure can't gaurantee nothin', but like I said, I think you'll be good. We'll just keep an eye on him when it comes to Colleen."

Sean left shortly after that.

Kathleen sat for a few minutes, watching everyone mingle. The buzz of conversation was occasionally interrupted by the happy staccato of laughter. Beer flowed freely and she watched Conlon as he worked. She felt gratitude. There had been signs he liked her.

A few people came by her table with words of encouragement. She felt such gratitude and a real connection to them, to the island, to be a part of something bigger than her, which somehow formed her. Seeing the musician's platform, she missed her fiddle terribly. Amazingly, she was going to get insurance money for the cello—she'd completely forgotten that she paid for that once a year. Somehow she'd replace the fiddle, but as a gift from her grandfather, it was irreplaceable. She could hear her mother admonishing her. "You can't call back the ship that's sailed, Katie." She sighed.

Of course her mother was right, but it's not that easy. Has Michael's ship sailed, she wondered? Her mood changed. She looked around. Still surrounded by all these people, she felt lonely. As she rose to leave, she resolved to talk with Michael about her uncertainties. Buoyed by the hope of the end of her problems with Tommy, she felt a surge of optimism and dared to hope Michael would return to Inis Mór. She found herself impatient for his call tomorrow morning.

The next morning she waited eagerly, but his call did not come. She waited the next day, but no call came. Nor the next.

Not ever.

TWENTY TWO

Juneau, Three Days Earlier

Marianne sat in her vanity chair facing the mirror. She had lightly applied eyeshadow and mascara, considered lipstick, and rejected the idea. What might it mean that she wanted to look nice for Michael? In three days since they'd met in the church, she sometimes felt like a boat adrift in an ocean of random thoughts about him and memories of their year together as juniors and seniors in high school.

They had laughed a lot. She would brush her hair for a couple minutes to look nice and he would tousle it up. She could never be mad at him for long. Their shared faith had been like a treasure that bound them together.

He was probably the smartest person she'd ever met. She never forgot how in Senior English he'd seen something in a Robert Frost poem that not even the teacher had noticed. *The woods are lovely, dark and deep.* "Couldn't this poem be about someone contemplating suicide?" he'd asked.

Marianne had never forgotten the discussion because she'd returned to the poem again and again in the months after her family moved so abruptly to Salem. She had plumbed the depths of the loneliness in the poem and the turn away from despair toward duty at the end—*but I have promises to keep, and miles to go before I sleep.*

Her promise had been to the baby growing in her and the duty to give it up for adoption. She'd held her for a few minutes after she was born, and when they took her away Marianne had cried for two hours. In some ways she had never stopped crying. It made no difference to her who the father was, although she hoped it was Michael's.

And now Michael was back in her life. She heard the sound of a car and him bounding up the stairs. This is going to be complicated, she thought.

He smiled as he entered. "Hey, Marianne. Wow, what a view."

They went to her large pane window that looked across Gastineau Channel to Douglas Island and the line of mountains that rose steeply to the peaks which for the moment were hidden in clouds to subtly step even closer.

She asked, "Did you ever climb every peak, like you wanted?"

He looked at her with a deep smile that reached his eyes. Oh, she thought. I remember that look.

"You remember that," he said, sounding surprised. "Yeah, I did. David, Jimmy and I climbed Jumbo one day the summer after graduation, really early, and hiked the ridges and peaks all the way to Anderson." He pointed to the last mountain she could see. "One of the best hiking days of my life." He laughed. "It was pretty crazy coming down Anderson. We ended up tromping cross country, coming out on North Douglas Highway all muddy. It was an hour before we got picked up hitching, and we'd already walked back three miles toward our car. Didn't think that one out too well."

At that moment, the sun broke through a small break in the clouds and lit up a part of the forest across the water.

"Michael, isn't that lovely? Let's find somewhere where the sun is shining. I want to stand in the light."

"Amen," he said. Marianne put on a sweater and grabbed a ski cap and light coat. He stopped at his car and looked up to her apartment. "Boy, that's really up there, gotta be as much as eighteen, even twenty feet."

"Sometimes I feel like I live in a fancy tree house. The quiet is nice, but I wish I had some neighbors. The guy next door waves, but not much more."

"It looks brighter out toward the airport. Let's head out the road to the glacier. Maybe the sun will be shining there."

They arrived at Mendenhall Glacier less than twenty minutes later, but the sun wasn't out. It's still so beautiful, Marianne thought. Curving down between high mountains on both sides and heavily crevassed, its face lay white and blue across Mendenhall Lake. Four miles back, rushing behind Mt. Wrather and far above the ice, the cliffs of the Mendenhall Towers thrust toward their two thousand foot height, peaks lost in the clouds.

Out of the car, Michael said, "Every time I'm here it makes me a little sad to see how it's receding. It's so much farther back than when we were together."

Marianne heard the hesitation in his voice at the end. She felt her anxiety return and consciously focused on their conversation. "Nothing ever stays the same, it seems. It's still beautiful, though."

Without words they began walking out the paved path toward Panorama Point. Marianne caught herself just as she was about to take his arm. Arriving at the end of the narrow peninsula a few minutes later, he started to speak, then stopped.

"What?" she asked.

After a couple moments, he said, shaking his head, "Nothing, really. It's just been a long time. I sure never expected to run into you." He took a visibly deep breath, as if making a decision. "I'm feeling kind of." Whatever he was about to say got cut off in a loud rumble, and they looked across to see a massive chunk of ice calving off Mendenhall's face. They stood mesmerized as the ice fell deep into the water, then bobbed back to the surface, pushing a large swell out in front of it. Smaller chunks of ice continued falling for some time.

"Oh, Michael, how very lovely."

"You don't get to see that much on Mendenhall. We're pretty lucky."

They stood and watched for a while as the swell visibly made its way toward them. Marianne waited for him to finish his thought, but he didn't.

As they turned back toward the car, the sky brightened to the west. She was about to ask what he'd wanted to say when he said with a small laugh, "Well, look over there, the sun is shining on North Douglas."

Marianne sighed. "I suppose we'll never catch up with it unless it catches up with us." And sure enough, before they even drove the three miles to the airport the sun had run off like a child playing tag.

Then Michael brightened, and said, "I know where I want to go."

"Where?"

"The beach off the end of the golf course," they said in unison and laughed.

He said in a teasing voice, "Do you remember my old '59 Impala?"

She smiled in memory. "You know I do. I loved the rear fins on that thing." There was a lot I loved about that car, she thought and felt herself blush.

"Any idea what those older cars got over newer ones?"

Something had changed in their mood and all at once, as if clicking into place, Marianne felt their old intimacy return.

"I bet you're thinking about the old bench seats that went all the way across. And me," she said, feeling a bit daring, "sitting right next to you."

He glanced over at her. "I felt like the luckiest guy in the school."

"You were the luckiest guy in the school."

They laughed together, and she wished that there was an old bench seat in this car. It was wonderful to laugh with him.

They drove through town, down South Franklin and out toward what had once been the Million Dollar Golf Course, so named because the sand course built atop the huge slag heap from the old AJ gold mine was reputed to have a million dollars of gold in the sand. The course was gone now, and the area was slowly building up with light industrial businesses that hadn't been there when they were young.

Michael parked a block from Schulter's, and Marianne thought back to that day with Johnny and the tension with Vince. She felt a little alarm now.

The beach lay on the other side of the new businesses. It wasn't long, a half mile at most, but the sand was nice. They walked to its edge.

He said exactly what she was thinking about. "This is the first place we kissed."

"What about up on top of the Knoll?"

He laughed. "Okay, fair enough. This is the first we really kissed."

"It's also where you first said you loved me, Michael."

He nodded slightly. "Yes." Almost a whisper.

They walked west a while and down to the water which lapped quietly against the sand. They were silent again. Marianne was thinking about something she almost desperately wanted to say, but wondered if it was going too far. She just decided, what the heck?

"Michael, can I tell you something really personal?"

"Sure."

"I never regretted, no, that's not right. I was always glad that we made love. It was really sweet. When things were really dark for me, I would remember us together and it would help."

He looked at her a moment, then surprised her by laughing out loud. "I'm sorry. I shouldn't laugh, it's just that I remember feeling so damn guilty, but all I wanted was do it again."

"Me too. Nothing like Catholic guilt." She stopped a moment for effect. "Every. Single. Time."

Their laughter startled a couple of nearby seagulls into flight. Michael picked up a flat stone and flicked it easily into the water. It skipped one, two, three, four, all the way to eight or nine times, then floated along the surface a few feet before dropping out of sight.

She said, picking up a stone, "Impressive, but watch this." She threw it hard. It hit the water with an audible splash and was gone. Kerplunk.

Michael looked away, trying to hold in his laughter. "I really hope your nursing skills are slightly better than that."

"You're going to need them in a minute if you keep on with that line of thought."

He turned back with a huge smile. Then his face became serious, saying, "I thought of you so much that first year, praying all the time for you. When I got to Seattle U, I wondered if you were going to college in Portland or somewhere else in Oregon. I even tried to see if you were a student at University of Portland. Then I gave up."

Marianne hesitated a moment. How could she tell him she spent the year at home having a baby who might be his or might be the daughter of a rapist? No one had ever known it might be Michael's baby until she'd told Sister Kris. Even as she realized the unfairness of it, she unexpectedly felt a moment of irritation toward him. Why hadn't he tried harder?

"Oh," she said, deciding to simply skip over that year, "I was down at University of San Francisco. What did you study?"

"I triple majored in history, literature, and philosophy. Took me an extra quarter."

She stopped and looked at him. Shaking her head, she said, "I guess it shouldn't surprise me, you were so darn smart. What do you do now?"

She was surprised when he said, "I fly, or flew, for Kenmore Air in Kirkland, near Seattle."

"Like your dad."

"Like my dad. Some friends of his completely paid for my flight lessons in his memory."

She interrupted him, "I remember that. You already had your solo when we dated."

"Well, I flew a lot that last summer, after you moved away. I had one hundred and fifty hours before I left for Seattle University and just kept adding to it in the summers, giving flight lessons to others. I thought I was going to be a university professor. I love literature, especially poetry. Maybe you remember that." She nodded. "But I love to fly more and flying up and down Puget Sound is a nice place to do it. I actually flew summers for Kenmore my last two years at Seattle University. It was a great college job. I looked kind of young, so I grew my beard. People trust a beard," he chuckled. "When I graduated, they asked me if I wanted to stay on, and I was there for ten years until, well," and here he hesitated, "well, you might have heard I was married and my wife died last year?"

"Yes, Michael. I heard it was a car accident and that you witnessed it." She shook her head. "I'm so sorry."

His eyes watered and he glanced out across the channel for a moment. She felt her heart breaking and started to reach for him, to hold him.

But he looked back. He spoke quietly, telling the story, all of it, including his part in her death.

They had begun walking back the way they'd come and passed the place where the car was parked. Michael stopped as he described throwing the stone at his wife's head. Marianne was stunned by the impossible choice he had faced, shaking her head and whispering, "Michael," as he looked at her. She reached and took his hand, and his look of gratitude was unmistakable.

They continued on. He said, "It was like nothing I could ever imagine. Finally I just needed to get away, quit my job and took off for Inis Mór, an island off the west coast of Ireland. I have ancestors from there. My Granny

Maeve had told a million stories about it when I was a kid, and I just kind of ended up there. It wasn't the most rational choice, I suppose." He stopped talking a moment. "I met some people there who helped me a lot and would probably still be there, but my mom had a minor heart attack, like I told you the other day. And here I am," he finished, looking back at her.

Marianne stepped up on a nearby log.

"Michael, I can't imagine." She glanced at him and was surprised to see how intently he was looking at her. A gust of wind blew by, swirling her hair. She pulled her ski cap lower around her ears and continued, "What was your wife's name?"

"Maggie. There were months that feel just lost to me. I was mostly just numb. Something would remind me of her, and I'd go crazy with grief. And anger. Just pissed off." He hit the last two words hard. "It's only been in the last few weeks that things have started to get better." He thought for a moment. "I met the right people, lucky me. Being back in Juneau has really helped, too."

Then he changed the subject. "What about you?"

Mariane hesitated again for just a moment. "Well, I was pretty much numb and depressed in Salem. After changing my major four or five times, I became a nurse. It took me six years. My parents were so patient with me. It was a good choice. I mean, helping others like nurses do has, I don't know, it's like my own pain has slowly healed or been transformed as I've worked with so many courageous people who overcome their own pain. I worked with cancer patients for seven years near Portland."

She shook her head. "People can be amazing with their inner strength as they face the last weeks of their lives. And the love I have been privileged to witness, the unfailing constancy of a husband and wife, or a parent and child, even as the presence of the one with cancer diminishes to a touch or a wordless gaze. Even in the last hours, when the sound of the heart monitor seems all that remains, the beloved stay, caressing a cheek and talking quietly.

Sometimes it seemed that the more that was taken away, the deeper became the love. I saw this again and again."

She stopped a moment, and Michael reached with an intimacy as old as the universe and as new as their unexpected reconnection, cupped her left cheek with his hand and touched her tears with his thumb.

She closed her eyes a moment and smiled. "Although it was always hard, it was all a blessing. But after seven years, I needed a change. Last year I finished up a program and am now a Family Nurse Practitioner. I would like to have my own office someday, but for now I am honing skills I would be able to use in El Salvador. I work one evening a week in the Emergency Room at the hospital and three evenings with newborn babies and their moms." Marianne stopped for a moment, looking south across the water to where an Alaska Ferry was slowly plying up the Channel. She remembered arriving in Juneau on a ferry way back in 1963.

"I lived with my parents for a long time—it felt safe to me. I've only lived on my own for the last two years. When you work full time and live with your parents, you can save a lot of money. As I told you the other day, I've been thinking about becoming a nun. I came up here for a couple reasons. There was something like a compulsion pushing me to come. To revisit what had happened. Everyone thought I was crazy, even my counselor was hesitant."

One of Marianne's feet slipped on the log, and Michael reached out and held her arm, keeping his hand on her elbow much longer than was necessary. She leapt lightly to the sand. "Thanks, Michael. Anyway, I see it all better now. We left Juneau so soon after I was raped, and for me, it cut me off too soon from what happened. I needed to see it, to almost confront the place where it happened, to walk on it and say, 'See, I am still here.'" She repeated the words more slowly, emphasizing each word. "I am still here. It's the best I can do, I mean…." She fell silent.

"You've never known who?"

"No." She thought about sharing with him Johnny's idea that it had been Vince and decided not to. What would be the point?

"Then I get why coming here was the best you could do and how important it was for you."

"Michael, thank you. I wish my family could see that. I also came because I wanted an opportunity to spend significant time in prayer, in a new place, where I wasn't affected, wasn't pulled by the life I had."

They began walking again. After a moment, she said, "Life." Michael nodded his head, saying nothing.

They were close together and it simply happened. Without thinking, Marianne put her hand in his arm. She startled and went to pull away. He reached across his body and took her hand, holding it in the crook of his arm. Then he let go, saying, "It's okay, I like it." He looked at her with a huge smile, and she wondered at his ability to move so quickly from their somber mood to delight. He said in what she recognized as his best Humphrey Bogart imitation: "Marianne, I think this is the beginning of a beautiful friendship."

She replied immediately, "Here's looking at you, kid."

She laughed freely and Michael stopped walking. "Wow, it's great to hear your laugh. I'd forgotten what it was like."

Marianne looked across the channel to Douglas Island. "I feel like I lost half my twenties and wish I could have those years back." she stopped a moment, shaking her head. "I got busy with work and lately helping my parents as they get older. Life is so much more serious to me than when we were young." She looked up at him. "It's nice to laugh with you."

They neared an old, rotting barge that sat like a misplaced freighter dock far above the level of the incoming tide.

"We used to play inside that thing when we were kids."

"That seems like a long time ago. Being kids, I mean. We had a big maple tree in our backyard…."

Michael interrupted her, "That was hollowed out in the middle and you could climb up inside the tree and come out way up in the air. When you were little, you used to try and touch the clouds with your hands, but you never could."

She looked at him, remembering how she used to reach for the sky. "Michael, how lovely that you remember."

He smiled at her, reached over and placed his hand on hers where it lay in the crook of her arm. "I remember."

They approached the barge. Marianne peered through a hole in the top into the darkness inside. "You went in there? You were nuts."

A couple large logs sat parallel to the waterline a few feet away, and they headed there. Like before, Marianne stepped on one of them. She looked across to him, almost eye to eye, aware how close they were.

He shook his head lightly. Took a deep breath again, audibly blowing it out. "Marianne, I need to say something. It's driving me nuts. I started to tell you out at the glacier. I want you to know, I want you to know that I never forgot you and always prayed for you. I even used to hope for a day exactly like today, where we could revisit some of our old haunts and just be together. It ended so damn fast back then. We never even got to say goodbye. And I have always felt terrible, so damn guilty about the last time we saw each other and I pushed you away. The guilt never went away, not completely. It sure came back strong when we met in the Cathedral."

She reached with her hand to his elbow and started to say something, but he insisted, "No, please, let me finish." His voice wavered a bit. "I am so very sorry for what happened. I mean all of it, but especially when I walked away. It was just wrong. I regretted it right off, but never got the chance to tell you. You were gone a couple of days later. And Marianne, I missed you so much. It hurt so bad."

He had turned sideways to her, and she pulled tightly on his elbow, turning him back. He didn't resist as she started to embrace him. The sun came out at that moment, bathing them in its light.

Momentarily blinded, she closed her eyes as she went to kiss him on the cheek—just as he turned his head. Their lips brushed. There was a long moment, like the silence before the applause at the end of a musical piece. Marianne opened her lips, and they kissed.

TWENTY THREE

They kissed deeply, but after a few seconds pulled back, lips touching, breath mingling. Marianne liked the taste of his breath. A particular quality of joy surged through her, and she almost cried as she realized what it was. She thought of the last line of a haiku she had read once: Forgiveness alights my heart. She lay her head against Michael's shoulder. He was slightly trembling. She pulled her head back, looking him in the eyes.

"Mmm. What did we just do?"

"Well, darlin, I'm pretty sure we kissed."

Marianne smiled and laid her head back on his shoulder. She sensed his strength, and as if reading her mind he lifted her right off the log, hugging her strongly. She gasped quickly, panicked. He immediately set her on the sand.

She put her hand to his chest, taking a ragged breath. "It's okay, Michael." She stopped. "I know you were just hugging me, but it's hard for me to feel overpowered like that. I react before I'm even aware of it."

He nodded his head.

Marianne continued, "I feel so fragile sometimes. It frustrates me when I think about going to Central America. It's dangerous there. How can I go if I can't even be hugged by someone I care about?"

He replied, "When we met, when you talked about El Salvador, I wanted to say, no don't go. The idea of it makes me afraid for you. But some people, I mean, maybe that is what God really does wish for you. If it is, a way will open, I believe that."

As Marianne sat down on the log she glanced down the beach, and her eyes were drawn to a man who stood by Schulter's Body Shop. It took her a moment to realize it was Vince. He stepped back out of sight behind the building, seemingly when she saw him. How long was he watching, Marianne wondered, hoping he hadn't seen them kiss.

Michael joined her on the log, and they sat silently for some time, looking across the Channel.

Finally, Marianne said, "Michael," at the exact moment he said her name, "Marianne."

"You first," she said.

He furrowed his brow a bit, looked down at the sand and was silent.

"Michael?"

"I'm a little nervous to talk about what just happened. I mean, I know you're thinking about being a nun. And I...."

Anxious again, Marianne interrupted him. "I can't tell how lovely it is to see you after all this time. It's as if out old friendship has returned. Do you know what that's like for me? But I've felt guilty, too, all these years, guilty for ever thinking you had raped me. I used to ask myself, how could I have done that? I mean, I know I wasn't being rational. I just lost my hold on life. But that don't take the feeling of guilt away."

"And I always, always, always hated the way things ended. God. Not seeing you again. I wrote a couple letters when we were in Salem but never sent them, thinking you were better off with me just out of your life." Marianne didn't add that the fact of her pregnancy and uncertainty about the father pretty much killed any chance she might have contacted him.

She continued, "I wanted to kiss you all day today, to just, to just." And she came to a stop, unsure what to say.

Marianne heard him sigh deeply. She continued, determined to try her best. "When we kissed, I felt for the first time that I was forgiven by you. It was like a benediction. Honestly, Michael, it's like a mountain has been lifted off my shoulders that I didn't even know was there."

He replied, "You don't need to ever, ever ask forgiveness from me. I was the one who turned away. It was just such a shock back then, you saying you'd been raped and then that you thought for a few days that I did it. I just reacted, it was like, how could you think that of me? I regretted it immediately and knew I would talk to you later. I really thought we'd be okay. But when later came, you were gone. Just...gone."

Michael stopped speaking for a moment, as if to control his emotions.

"Kissing you was, I just knew that you couldn't do that if you hadn't forgiven me."

Marianne shook her head, saying, "It never occurred to me you might think that way." She looked at him impishly. "It was pretty nice." She blushed, but didn't care.

Again, Michael surprised her with a laugh. "Ooh, it was nice alright. I was curious if it would remind me of kissing you before. But it didn't. Too far in the past, I guess."

She nodded her head. What she said next was hard to say, but she felt the truth of it deeply.

"Michael, this is so, I mean, I haven't." She stopped, thinking. "I'm not a tease, but I." She stopped again.

Michael was nodding his head. "I think I get you, Marianne. You're still thinking of being a nun."

She closed her eyes and nodded emphatically. "Yes."

He continued. "When we kissed, I felt you pull back after a few seconds and was grateful. Well, not entirely grateful. Maybe only a little grateful." He laughed. "At the end of the day it was a kind of chaste kiss, as such kisses go."

Now it was her turn to laugh. "I'm not sure Father Melbourne would have found that a chaste kiss. But why grateful?"

"There's another woman," he said with a small smile.

Marianne hauled off and hit him hard on the shoulder, but smiled herself as she said, "Men. You're all alike. Troglodytes, the whole bunch."

Michael looked at her impishly. "Well," he said, drawing each word out, "I'm not the one two-timing Jesus."

It took her half a moment to get it, after which she literally fell off the log, laughing.

When she righted herself, she said, "Maybe we're lucky to be Catholics, I mean, we understand ritual. I feel like we just experienced the most beautiful Sacrament of Forgiveness ever."

Marianne was relieved and felt free. She trusted Michael in this moment completely. "If there's another woman, why kiss me?"

"Oof. Honestly, I'm not entirely sure. Well, for one, I just wanted to kiss you. You do not look like Godzilla, and you do not smell like a garbage dump." He raised his eyebrows quickly two times, like a slapstick actor, and she shook her head with a smile.

"And it would be more accurate to say there might be another woman. Her name is Kathleen, and I met her on Inis Mór. I haven't even known her that long. Anyway, maybe I felt a little reckless. I'm not perfect, I guess. But there was something else, most important of all, and I felt it all afternoon. I wanted to reclaim the goodness of what we had, to erase that ending."

"Yes," she exclaimed. "I know what it feels like to carry something inside, and it was terrible to be suddenly cut off from you. Even on top of everything else that happened, I so regretted the way it ended for us.

Something felt unforgiven—not about you, not even about me, but just what happened. Maybe we," and she slowed down, amazed at her thought as it emerged as from a fog, "maybe we need to forgive God. And what would all the great philosophers say to that?"

"Wow. Marianne, what an idea. Most people for sure would just dismiss it."

He was silent a moment, then continued, "What would philosophers say? That God is Pure, Perfect Act, untouched by the vicissitudes of our lives. Impassable. And there are good reasons to think that. But," and he reached out in an intimate way and touched the chain just visible at her collar, at the end of which lay her crucifix, "Jesus changes everything, no? In a way I don't fully understand, I think Jesus allows God to suffer with us. Really and truly, to know what human suffering is like because he suffered as a human."

"Michael, what a lovely thought."

"Well, it doesn't always help, like when you want God to make something happen." A tone in his voice prompted her to look closely at him. A line creased down the middle of his forehead. She thought of his wife, Maggie.

They stood up and began walking back toward the car.

"Tell me about her."

He misunderstood. "Kathleen? She's soulful. Not religious, exactly. She listens like no one I've ever experienced—I think of a lake without a ripple, under the sun." He gestured with his hand, as if drawing it across a flat pane. "Perfectly reflecting mountains and the sky. But she can also get pretty animated, feisty, riled up even, when something happens that is flat wrong. I could imagine her sometimes saying things she regrets or has to apologize for. She's a seriously talented cellist and plays a mean fiddle. We sang and played together a couple times at a local pub. It's wonderful. People all over the island come to listen. She waits tables and sings and plays on the weekends. She's content, and there's something really attractive about that."

Regret stabbed her so quickly, Marianne stumbled. Michael took her hand and put it back in his arm. They spent a domestic evening together. After buying food at Foodland, they prepared a dinner salmon and salad, eating at her small table placed next to a window that, like the large living room pane, looked west toward Douglas Island. It was dark as they did the dishes. Despite her earlier words, their comfortable domesticity brought forth feelings for him.

He asked when they were done, "Do you have a guitar?"

"I do, it's an old Guild that my dad gave me. I don't play well, but I keep practicing. I was surprised when you said you performed with Kathleen in Ireland. But you did used to sing a lot." She added in a teasing voice, "I seem to remember you joining the choir in the middle of your Junior year because there was a girl in it you liked."

"Well, and it worked, didn't it?"

Marianne got the guitar. Coming back from her bedroom with the instrument in her hand, she said, "When did you learn to play?"

"I picked it up my freshman year at college. I took lessons a couple years at Seattle University."

After a little tuning, he played a G chord, and a simple riff. "It has a nice sound—lots of bass, but it doesn't dominate the higher notes."

Michael quietly doodled as they chatted. At one point they grew silent, and he played more seriously to her listening. Marianne closed her eyes and relaxed into the intimacy of the moment, suffused as it was with the goodness of who they had been and might have been. The question emerged unbidden, as if it had its own will.

"Do you remember our song?"

Michael stopped playing and considered her for a couple seconds. "Of course I remember, Marianne."

He played a few chords, then began fingerpicking the melody as he sang the first line of "Let It Be Me."

Immediately realizing she asked too much, Marianne reached out and touched his arm. "Michael, I'm sure I should have asked for that. Perhaps it isn't wise."

It was almost intoxicating to be here with him—not to claim him in any way, but this kind of closeness with another was a thirst she hadn't fully felt until meeting Michael again. She thought to apologize but realized she wasn't sorry.

Michael nodded his head. "I think you're right."

She worried they would be uncomfortable after that, but they weren't. They chatted on about his mom, Kathleen and Inis Mór, and she mentioned having spent time with Johnny and Evie. An hour later, he was about to get up and leave, but she asked him to sit a moment longer.

"I had a lovely day, Michael. Seeing you again is," she shrugged her shoulder, "what can I say? I don't want to do anything either of us would regret, and I feel like we're going to be walking a fine line. I'd like us to be friends. I guess it's that fine line I'm worried about."

"You know, like I said earlier, I used to dream about a day like this. I still can't believe you're here." He looked thoughtful. "Look, I know what you mean, I won't pretend I don't. Honestly, I'm not sure how much longer I'm going to be in Juneau. Mom seems better. I'm going to call Kathleen in three days and talk to her about returning. But I'd love to spend time with you, and we'll just, well, not step over that line?" It came out as a question.

She said, "Well then, I know what I'd like to do if the weather cooperates. Go hiking up to Granite Creek Bowl. I've never been, and I remember you saying there's frequently bears there."

"Great idea. I was headed up there just the other day and kind of got interrupted. When can you go?"

"I work this week Sunday, Monday and Tuesday. Maybe before then?"

"I can't tomorrow, I'm taking Mom to the doctor. Friday? I could come by and get you, or we could meet at the trailhead. Say, eight?"

"That's perfect. Why don't you come get me?"

"Okay then." They got up and at the door he stopped. She was standing a couple feet away. Marianne felt his uncertainty, so she acted, going to him and hugging him. She felt his kiss on the top of her head. Did she imagine it, or did he press his kiss a little longer than necessary? They said goodbye and he was gone.

Fifteen minutes later Marianne was sitting at her vanity. She raised her hand and touched her lips, remembering. All at once, she had the feeling of being watched. Her loft apartment was so high up, she never thought about closing the curtains. She went to the window. She was too high up to be seen. Even the top floor of the house across the street was lower. Unless someone were in the woods. And who would do that? Accustomed as she was to unnecessary anxiety, she dismissed her feeling, saying to herself as she often did, "Nerves."

Still, she pulled the curtains.

TWENTY FOUR

Marianne dipped her hand in the holy water and made the sign of the cross as she entered the church. Two elderly women were leaving and conversing quietly as she genuflected next to the pew. In the background the door to the church quietly opened and after a long moment closed.

Instead of kneeling, she sat back. Four days ago Michael had been a happy memory colored darker by the ending. Now he was a presence that felt like waking from a pleasant dream. There were some things she hadn't told him yesterday. It was the first time she had kissed a man in four years. It was the first time she had kissed a man without feeling a small urge to pull away since she'd been raped. She had not told him of the stab of regret when he'd told her about Kathleen.

And while it was true that the kiss had not drawn her away from her growing longing to go to El Salvador, she had also come to see Sister Kris's concern that her desire to be a nun might be partly based on a fear of men. Yesterday, except when he had picked her up, she had not been afraid. This lack of fear seemed to open up possibilities.

Marianne sighed. Had the return of Michael not altered the question of being a nun? She'd learned the importance of honesty in her self-reflection. This had been essential in her slow recovery from the rape. Sister Kris's warning came to mind: Unrecognized fear of men had resulted in some very unhappy nuns.

She wanted to serve God as fully as God would wish for her. It was not easy to give up the idea of a husband, of children. But in the last couple years she was attracted more and more to the idea of living in community with other women who shared her passion to serve Christ. She hadn't liked it when Sr. Kris had challenged her to search her heart and be certain that she was free of the impediment of fear of men—to assure that this fear was not affecting her judgement. She was seeing Sr. Kris in four days, and it would be a good conversation. Meantime, she would pray and ponder.

All at once she needed to get out of the confines of these four walls, beloved as they were. As she headed down the aisle a squeak drew her eyes to the balcony, but there was nothing to be seen. Old buildings, she thought. It was cool outside and damp from a rain that had stopped for the moment. Clouds hung like frayed sheets over the cliffs of Mt. Juneau. It looked brighter to the south, so Marianne decided to chance a walk back to Basin. Coming up to Sixth Street she realized her umbrella lay back in the Cathedral so she hurried back, walking quietly into the church and up to her pew, noting out of the corner of her eyes someone was now sitting toward the front on the right side of the aisle. Her umbrella was under the pew. Reentering the aisle, she looked across to the person, and her heart skipped a beat. Vince. The man Johnny thought had raped her.

Like a rudderless boat coasting onto the beach, she came to a stop. Heart hammering in her chest, she looked at him for several seconds. He had a blank look on his face. She realized how large he was. Finally, at a loss for what else to do, she quietly said, "God bless," and gave him a small smile just before turning to leave.

His presence in the church had unsettled her a bit, but then she felt relief. Vince praying in a church—that is a good thing, no?

A couple hundred feet past Second Bridge, Marianne turned off the road onto a track that led to one of Michael's favorite spots in high school, a small place along Gold Creek called The Stump. She was a bit surprised to see that the old stump was still there. She semi-squatted next to the creek and put her hand in the water, palm up, bringing the water to her mouth. Wow, it was cold, but tasted good. Pure. She saw a person walk by up on the road—not too much foot-traffic this time of afternoon.

Almost every day there were newspaper articles about the violence in El Salvador. About the poverty and sickness that came with war in an already poor country by an army financially supported and trained by the U.S. What had Michael said to her yesterday? If God really wanted her in El Salvador, a way would open. But she had no idea how she could ever be rid of her anxiety and fear. She was much better than say five years ago, but that was still a far cry from not jumping in fear every time someone said "Boo". Or, every time someone picked her up in a big hug as Michael had yesterday.

Michael. In her soul's long dark night, she had never doubted that their love had been real. Indeed, there'd been days when those memories were the moonlit sliver of the only light that penetrated the darkness. God never seemed to answer her prayers, but one day she'd had the epiphany that her memory of Michael might be the very thing which God supported her. She laughed now—didn't seem like much. But the last couple years she'd also begun to sense a new depth to her compassion, rising like a Phoenix out of the fire of her pain and the profound depth of love she experienced as an oncology nurse.

Like a resurrection.

She could no longer turn away from suffering. Why El Salvador? Marianne had no answer. It was simply so. She thought again about what Michael had said, that a way would open for her.

There he was again, in her thoughts. She read all the time about older people who looked up their first loves. Sweet stories. After spending yesterday with Michael, she knew a little how that felt. He was still smart, funny, thoughtful. Good looking. God, his eyes. She'd wanted to run her hand through his way hair and still couldn't believe they had actually kissed. But there'd been a hesitation to his happiness, an underlying grief she sensed even before he explained about his wife Maggie. Why do we have to suffer?

There was one more thing she hadn't told him. Her—their?—daughter was sixteen now. Occasionally Marianne dreamed of her and thought of her always as Michaela. She was tall, with Michael's blue eyes, her blonde hair. In the dreams Michaela seemed to float rather than walk. Marianne would approach, and sometimes Michaela would turn and smile. But she remained ever elusive, always just out of reach.

Marianne made her way back from the Stump to Basin Road, headed back to Second Bridge and pulled herself up into the flat area where she'd been raped. As often as it took, she was going to return to the place until this might help her healing. It occurred to her that this could be like picking at a scab, but it was as she said to Michael yesterday. As long as it took, she was going to stake her claim in the very place of her near destruction.

I am still here.

Marianne stopped halfway across Second Bridge, gazing up and around, surrounded as she was by the high ridges of Mt. Roberts and Mt. Juneau. A mile to the east one long ridge dropped down from Roberts. Gold Creek started a couple miles back in that direction where Perseverance trail ended. How lovely, she thought. Decisively, she turned from the beauty, walked to the end of the bridge, and up into the forest where she'd been attacked.

Vince was unsure what the hell was happening. He knew Marianne's daily patterns and had waited by the church. She'd shown up at the usual time. But staring at the back of her head was getting boring. When Marianne had left the church, Vince walked down into the sanctuary, drawn to a statue of Mary and Jesus.

Everything about this place was odd, the smell, the candles burning, the statues, the several paintings along the wall. That damn cross in the front.

An idea occurred to him with surprise. He liked the quiet. It was here that he thought about his mom and how helpful and kind she was. About how much he liked his job, the pride he felt when receiving compliments from the owner, Roger, and his luck at getting the job in the first place.

He'd discovered in the last couple weeks he knew something of the church stories. His grandma used to read them to him. He'd forgotten. The statue next to him was Mary holding her baby Jesus. Jesus had been killed on that cross. Looked like a damn shitty way to die. He found it hard to look at. Somehow this guy was a hero. Didn't look like a hero to him. Or like a two-bit chump. He wouldn't last five days inside. He remembered more. Jesus couldn't have run. Someone'd had a sword. Jesus told him to put it away. Vince thought of his hidden gun. Ain't no one'll take that from me.

A person came quietly up the aisle. He watched as Marianne bent over and picked up an umbrella from under the pew. She glanced his way as she reentered the aisle, then looked again more closely. Clearly startled, but not afraid. He knew what afraid looked like. She stared at him for a few seconds—it felt like an eternity. With a "God bless," she was gone.

After she'd left, he sat as still as the statue next to him. It had been seventeen years. The memory, the sheer excitement of what he'd done to her had seen him through some of his darkest days in prison. She was still a looker, damn, but something was different. In him. It hadn't really pissed him off when he'd seen her yesterday during his work break on the beach with Flaherty. He thought back to what he'd said to Johnny a couple days ago, about how he wanted to fuck Marianne again. He hadn't meant what he'd said, not really. Not like he used to. He'd spoken mostly to piss that warhoop off. And he'd succeeded there.

He looked again at the wooden statue of Mary. She was glancing down at an infant in her arms. There was a look in her eyes he'd seen in his mom's eyes.

Kindness.

Vince got up so quickly he banged his knee on the pew in front of him. Outside, he headed along Fifth and decided he'd tromp up Starr Hill, take the shortcut over the ridge to Second Bridge. Maybe head up Perseverance. His thoughts were interrupted about halfway up the block. A female voice.

"Sir. Sir."

He turned. Stroller Woman was standing in a yard.

"Can I ask your name?"

"It's, ah, Vince."

"Vince." She said his name as if it were a jewel she was turning over in her hand. Her eyes sparkled as she looked at him. "My name is Diane. I don't want to go on and on, but I'm so glad you passed by. I wanted the chance to properly say how grateful I am. Benji, my boy, he just pulled away from me the other day. I wasn't ready. He's never done that before. I don't know what would've happened if you…." She stopped for a second, swallowing. "You saved his life. There's no way I can ever tell you how grateful I am."

Vince fidgeted a bit, having no idea what to say. He blurted out what he'd heard once in a cowboy movie. "Anyone would have done."

"But you did do it. You ran out in front of that car to help my son."

"Well, then, you're, you're welcome." He added, "Ma'am."

Unsure how to extricate himself, Vince nodded his head and walked off. He walked with the mindless cadence of his childhood's hatred, powerlessness and anger. Like a million times before, up East, turn right, up Starr Hill and up the old switchbacks to the ridge.

At last, Vince stopped.

He turned away from the deer trail that led down to Basin and Second Bridge, tromping a short distance through the underbrush to a large rock. Bossman Rock. His private name. His place. It had been years since he'd been there.

Vince sat on the large boulder and noticed he could still see through the trees out across Juneau to the Channel. He used to come here a lot after his father would beat him. Probably not a week'd gone by and he could still see where he hit the rock over and over as if it were his dad's face, until the wood handle broke. He stood and walked a few feet. There it was, the rusted hammer head, right where he left it more than twenty years ago.

Vince sat on the large boulder and noticed he could still see through the trees out across Juneau to the Channel. He used to come here a lot after his father would beat him. Probably not a week'd gone by his whole time being a kid that hadn't happened. Once Vince brought a hammer with him to Bossman, and he could still see where he hit the rock over and over as if it were his dad's face, until the wooden handle broke. He stood and walked a few feet. There it was, the rusted hammer head, right where he left it more than twenty years ago. He picked it up.

Vince gazed at it a long time, finally setting it on top of Bossman. Random thoughts fired in his head. What the hell was happening? Fuck it, Vince thought. Fuck my dad, fuck my mom.

He stopped. He really didn't feel that about his mom anymore and laughed bitterly. So, just Dad. Fuck you.

His eyes returned to the hammer head. An idea came into his mind. He liked it. He would get it when he returned. Retracing his steps, he started slowly down the deer track. Gold Creek filled the narrow valley with its sound. Once he caught a glimpse of Second Bridge through the trees. To his left, a startled deer bounded away. He couldn't turn his eyes from its graceful leaping flight.

He had a job he liked. He didn't hate his mom any more. With an inner startle, he realized that he didn't fantasize as much about Marianne as he had and laughed self-deprecatingly, thinking, if I could just get that damn warhoop out of my life, I'd be almost normal. But thinking of Johnny brought back his old anger. He settled into it like a comfortable pillow.

Vince came to the bottom of the deer trail and made his way carefully through a thickness of Devil's Club, dropping into the flat area where years ago he'd raped Marianne. He came to the very place and stopped. Back then, he hadn't planned it. He'd spotted her and was able to see that the road was empty. Hardly anyone came this way back then and even now, this time of the day, few hiked back here. Still, it had been a risk he'd gotten away with.

His thoughts were interrupted by a noise. He looked up and immediately edged behind a large Hemlock. He was shocked—coming straight in his direction was Marianne. Without a thought, just as he had seventeen years earlier, his eyes took in the whole length of Basin Road.

As then, no one was in sight.

TWENTY FIVE

The Same Day

Michael had woken early to a dream-image of a whale disappearing below waves, the first whisper of poetry since Maggie had died.

Marianne—what a wonderful, unexpected and complex thing meeting her was. She wasn't the same. Marianne had possessed a kind of sassiness in high school he hadn't noticed yesterday, and there were moments of uncertainty, of hesitation, almost frailty, that were new. Understandably enough.

He'd read once that *suffering is the face of love in a world full of sin.* Marianne possessed a quiet quality of compassion that had softened the scar tissue of his still wounded heart yesterday. She might not even be aware of it. He wondered at the cost of it for her.

She was still as lovely as anyone he'd ever seen and was right to have spoken of a fine line for the two of them. The combination of their shared history, her fragility and strength, the pleasure of conversation with her and her physical presence had floated before him every instant they had spent together yesterday. The kiss had been unintentional, but he'd been more than willing. As they held each other afterwards, he had almost wept to have shared the kiss. It really had been a healing of that awful rupture sixteen years ago.

Given that Maggie had died less than a year ago, Michael was struck by the incongruity of having needed forgiveness from a woman he hadn't seen since 1964. He hadn't even been aware of the weight of this guilt.

Michael heard the door to the house open and close. His mom, returned from her morning walk. He stretched and looked around his small room, eyes lighting on the built-in desk his dad had built on which he'd made models as a kid. He'd loved reaching out his dormer window on cold winter mornings and breaking off a huge icicle. There wasn't much to do with it once he had it—bite off a chunk or hold it up to the sun and see it gleam like a diamond. Feel the freeze in his fingers.

"Hey lazybones," his mom yelled up the stairs. "You're missing the best part of the day."

"You look tired, Mom," Michael said as he finished his bowl of cereal a few minutes later.

"Yes, honey, I am. That walk tuckered me out. But I made two miles."

"I'm going to head up to Roberts. Maybe stop off at the Williams' on the way."

"Johnny? I heard he's struggled since Vietnam and has been in Angoon for years. Say hi to his mom. I'm going down for a nap."

"Okay. See you later." He headed back up to his room. Michael had something he'd wanted to give to Johnny for a long time. He wondered how welcome he'd be.

Nevertheless, Michael folded up the poem, stuck it in his jean pocket and left the house quietly.

Approaching Johnny's house, Michael decided to head up the mountain and stop on the way back, but at that moment the front door opened, and Evie stood there, looking at him with a crooked grin on her face.

"Mike Flaherty, as the salmon runs, I swear you are good to see. I never thanked you for a couple days ago—I think that murdering bastard Vince was about to get the best of Johnny and me."

Michael winced inwardly at her description of Vince.

"Evie, it's sure been a few years. You look good." Which was true. She was tall and slim with medium length black hair and expressive eyes. A great high school runner, he remembered. She had a direct way about her that he'd liked in high school. He noticed the fading bruise on her cheek.

"If you're here for Johnny, he left a while ago, up Roberts."

"Huh. Just where I'm headed."

Evie looked at him a moment, then seemed to make a decision. "You'll not find him, but I can show you where he is."

Michael wasn't really looking for company, but he didn't mind. He'd like Evie in high school, and it would be good to catch up. He wasn't so sure about Johnny, given how their friendship ended. The plan had been to just drop off the poem and go after a few minutes of polite conversation with Johnny and his mom. To see him up Roberts would be more complicated.

Evie came back out a couple minutes later, her black hair pulled back in a ponytail. Coming down the stairs she said, "Running Water. That's what Uncle Walter called you. He used to joke that it sounded more like a Plains Indian name. But you were always going a hundred miles an hour, yet brought life to people. Especially the older people you used to visit."

Michael thought back fondly. "Visiting them was kind of a church thing at first. Then I discovered they had really interesting stories and lives. Like Uncle Walter. My God, could he tell a story. Anyway, it was never a bother to help them with errands, keep their walks shoveled in the winter." Michael shrugged his shoulders. "Buy groceries. I still think of them. They are all dead now, except Mrs. Mahoney. I saw her a couple days ago."

"You are a good man, Mike." There was a slight hesitation. "We were all sorry to hear about your wife."

"Thanks Evie. It's been a long hard year, but it's getting better. It helps being in Juneau."

Evie led him along the side of her home to a narrow track rising up behind the small backyard. Salmonberry bushes lined both sides of the narrow way as they ascended. Near the top of the ridge, they went by a massive boulder. Big enough to call it what it was, an erratic, Michael thought. He noticed that there was an old rusted hammerhead sitting on top of the boulder. They tromped through thick underbrush for a couple dozen yards until they came to the actual Mt. Robert's Trail. The deer track continued down to Second Bridge. As he turned away, Michael saw someone almost at the bottom of the narrow path about to cross through the thick stand of Devil's Club.

Michael said, "So, how are you?"

"Pretty good. Mom is getting older, and I help her a lot. I've been behind the bar at the Imperial for a few years, get good tips. I'm thinking of going back to school, become a teacher. I like kids and think I could make a difference. I'd have to leave Mom, though, to get my degree and don't know how that would work."

Michael nodded. "Yeah, that'd be hard. My mom had a mild heart attack a couple weeks ago. She seems okay, but she's fatigued. I worry about her a lot."

"Oh, Mike, we hadn't heard that about your mom. I'm glad she's better. Hey, is it true you're a pilot in Seattle?"

Michael half shrugged his shoulder. "Yeah, although I took a leave of absence."

All at once, Evie stopped. "You said it was helping you to be back home. It's the opposite for Johnny. He's struggling again from his war experiences since he got to Juneau. We've always been close, but I feel him pulling away. I think it's tied with Vince Murdoch returning here—he got out of prison a few weeks ago. Johnny has this idea he's going to do something to us. After that fight back Basin, I wonder if he's right. Johnny's irritable, sometimes really angry. He's says he's getting bad dreams like he hasn't in years. I'm worried. Honestly, I don't know if he's going to be glad to see you.

"He was my closest friend, once."

Evie shook her head. "I never took to what you did, Mike. But I would not have ended my friendship with you. Johnny, though," and she shook her head, "never been one to paddle in someone else's canoe. Not exactly a strong point of his." She pursed her lips, then said quietly. "He could use your friendship right now."

The pair turned and started back up the mountain. Tall, gnarled Sitka Spruce rose to either side of the sometimes muddy trail. Michael took a deep breath. It smelled damp, of all the plants of the forest, of the fallen trees giving themselves back to the earth for the furtherance of all things. It smelled of home.

They arrived eventually at a smaller trail that cut to the left. Evie set a good pace. Unexpectedly, she turned up the steep slope onto a deer track. As they ascended, Michael began hearing a distant repetitive tap. Gradually he realized it sounded like a hammer hitting nails. The slope flattened out. It took Michael a couple seconds to realize what he was seeing. A huge Sitka Spruce had fallen into the large flat area and its branches had been removed. Johnny was carving a Totem Pole.

Michael wiped at a mosquito. Johnny was wearing a pair of jeans, a long sleeve plaid work shirt and gloves. A baseball cap rested atop his head. He was sweating and did not smile as they approached.

Johnny looked at Evie, shaking his head, eyes turned to Michael as he spoke to her. "Dammit, Evie. This is about the last guy I ever want to see."

"You could at least thank him for the other day. He saved our skins."

"Wouldn'a had to, you didn't get in my way." Abruptly, Johnny dropped his hammer and chisel, took off his cap and wiped his forehead.

He said, "Alright, Mike. I got to admit, Evie and me, we were in trouble with Vince. I'll give you my thanks for that, alright? Now, just leave. Don't want anything to do with traitors."

"I wish we could put it behind us, Johnny."

"Your doing, not mine."

Michael raised his arms helplessly as he said, "I brought something to give you." He took the poem from his pocket and held it out to Johnny.

Johnny looked down at Michael's hand and back up. Not a nice smile. Michael thought. When he didn't reach out to take the poem, Michael said, "Well, I'll leave it for you," and walked over to the log. Looking at the various, half-carved animals emerging in the wood reminded him of Michaelangelo's *The Prisoner's* at the Accademia Gallerie in Florence and the way the men seemed to be struggling to emerge from the marble. He clearly saw Frog and Raven. Maybe Wolf. He set the paper on the log and weighted it with a stone.

"Very nice," was all he said, and left. He heard someone following him down the slope and wait when he got back to the trail. Evie joined him.

"I was afraid of that, I'm sorry. What was it you gave him?"

"A copy of a poem I wrote a few years ago in memory of your Uncle Walter."

"Oh Mike, that's really nice. Now I'm even more sorry. Could you get me a copy, in case Johnny doesn't even read it?"

"I'd love to."

They parted on that note. Michael moved quickly up the long switchbacks, the sound of Gold Creek gradually receding. As he hiked above where the initial settlers of Juneau had cut them down, the trees grew massive, rising like cliffs above him. The quiet was broken only by the occasional distant sound of small planes.

He found himself thinking of Kathleen, especially their last day together in Galway and on the ferry back to Inis Mór. It seemed so long ago but had only been a couple weeks. His heart longed for her. The kiss yesterday with Marianne had not changed that.

When had Kathleen captured him? Singing together? Snuggling on the ferry after their afternoon in Galway? He thought of the moment Colleen had gotten on the plane and the tears in Kathleen's eyes as she said goodbye to her friend. She'd done everything for her, including giving her money. He thought back to the hazy memory of her holding his bleeding head in her lap, that horrible day at Dun Aengus. But of course, love is not a calculation, a multiplication table of positive qualities divided into the negatives. Michael believed there was some inner secret that drew people to each other. Psychiatrists and biologists had their ideas, but all their theories did not add up to the *experience* of love. Then he smiled. He had a friend in Seattle who told him he'd married his wife for the smell of her hair. Kathleen's hair smelled really nice.

A raven squawked and several others rose up a hundred feet in front of him. The trees grew shorter. He emerged from the forest a couple minutes later and quickly hiked up the switchbacks to the Cross.

More than fifteen feet high, the Cross stood on the top of a small ridge overlooking Juneau 2000 feet below. It was an icon of his childhood. He sat on a nearby stone, greeting a couple of descending hikers.

He made a decision. He would return to Inis Mor next week. The plane ticket would be expensive, but this was more important than money. He needed to see Kathleen, to find out if she might feel for him what he felt for her. As they'd agreed, he would be able to call her late tomorrow night.

It was another half hour to the top, up and over three high rolling ridges. Michael hiked swiftly, enjoying the strength and endurance of his body. From the peak he looked over Gastineau Channel to its end seven miles south and farther to Swan Island where he'd hunted deer with his dad. Gazing back toward Juneau he saw Johnny coming ten minutes before he arrived. He too was moving fast and shook his head as he walked up.

Johnny said, "I'm no poet, but what you wrote is good. You're right, Uncle would be happy to see what is happening today with the language and all."

"I'm glad you read it, Johnny. He was an amazing guy. Man, he could tell a story."

Johnny abruptly changed the subject. "Why'd you do it? You betrayed our whole family."

Michael shrugged his shoulders. "Nothing has changed, Johnny. It was the truth as I saw it."

"Murdoch killed my dad. It was his word until you took the stand and agreed that he probably didn't intend to kill dad, just beat him up. He'd still be in for murder, but you helped get it lowered to manslaughter."

Michael's voice shook a bit as he said, "I was stuck, Johnny. Like no matter what I did would be the wrong thing. I wanted to lie, even thought I would. Right up to the moment the question was put to me. And I couldn't." Michael shook his head. "I just couldn't. I'm sorry."

Johnny said forcefully, "God damn it, Mike. You were my fucking friend. That bastard killed my dad. That should'a mattered more." Johnny's hands shook. Michael had rarely seen such intensity in another's eyes. Seconds passed. Johnny closed his eyes, raised his head to the heavens, and screamed, his arms bent at the elbows, fists clenched. Taking a couple deep breaths, he opened his eyes.

"Johnny?"

"I don't think I'm made to be happy. Never have been."

"You seemed happy enough when I knew you."

"No, you're right, but that's been a long time. Vietnam. Fucked me up. Get these adrenaline surges, I'm looking around for enemies my mind knows are not there. My whole body reacts wrong—it's like I don't fit into any regular world. Lived in Angoon for years, didn't have to interact much with people. Things were better there. But when I heard Vince was out and back in Juneau, I came home. He wants to hurt us, Mike, I'm sure of it. But all my old damn shit is back. And that asshole would still be in jail if you'd just shut your mouth." Michael raised his hands but found he had nothing to say.

Johnny sat down right next to the small formation of rocks that was the highest point of the mountain and waved Michael over. His eyes were so brown as to be almost black, and they looked anguished at the moment.

"I got too much pride. That's what Mom says. Reading that poem, I remembered how much Uncle liked you. I've been thinking on that all the way up here." He looked up at Mike. "What I mean to say is seeing you is a good thing. It's hard to admit—I need to do something, get help. Anger's been getting its claws into me more and more. But this Vince thing has to end first."

Michael closed his eyes, running his fingers across his forehead. "Man, Johnny, I am sorry about Vietnam."

A moment of quiet into which Johnny finally said. "Thanks, Mike. Hey, you know Marianne Greene is back in Juneau?"

Michael smiled and nodded his head. "I ran into her, and we spent the day together yesterday. We're hiking Perseverance tomorrow."

Johnny let out a strong breath. "I took her on a couple dates. She's sweet, but too damn edgy for me. And her political ideas—crazy, you know?"

Michael interrupted with a laugh. Johnny looked over.

"I'm sorry, but that's good, you saying she's too edgy."

Johnny nodded his head and smiled. Michael noticed how Johnny's face relaxed. It felt good to be talking to his friend again. They had hiked and hunted and fished together for the three years of their friendship, and run together in track. Except for Maggie he'd never had a friend since that he felt as close to.

Johnny interrupted his thoughts. "Okay, that's funny, but I worry for her. Mike, Murdoch was the one who raped her. I think she's in danger, too."

Michael listened with increasing dismay as Johnny explained.

"Jesus Christ, Johnny. She didn't mention any of this to me. We were down by Schulter's yesterday."

"I tried to get her to get a gun, and she just about took my head off. Maybe you can smarten her up."

Michael shook his head, thinking. He was glad he and Marianne were hiking together tomorrow. He could find out what she was thinking.

"Thanks, Johnny. I'll talk to her."

They got up and headed down, moving quickly, chatting more and more comfortably about their common past. In just over an hour, they were back at the narrow deer track.

As they started up, Michael asked, "Johnny, why way up here in the woods? And that tree is not cured at all. Won't it crack and distort as it dries?"

Johnny answered with humor, "You always were so damn smart, I felt like you knew everything. Did I ever win an argument with you?"

"Well, once or twice you did score a minor point." they both laughed.

Johnny returned to Michael's question. "I like to go cross country, and old man Sweeney told me there was a forgotten tunnel in the old mine up here. I came across the tree looking for it. I know it's not ever going to be anything, the wood is too wet and all. It's a chance to see if I got any of my old carving skills, I…."

Johnny stopped talking. Michael halted, puzzled. Then he heard it. Voices and laughter. The sound of chopping. Johnny took off running up the steep slope. Michael followed and was right behind Johnny as they came to the flat area. Three kids were at the Totem Pole, looking to be eleven or twelve years old. One was hacking at it with Johnny's hatchet. Another was standing on it, jumping up and down. A third was just zipping up his pants, having peed on it.

Johnny was fast, but Michael had been the State 220 and 440 champion as a senior in high school. He pulled quickly alongside Johnny and yelled at him. "Johnny, they're just kids." He thought to get in front of him, but Johnny pushed him aside at that moment. Michael stumbled and fell and Johnny surged up to the boys who were scrambling over to the other side of the trunk. Michael was about fifty feet away, rising to his feet as Johnny picked up the hatchet.

TWENTY SIX

The boys were sobbing.

"Johnny, don't," Michael yelled.

"Don't you move," Johnny screamed at the boys. With another scream, he threw the hatchet at a nearby spruce. It tumbled across the space and stuck with a powerful "thwack" in the tree. Johnny peered at the hatchet for a long moment, then turned and glared wordlessly at the boys. Michael walked up to the small group.

The trio began yammering in a riotous cacophony, reminding Michael of a symphony tuning their instruments before a performance. He heard a lot of "sorry" and "mister" and "didn't mean nothing." Finally, they quieted down.

Johnny checked his totem pole. Michael did as well. The figures, except Raven, were ruined, deep notches where the boys had taken the hatchet to the faces. The pungent smell of urine assaulted Michael's nose, the thick liquid slowly seeping into the damp cracks of the spruce.

Johnny spoke again. Michael could hear the stress in his voice.

"How did you find this place?"

The shortest of the three answered, "We heard there was an entrance to the mine up here somewhere. All the easy ones have been caved in by the city. We just wanted to get into the mine and were looking around and found this." Johnny looked over at Michael and shook his head. It could have been us twenty years ago, Michael thought, although he was certain they would have never vandalized a carving such as this had they come upon it.

"Why the hell did you do this to my carving?"

The same boy spoke up. "Don't know, it…we just kind of did it. It was like…what're you going to do to us? We're real sorry." The boys voice cracked and he stopped talking.

Johnny sat down, putting his head in his hands for a moment. He said something to himself, but Michael overheard it. "Not kids. Not again." What does he mean, he wondered?

"You think it's fun to wreck someone else's work?"

No one answered. Finally the tallest of the three spoke up. "It, we," and then he ran his words quickly together. "Are you gonna hurt us? We didn't mean nothin'. We didn't think about it…." Like a balloon deflating to a tiny flatness, the boy's effort at explanation petered out.

Johnny let out a deep breath, emphatically whispering, "Fuck it." Followed a moment later by, "Fuck!" The boys jumped. He stood and turned on them. Michael felt a rising alarm.

Johnny moved away with a snort of disgust. Looking at Michael he said, "I have no goddamn idea what to do," raising his eyebrows and shoulders as if asking a question. Michael noticed that the boys seemed to be calming down.

Johnny spoke to them in a tense voice. "What are your names?"

They gave them to him. Johnny continued, "You know what I feel like? I feel like beating the shit out of you."

Amazingly, at that moment the largest raven Michael had ever seen dropped out of a nearby tree and landed at the far end of the carved spruce.

Johnny looked at it and laughed. "Raven," he said.

Michael saw the tension visibly leave him. On the other hand, the boys looked at the raven as if it were a demon from another world. Fear returned to their faces.

Johnny glanced at Michael again and gestured at the boys with his left hand, as if to say—well, what are you going to do?

Michael indicated Johnny with a movement of his head. His words felt wooden, not sufficient for the abuse of his friend. "This man fought in Vietnam. A man he loved, his uncle, died during that time. He was carving this in his uncle's memory. Any of you ever build something you cared about?" The short one who'd spoken first slowly nodded his head.

Johnny spoke again, disgust in his voice, "Just get the hell out of here."

The three immediately ran off. At the top of the slope, one of them turned, coming back within about fifty feet. "I'm really sorry, sir." Johnny nodded his head, and with a look of relief the boy was gone.

"Brave kid," Michael said.

Johnny surprised him with what he said next. "This destruction feels like what happened to our whole people. Uncle was the most dignified man I ever knew. But there was a deep sadness in him. He told me once, when he was a child in Yet Hit every man and woman could learn everything important there was to know. Everybody had a place and a purpose. I've tried to walk in his footsteps. But sometimes it feels like, what's the point? We'll never be the way we were. I'm so tired. So tired."

The raven hopped halfway up the log. Johnny took some bread from his pack and threw it to their black friend.

"You know ravens can mimic other birds and animals? I've heard them sound like a grouse, like squirrels, once like a wolf. They're damn smart. I don't know what those boys thought when Raven—that's his name—showed up. Looked like they feared I had magic powers or something. I've been throwing him food for weeks. He hasn't eaten from my hand, but he's come close. Nice timing, when he dropped out of the tree. Jesus, he's almost as big as an eagle."

Michael chuckled, saying, "It shocked me, very dramatic. It did seem like you'd conjured him up. And that hatchet throw, holy shit."

Johnny laughed. "That was pure luck—I bet I could throw it one hundred times and not do it again. It was impressive, though, wasn't it?"

They sat quietly a few seconds. Raven flew up into a nearby tree. Finally Michael said, "You had me a little worried for a second there."

Johnny said, "Sorry about pushing you. I was glad you called my name. What I mean to say is, nothing was going to happen, but I was pissed as hell. Your calling out kind of anchored me. Feel a bit like I let them off easy."

"I don't know what more you could do."

"Wanted to smack them around a bit. Jesus, I didn't take any shit when I was a kid. I'd have just fought them."

"It would have cemented the idea of violence in their heads."

Johnny reached down, picked up a stone, and threw it into the woods. He glanced at his friend. "You're starting to sound like Marianne."

Michael laughed. Johnny joined in a couple seconds later. Michael said, "She might be smarter than you thought, hmm?"

Johnny just shook his head. "She's a golden child. Should'a tried my childhood."

Michael disagreed. "A golden child? Maybe when she was a kid, but do you remember what happened to her? I'm sure she's given her ideas a lot of thought."

"Ain't gonna help her much if Vince shows up. You gotta talk sense into her."

Johnny looked sour and changed the subject. "Well, this whole damn log is wasted. It wasn't ever going to be anything anyway. Like you said, the wood isn't dried. Do still have my carving skills, though. Don't know that Tlingits can ever reconnect to the world of nature as we once did, but Uncle told stories to keep our people alive. I am going to carve. Least on my better days, I think this is a worthy thing."

He gathered all his equipment in his pack. As they dropped from the deer path onto the trail, Michael glance up and saw the boys in the distance just going around a curve. The tall one looked back, nudged his friends and yelled at the top of his voice, "Hey. Screw you, you damn Indian."

Later Michael would think about this moment, when he snapped. Perhaps it was the stress of Maggie's death working its way out again. His worry about his mother. Maybe the tension of not knowing what Kathleen was thinking and if Tommy was still bothering her. Perhaps some residual guilt at having spoken up for Vince at his trial, and the effect it had on his friendship with Johnny. Or all of it together.

Whatever it was, at the boy's words, Michael erupted like an exploding volcano. The boys saw him coming and took off. They had a substantial lead, but Michael had been the fastest runner in Alaska when he was eighteen. The chase was on.

In twenty heartbeats, MIchael got to the curve, anger fueling his feet. "Mike," Johny yelled behind him. "Mike, stop." He ignored the voice, remembering the time he had run two hundred twenty yards in under twenty one seconds—he was moving faster now, he was sure. With a perfect purpose, running with the pure strides of his genetic gift, he felt like a fighter jet closing in on a single-prop puddle jumper. The boy who had yelled, knowing he was caught, left the trail and headed off into the woods. The other two kept running down the trail.

This jolted Michael out of his unthinking focus, and it felt like someone was pouring the elements of his person back into a container that had been emptied of all but blind anger. He stopped, breathing hard. A few seconds later, Johnny came running up, huffing himself.

"On Uncle's grave, I think you could outrun a bear. Mike, what the hell got into you? What were you going to do if you'd caught that kid?"

"Let's just get back."

"Right."

The weather stayed sunny and cool. At one point the pair stopped simultaneously.

This is right where we met. I was coming down, you headed up." said Michael.

"We were like two eagles around a carcass."

"As I remember, you didn't seem to wary—you said, 'Hey white boy.'"

Johnny smiled. "You were just as quick coming back at me—'Hey, Indian.' And you told me you'd seen a sow with her cubs up on the high ridges. I thought you were kind of stuck up in track, but I liked you after that."

"I think I did kind of have a big head in track."

Johnny said, "I appreciate it."

Michael looked at him quizzically. Johnny continued. "That you chased that asshole kid. That you got my back again."

They continued their reminiscing, a half hour later taking the nearly negligible path that led to the William's back yard. Walking by the erratic, Michael noticed that the rusted hammer head was gone. Someone else comes this way, he thought. He wondered who had taken it, and why.

TWENTY SEVEN

The next morning

He rose at 5 AM. Might be a big day. Patience. That was his key. But he felt his calm reserve leaking away, like a pinhole in his car radiator. He was heating up. He'd been watching her for three months. She closed her blinds now at night. Dammit, couldn't see anything anymore. Her landlady, the old windbag, Mrs. Smith, was in the hospital. How hard it was to pretend he liked her. Jesus, small towns, you could learn anything about anybody. Even knew she was getting her gallbladder out. He needed to act in the next couple days. If Marianne left her apartment, he'd go in today. It was perfect—the nearest house was at least two hundred feet away and down a steep incline. Lots of trees in between. He'd never had such an easy set-up. What a fucking babe. Couldn't wait to see the life leave her eyes. She'll be the best ever. Today, or tomorrow. He had no trouble waiting. It was the key to his success. He laughed at his joke—the key.

And he knew what to do about the dog.

Marianne woke up and stretched deeply as she glanced at her alarm clock—just after 6:00. She got out of bed and headed straight for the kitchen. Ten minutes later she sat at her table, drinking her first cup of coffee, scratching behind Skippy's ear until he sat down. She thought of yesterday afternoon, when she'd returned to the woods where she'd been attacked and realized that whatever healing waited for her lay in the future, not in the past. She'd stayed there for a few minutes and a generosity of spirit for which she claimed no ownership entered her like a tender-taken breath. She'd prayed for the man who'd raped her, Vince or whoever he was. She'd briefly cried and let the tears fall into the spot where she'd been thrown, battered, bruised, bleeding. Marianne saw in that moment how fragile her life was and how utterly dependent she was on God.

Before she made breakfast, she sat in her "prayer chair" and said a rosary. As always she started with Mary's words to the Angel Gabriel. "I am the Handmaid of the Lord. May it be done to me according to your word."

St. Ignatius of Loyola's words came to her: Do not prefer sickness to health, wealth to poverty, long life to a short one, but desire only that which will bring one closer to Jesus. For God, as Ignatius was fond of saying, can be found in all things. Smiling, she got her drawing materials and set to drawing Ignatius at Monserrat, where he'd given his life totally to God.

Marianne heard Michael bounding up her stairs at 8:00 sharp. She smiled to herself at his energy. He came in and beamed a smile at her that drew one from her.

"Marianne, you're a sight for sore eyes."

She took half a bow. "Well, and I'm glad to be of service. I just need to get my hair under control. Would you like coffee?"

He declined and a couple minutes later she came out of her bedroom, hair back in a ponytail. He was looking at her drawings and complimented her on their beauty. She grabbed her day pack, and they were on their way.

It was a cold morning, but the sun was out and they both shed their heavier sweaters within minutes of leaving the trailhead. It rose steeply at first, and the pair were quickly above Gold Creek, penetrating east into the narrow valley between the long ridges of Mt. Juneau and Mt. Roberts. Marianne pointed out several mountain goats high on the green slopes to Michael. In no time at all they came to Ebner Falls and hiked down to it. The waterfall stair-stepped its way down a couple hundred feet with tremendous power.

"Marianne, let's sit a minute."

She noticed the serious look on his face and thought back to high school, when they'd discussed whether to make love or not.

Michael continued. "I saw Johnny Williams yesterday"

"Oh, Michael, I hope it went well."

He nodded, "It did. I'll tell you later, but he told me about Vince."

She pursed her lips. "Well. I never told you that Johnny thinks he's the one who raped me, but I…."

Michael interrupted her, putting his hand on her arm. "Stop a second." He sighed deeply, resting his forehead in the heel of his other hand for a moment. She was startled by the concern in his eyes when he looked up.

"I don't know if this is right, but who else would tell you? Marianne, he did rape you." He explained about the fight between Vince, Johnny and Evie and how both Johnny and Evie heard Vince say he'd raped her and that he was following her.

She closed her eyes, aware of her breathing. Again, tears flowed and again she let them run down her cheeks. Michael moved closer, and without opening her eyes, she leaned into him and put her head on his shoulder. They sat that way for a couple minutes. Kathleen or not, Marianne was aware of the comfort of his arm, the warmth of his body against hers.

With a deep sigh, she raised her head.

"I need to think about what to do. For certain I'll talk to the police. Not that they can do anything, but it's important he's aware the police know something. Maybe it would stop him in the future. But honestly, for me, if he's following me, I think it's not as important." She told him what had happened the day before and her epiphany.

"And so," she finished up, "I think it probably doesn't matter. I'm going to be leaving Juneau soon."

It's going to be hard to say goodbye to you, she thought, wondering what she might do if there were no one else in the picture. An old adage popped into her thoughts: All is fair in love and war. She laughed quietly, shaking her head. She could never do that.

At Michael's questioning look, she said, "It's amazing how we found each other, and it makes me kind of sad that, well, it would be ever so lovely to stay in touch. I know people say that all the time, but I mean it."

"Yes, It's funny, I decided yesterday I want to return to Ireland right away. I'm calling Kathleen tonight to tell her."

"So, we're both leaving."

She stood and Michael followed suit. When they got back to the main trail, Marianne saw the sign where the way up Mt. Juneau branched off to the left and said impulsively, "It would be lovely to go up Mt. Juneau instead."

"We've got the whole day ahead of us. Sure, let's do it."

"Hold on a sec, she said. "What we were just talking about? There's something else. A couple times I've gone into my apartment, and it feels like someone has been in there."

Michael's head shot around. "What?"

"I don't know, once there was a slight odor. A time or two it seemed like a couple things were moved, just a bit out of place. I mean, that's crazy and I could be wrong about things out of place. It hasn't happened since I got Skippy."

Michael thought a moment. "How long do you think you'll be in Juneau?"

"Two weeks for my job, that would be the soonest. I've got no lease on the apartment, though I'll probably pay an extra month to help Mrs. Smith."

"Well, I can wait two weeks to go to Inis Mór. I'll arrange on the phone tonight with Kathleen the day I'll fly out. You can stay with us, me and my mom. There's lots of room."

She thought about being in the same home with him for two weeks and chided herself.

He mistook her hesitation and said, "I'm sure my mom won't mind. Tell me you wouldn't be relieved."

She hesitated a moment longer, "Truth is, after what you told me about Vince, I would be relieved."

"We'll start tonight, get most of your stuff moved. I bet we might even talk Johnny and Evie into helping us."

"Are you sure your mom won't mind?"

"Not a problem, she's got two extra bedrooms."

"Thank you, Michael."

They moved at a fair pace up the switchbacks and across the long flat traverse above the cliffs, to the point where the trail turned onto the steep upper slopes of the mountain.

Looking up and up, Marianne glanced sideways at Michael, furrowed her brow, and asked, "How much further from here?"

He responded, "Maybe twelve hundred feet, straight up."

She looked bemused. "Whose brilliant idea was this?"

"Well, there's just the two of us, and it wasn't my voice that said," and he spoke with a fair imitation of her, "'Hey, Michael, wouldn't it be lovely to go up Mt. Juneau?'"

She pushed him playfully on the shoulder and said, "You dare to mock me. I'd race you to the top, but I wouldn't want to hurt your male ego." And laughing, she started up. After a half hour, she came to a stone formation and chose to go left around it. Michael went right and was waiting for her at the top of the rocks. "And what were you saying about a race?"

Michael led now, pulling a bit in front of her. At one point Marianne yelled up to him, "Michael, this is beginning to feel a lot like work." He laughed. A few minutes later Michael scrambled up another steep rock formation, waiting for her at the top of it. She arrived next to him a minute later, breathing deeply. Looking up, she said, "Not far now. Wow. I forgot how steep this is."

"People turn around because they're nervous about the descent."

"Eh, it's not that steep." Michael was looking down at Juneau. She took several quiet steps past him and then pointed down the mountain. "Is that a bear?"

He turned and looked. "Where?"

Marianne was fifty feet above him and moving fast when she heard his exclamation. "You dirty dog." She didn't turn back and moved as quickly, determined to beat him to the top. A couple minutes later she reached the flatish peak area and turned and laughed. "Beatch'ya," she crowed.

He was a few feet behind her and glared in jest. "Ech, never trust a woman, that's my new motto."

The pair walked to the other side of the flat area, where the mountain sloped steeply away to the north. They looked over the airport, Auk Bay and Lynn Canal all the way to the Chillkat Mountains, which were dusted with snow on their peaks. In the far distance Michael pointed out fifteen thousand foot Mt. Fairweather.

Impulsively, Marianne raised her arms above her head and exclaimed, "A good hike is the best medicine."

They put back on their heavy sweaters and silently took in the view. Marianne put her arm in his and they stood contentedly. Michael pointed off to the east. "There's snow on Observation Peak. Most likely in town before Halloween."

"Do you still go to Mass?"

"Most of the time. Sometimes I get this spiritual hunger for the Eucharist, and I even go to daily Mass for a while. Weird, huh?"

She disagreed, shaking her head. "I'd go to Mass everyday if I could."

"Well, if you become a nun, you'll be able to." He paused a moment. "I haven't gone much since Maggie died. I need to get back to it."

Marianne walked over to the small raised area that was the actual peak, taking a light rain coat out and putting it on. Michael followed her.

"Actually, I'm still not sure about becoming a nun, but I am about El Salvador. It's just become clear to me that to fully give myself to Jesus means going there."

He looked at her and shook his head. "You really are something, Marianne Julia Greene."

"Here's looking at you, kid."

Michael pointed to the ridge. "You want to walk it? Probably adds three hours to the day, but we've got time."

"That sounds lovely. I'll have to watch my water, though. I have just over a quart left."

"You can just drink out of the creeks here."

"Seriously?"

He nodded.

Marianne raised her eyebrows and shoulders. "All right, let's go."

His satisfaction was almost sexual as the lock opened for him. Easiest entrance ever. His locksmith grandfather had taught him everything. He had a talent for it. The key to his success.

The dog came barking at him. He walked up to it and tazed him. Back outside he finished the job and threw its body into the bushes.

No one had seen him because there was no one to see him. Up the stairs again, he closed her door. Standing just inside the door, he took several deep breaths, filling his nose with her smell. He saw the rosary and laughed, wondering if she'd noticed he had moved it and what she thought if she had noticed. He breathed her in one more time, eager for the smell of her fear. He'd take his time. He would have all night.

Three hours later Marianne and Michael dropped down into Granite Creek. Unusually, there were no bears. At one point the creek flowed into a matted area and divided into dozens of rivulets. Marianne was tired, but elated. It was so beautiful, the water glinting in the low sun as they walked among and over the softly burbling rills. She thought, thank you God for this perfect happiness.

Michael interrupted her thoughts. "This is so nice, let's sit a minute."

They found a large stone in the midst of it all to sit on.

"Michael, it really is a relief to be moving to your mom's place. I hadn't realized how much my sense of being invaded was bothering me. I'm so used to feeling anxious while my mind knows it's not necessary. I was kind of dismissive, but on a deeper level I guess it did bother me."

"To use your word, it would be lovely to have you."

She looked at him impishly. "And how am I doing with the proverbial fine line?"

He pushed her shoulder with his. "You're a bit flirty," he said as he smiled, "but it's nice being flirted with by a beautiful woman."

She felt her face flush. "Now who's flirting, hmm?" She sighed happily. "But, I know. It's been so long since I've been this way, I almost forgot what it's like." God help me, she thought. I wish this could continue.

They sat shoulder to shoulder for several minutes, the low, cool October sun on their faces, the creek burbling around them. Finally they looked at each other, nodded their heads and rose.

"Let's go get you moved safely into my mom's home."

Two hours later, as the sun fully set behind Douglas Island, after having checked with Michael's mom and stopped off to get Johnny and Evie, the pair arrived back at Marianne's apartment. Evie and Johnny would show up in a half hour or so.

Marianne unlocked her door, almost mindlessly scrunching her nose as she went inside. She crossed the kitchen area while Michael went to her CD player, asking, "You want some music?"

"John Denver?"

Marianne was just noticing that Skippy hadn't greeted them when she heard a puzzling noise, as if something fell.

"Michael, what was that?"

"Michael, did you hea…."

She stopped in shock at the edge of the room. A large man dressed all in black, in a mask, was standing over Michael, a baseball bat in his hands. It was raised, and the man brought the bat down hard on Michael's back.

Marianne whimpered. He turned, and she noticed his gloved hands were holding the bat, a gift from her brother David. Michael lay unmoving on the floor. There was blood around his head.

The man's eyes were visible behind the mask. Marianne glanced to the door. He saw that and walked quickly to cut off any possible escape. She moved over to Michael, never taking her eyes off the intruder. Marianne knelt next to him, but before she could check his head closely, the intruder spoke.

"Get away from him."

Marianne rose. Twenty feet separated the two.

"I said, get away from him."

She did not move. To her horror he pulled a gun from behind his back and spoke again. "No one'll hear you, bitch. Mrs. Smith's in the hospital. You can scream all you want."

Marianne's chin quivered and her hands shook. She wondered how he knew about Mrs. Smith and felt panic rising.

He pointed the gun at her. "Move over there," he said, indicating the bedroom door.

Peace flowed into her and everything became clear. This is what my life is to come to. To die standing over Michael. She glanced down at him but could not tell if he was breathing. Her choices for survival were non-existent. Her choice for love seemed to expand right in front of her, as if a mirage had suddenly become real. She decided, speaking her wild choice in her heart.

Michael, I will not abandon you.

He pointed the gun at her head. She heard the clock tick a single time. Touched her hand to her lips, remembered her kiss with Michael and took out her rosary. Raised her eyes. Asked nothing.

In that moment, all fear left her.

"No, I will not leave him."

He'd be moving again, a while after he murdered her. Head east, maybe New England. This would be his fourth one. He was smart. And very careful. No one ever knew.

He'd wanted to rifle through her clothes, smell her perfume, touch her things. But unlike his previous visits he did none of this and waited with the patience of a stilled tiger. Finally, the key in the door. Another voice, shit. Saw the bat. Picked it up. The guy never saw it coming, just the way he liked it. Total control.

And now the bitch wouldn't do what he said. The tiger tensed.

"Goddamit, do what I fucking say—move, or I'll blow your goddamn head off."

She flinched, but kept her eyes on his. "Hail, Mary, full of grace...."

He lost control—this fucking bitch wouldn't do what he said. The tiger leapt. Taking a step closer, he raised the gun and shot her.

Her head jerked back and to her right. She fell across the man, lay still. Seconds ticked off the clock. You stupid cunt, he thought. He walked over to the pair. Her head was covered in blood.

Unexpectedly, sirens. Coming closer. What the fuck.

His mind was calm but lightning fast. Had to be someone was downstairs who called the cops a couple minutes ago. No other way they could be coming this quick. Gotta move now. The death of these two meant nothing compared to his being nabbed. He raced down the stairs and barged into the old windbag's house. It took one kick to get through the front door. Move, move, move. A middle-age woman ran away from him into the kitchen. He was on her in two seconds. He hit her hard in the face, one, two, three times. She fell unmoving on the floor.

In two seconds he considered. If the guy was alive upstairs, no sense killing this old bag. Murder gets pursued much more than assault. Leave her alive.

Move. Move. He sprinted across the street to the house he was renting. Gotta be fast. On a large piece of plastic already set out just inside the door to his garage he ripped off his clothes, mask, gloves, everything, and put it inside the plastic. Even his shoes. And the gun. He wadded it all up, putting the whole thing inside a Hefty garbage bag. Naked, he took it into the kitchen.

He always prepared a hidey hole. The high kitchen cabinets were mounted on twelve inch soffits. Months ago he'd made a secret hiding place in the soffit. Earlier in the day he'd taken all the bowls, plates and shelves out of the cabinet. On a step ladder he'd reached up with his hand and pushed the false top of the cabinet up and angled it out. Now he squished the bag into the hollow soffit and off to the side. It took some doing. Replaced the false top and put everything back. A police siren right outside. He dressed quickly, opened a magazine to an article he'd read earlier that day. Put his stereo headphones on the chair. Knew which song it was set to. He went to the door and walked outside, looking the part of a curious neighbor. Two cop cars pulled up at the bottom of the stair to her apartment. Tense voices. Someone yelled. When the cops finally came to him, he would know what to say. He'd been reading with his headphones on. Not seen or heard anything. If they asked, they'd be welcome to come in and look around.

A third car arrived and two Indians got out, a man and a woman. A brief conversation with a cop and the Indian guy lost it. He jumped back in the car and tore off down the hill, leaving the woman crying in his direction to stop. Then she took off running. There was another siren. He'd thought of everything. It hadn't gone the way he hoped, but his bases were covered. He'd wait a few months to move and the hunt would start again. Like a spider building its web, he thought of the future. He could be patient. It was the key to his success.

Key, good one, he thought.

TWENTY EIGHT

Evie drove down Starr Hill toward Marianne's apartment. She said, "I'm relieved

Marianne's moving in with Michael."

Johnny nodded his head, feeling the same way. "I ask Michael to talk to her, and twenty four hours later she's moving. Glad she listens to him. She never listened to me."

"Come on, Johnny, you can't expect someone like her to just go buy a gun."

Evie turned right at Harris and headed up to Seventh. They drove by Vince's apartment. Johnny nodded toward it as they drove by. "You think he's going to just say, 'Oh, I'm sorry, I guess I won't rape you again and kill you this time.'" He felt his frustration at Marianne and anger toward Vince sink its teeth into his mood.

"I don't know Johnny. I don't know what the answer is. But she made her choice."

She looked over at him. "Is fighting working? What if we, I don't know, met with him for coffee. Talked. We don't even really know what he is thinking."

He held her gaze, wondering if she was out of her mind. Finally, he shook his head. "He told us what he wants to do to Marianne. You were there. He hated us sixteen years ago and nothing has changed."

She couldn't keep the sarcasm out of her voice. "So what's the game plan, Johnny? You're going to beat him up until he leaves us alone?" Evie laughed with a bitter sound. "That sounds like it'll work. In the meantime, you're all knotted up in anger, and it feels like it's getting worse. How will this end, Johnny?" she finished, slowing down at the end.

With one of us dead, he thought, because there was nothing more to say, "Look, Evie. I know you're worried, and I know I've given you a reason. Let's just help Marianne move. Maybe even enjoy us all being together."

She nodded her head. They drove down the steep curve of Goldbelt and turned onto Calhoun. As they started up into the Highlands, Evie asked, "Are those flashing lights?"

A blinking light was striking the trees and then leaving them in the dark. Again and again and again. They turned up the long narrow street to Marianne's apartment.

"Oh my god," Evie said in a shocked voice.

Johnny said, "What the hell," at the same time. Two police cars sat with lights flashing in the parking area in front of Marianne's apartment. The door at the top of her stairs was open. A couple of officers were standing by a car, one of them on the radio. Another stood at the bottom of the stairs with a fourth one at the top.

Evie sped up and parked close to the commotion. Johnny leapt out and sprinted toward the stairway. He was stopped by a uniformed officer. Evie hurried up as Johnny yelled, "What's going on? Those are out friends up there."

"Sir, you need to stop," the officer replied.

Evie grabbed his arm, pulling on him. He knew his eyes looked crazy. He was shot through with anger.

"Johnny," she said, "Johnny, get away."

He glanced at her and took a breath.

Evie asked, "Are they okay?"

"Ma'am, I really know nothing."

"Sir," she implored, "Our two friends are up there. Can't you tell us anything?"

The officer looked at her. "There are two people in the apartment, and they were attacked." He hesitated. "I don't know how bad. Pretty bad I think."

"Are they alive?"

Again, he hesitated. "That is really all I know, ma'am."

Johnny saw the keys in Evie's hand and snatched them from her, sprinting for the car. Adrenaline hit him like a slap of ice cold water.

Johnny sped over to the Gold Creek bridge at fifty miles an hour and up the hill to Calhoun Avenue. He braked hard at the top of the hill, slewing sharply to his left onto Goldbelt, slamming into the stone wall on the other side of the street. "Come on, Goddammit," he screamed as his car strained to accelerate up the steep curving road. He smashed his fist into the windshield, cracking it. "Come on."

His rage was so overpowering he could scarcely think. His worst fears had come to pass, except it was his good friends who had been attacked, not his family. A raw, battle-familiar energy coursed through his whole body. Hands shook on the steering wheel. He topped Goldbelt. Knew he needed to go slow—cars lined the right side of the already narrow street. He floored it. Someone yelled at him to slow down. Fuck you.

Helicopters. He looked up through the windshield for their lights. They're not really there. Focus. Vince. Pictured his face. Yelled at the top of his voice. "Aaauuuugggghhhhh!" Four blocks now. Punched the gas as he screeched left onto Seventh Street.

Vince was tired. He put away his tools and walked to the door with the boss man.

"Long day. I'm beat."

"Vince, thanks for staying late the last couple nights. We've completely caught up and can go back to a sane schedule tomorrow."

He felt a deep sense of satisfaction. "No prob, Roger. I can use the overtime. It'll be nice to get home, have a shower, have a beer."

"Well, you earned it, but don't get used to the overtime." The pair laughed companionably. "Get that hand cleaned," he said, indicating a cut on Vince's left hand.

Roger stopped and put a hand out to the larger man's shoulder. "Vince, you've worked out good," he continued. "You're my best worker. I guess I just want to encourage you to, well, keep this up. I'll say this, I'm glad I took a chance on you."

Vince felt his throat tighten and fought to control his emotions. "Thanks, Roger. I'm really, well, thanks."

Vince liked Roger. He was fair with his workers. Honest with his customers. Roger had given him an opportunity. Vince realized how lucky this was. Rolling his shoulders a bit, he got into his old Impala, headed into town and stopped at 20th Century to buy a six pack and chips. He thought of his mom as he parked and decided to buy her something nice with the extra money from the last couple days. With that thought, he entered the front door of the apartment building, walked up to the second floor, and let himself in.

"Hey, Mom," he called out as he hung up his coat and walked through the small entrance hall to the living room. His mom was not there. He came alert, sensing something was off. He heard a kind of muted shout from his mom's bedroom—then Johnny Williams raced out of his bedroom and headed straight for him, silent as a hawk dropping on prey.

"Ma'am, do you know the identity of the people upstairs?"

Evie watched Johnny tear down the road. She was worried sick for Mike and Marianne. Were they dead or dying? But she was filled with dread for her brother and knew where he was headed.

The officer's question brought her to herself. "Michael Flaherty and Marianne Greene. Officer, I have to go."

Evie started running. She heard the officer yell but did not stop. I can get there in time, I can do it, she thought as she ran. I am a state champion runner. I can take the shortcut. Faster, she thought, even as she knew she would be too late.

She almost sprinted down the streets and out of the Highlands. Calm now, she thought. Get your pace, and don't let go. She came into her rhythm, feeling like she was on the crest of a wave. As she turned into the shortcut through Evergreen Bowl, she thought of the steep three hundred yard climb in front of her up and out of the park. She would be there in a minute. I will not submit, she thought, remembering the pain of her State winning the 5K Cross Country race as a senior in high school, when she'd run almost a full minute faster than her best previous time. I can do that again, she thought. For a second, doubt entered her mind, and she voiced her refusal. "No."

Find your eagle heart.

Evie hit the bottom of the steep hill running like a deer in flight, remembering Uncle's affectionate nickname for her, Windrunner. Let it be so, she thought and then gave herself over to every hard stride as she raced up and up and up toward Seventh Street.

Johnny hit Vince hard in the chest with his turned shoulder, driving him back into the wall. His breath went as Johnny punched him several times in the stomach. But sixteen years in prison had hardened him, and he smashed his fists on Johnny's shoulders, pushing him back. As Johnny came in again, Vince rocked him with a fist to his head, just as Johnny's fist exploded into his face. He heard and felt the crack of his nose. A movement drew his eyes, and he saw for a half-second his mom in the doorway to her bedroom, a rag duct-taped across her mouth, her hands looking to be tied behind her back.

With a roar, he spit out blood and raced at Johnny. The two crashed to the floor. Vince kicked out, hitting Johnny in the head as the warhoop rose to his hands and knees. Again Johnny hit him in the chest, but this time Vince had time to brace himself. As Johnny came into him, he took a half step back, turned, grabbed Johnny's body, throwing him into the wall. He followed right after him, but Johnny was unbelievably quick to rise, punches coming at him in flurries. He felt a sharp pain in his rib area and suddenly had trouble breathing.

They fought without words, breath rasping harshly, their hatred as implacable as the unchanging laws of nature. Vince backed up, but could not get away. Johnny got him up against the wall. He tried to counterpunch, but the damned Indian was too close. He was losing, and he knew it. He pushed Johnny away, but the bastard came right back. Vince landed one good punch to Johnny's face before he was once again too close. Another pain in his rib area. Vince began to panic. He ran at Williams, trying to grab him in a bear hug, to fall on him. The pair grappled, locked together like two bull moose. Using his superior strength, Vince turned his adversary to the wall, and ran him into it. Again, the asshole dropped his hands, slugging him repeatedly in the stomach and rib area. More intense pain, and he was forced to let Williams go. Johnny came at him. Vince hit him in the head, but his punch was weaker. Although far from done, Vince knew he was going to lose this fight. Desperate, he pushed Johnny away.

As Johnny rushed in again, his mom ran into Johnny from the side, and he stumbled just a bit. She fell hard to the floor, unable to use her hands to stop her fall. Vince took two quick steps and smashed Johnny in the face before he could recover his balance. Johnny fell, and Vince kicked him in the jaw. The warhoop tried to rise. Vince kicked him again, and again, and a third time in the stomach. Johnny stopped moving.

Vince was rearing back to kick him again when he sensed a presence. The sister stood swaying in the open doorway. He spit out blood, breathing harshly, sharp pains in his ribs keeping his breaths short. Feeling dizzy he asked, "Why, why the hell di-did your asshole brother come here?"

The sister, Evie, he remembered, was panting deeply and swayed again. Sweat covered her face. She spoke between her own panting breaths. "Our friends were attacked tonight. You might know them, Marianne Greene. And Michael Flaherty."

His thoughts reeled. Williams thought he'd attacked Marianne. Vince briefly regretted his words before the fight last week with Johnny back Basin. Just to piss him off. Hadn't meant them.

His mom had risen off the floor and was sitting and crying in a chair. He looked down at the body on the floor. There was blood everywhere on him. I probably look the same, he thought. He looked back at Evie.

"I didn't do it. Was at work until I got home—was at work until I got home—you can call my, my fucking boss, if you want."

Johnny started to move and Vince moved to kick him again.

"What are you going to do to him? Vince, please stop, don't hurt him anymore."

He looked at her, saw the pleading in her face. He remembered how fearless she'd been last week up Basin. Realized he could hear sirens, getting closer. Looked at the Indian bitch. She held his eyes.

"He deserves to fucking die," was all Vince said.

And he backed away.

With a sob, she ran to her brother, cradling his head, softly saying his name over and over. "Johnny, Johnny, Johnny. Just breathe, Johnny. Breathe."

TWENTY NINE

Kathleen glanced at the clock as she drank her second cup of coffee. Michael called religiously at 7:00 in the morning, 11:00 at night in Juneau. She'd decided to tell him without reservation of her feelings, starting with that last morning when she'd sped too late to the ferry terminal in Inis Mór and the restless loneliness that had surged like a rogue wave as she watched the ferry disappear in the direction of Galway. That she wanted him to come back. If he didn't feel the same, well, it was time to know that.

As the clock reached 7:00, she drummed her fingers on the table and tried to read from her book.

7:01.

7:02.

A few minutes later she gave up any pretense of reading and walked into her living room. She had a fiddle on loan from a friend, but the space where she'd kept her cello sat empty as if someone had sawed off her hand. She'd become edgy these past three weeks, missing the newness and hope of Michael and the joy that playing the cello had daily brought to her life. The destruction felt like an attack on her soul. She found herself wishing something worse had happened to Tommy.

It was after 8:00 when Kathleen sighed and rose from her living room couch. Michael had never been late. She went to the loo and of course just as she was peeing the phone rang. She set her head against the wall at her stupidity. Kathleen realized she didn't have his mam's number and would have to go to the Post Office, and get the Juneau Operator to dial Michael.

It rang again a couple minutes later, and Kathleen leapt to answer.

"Katie, it's Sean Conneely. Colleen tried to ring you a few minutes ago. Listen, Tommy's gone missin'. He didn't show for work these two days now, and Colleen says he called, drunk and incoherent, but he threatened ya twice. I don't know but he might mean ya harm. Soon as I hang up, I'm comin'. I think my Conlon is already on the way. I wanted you to know right off. Lock your doors until we're there."

Kathleen felt goose bumps on her arms, and her heart pounded. "What did he say?"

"Ah, Katie girl, I'm not knowing that then, but Colleen sounded right scared enough."

"What about Aoife and Colleen? Is someone with them then?"

"Yes, Kevin Mullen is already there. Get that door locked now."

Katie immediately locked both doors. She looked out her living room window. Clouds were scuttling in from the west. The long stretch of fields appeared empty, but she knew the walls provided more than enough hiding places. Conlon's arrival was a relief. Sean was only a minute behind his son.

Sean said, "I have no idea what he's about, Katie. You did a good thing with him the other night. But we can't control another's actions. Maybe you should move back with Aoife for a couple days?"

"I've been so long away from my life, what with Michael gone and my cello. Let's wait and see what happens. I would like to stay here if it's possible."

Sean nodded, heading to the front door. "Well ya think on that lassie. Ya need to be right careful now. It could be Tommy needs help, maybe fell somewhere and hurt himself." He stopped at the open door and looked back at them. "Or worse. I'm meanin' to look down along the back of the island and the coast road. Wanted to be sure you were looked after first. But this afternoon the weather is supposed to get fierce altogether, so I'll be goin' now."

Kathleen and Conlon looked at each other for a couple seconds after he left. It all felt unreal to her, but the look on his face gave her a pause.

"Conlon, could you walk the line for me, make sure he's not about?"

He nodded his head and went out to check around her home. The corners and spaces of her beloved home now seemed threatening. She looked out the back window for Conlon, saw him up near the top of her property.

When her phone rang, she damped down hard on her hope it was Michael. It was not.

Aoife said, "Love, I had to be callin ta see that you're okay. Colleen is all in bits. How are ya then?"

Kathleen sighed, grateful for her friend's concern. "I'm a little better. Conlon's here with me, he's out checking the property. It's frightening, when I think of the rage I saw in Tommy's face up at Dún Aonghasa last week. It was only there a moment, but it was ugly."

"You should think on callin' the Garda."

Kathleen nodded her head. "You have the right of it then." She looked at the counter and saw the note Michael had written her the night before he left.

As if she read her mind, Aoife asked, "How then is Michael? His mam?"

"I don't know. Well, I do know his mam is better. He calls regularly, always right at 7:00 in the morning, every other day. I asked him four days ago to wait, told him I was going to be off island for a few days. I guess I kind of lied to him, but I wanted to be sure this whole Tommy thing was finished and done, you know? And now, look, it's worse than ever." Kathleen frowned sourly. "He didn't call today. He's never missed a call."

"Oh, well then Katie dear, there be a lot of good reasons for that. Try not to worry your head now. You'll see, he'll surely call in the morning."

Conlon returned with a shrug of his shoulders.

Kathleen said to Aoife, "Conlon is back. Thanks ever so much for your call, and you take care. Aoife, you are such a good friend."

"Oh we'll be fine. You're the one who needs to watch herself. Katie, ya are a light in my old age. Goodbye and we'll be seein' each other soon then."

"Bye bye, Aoife."

Kathleen turned to Conlon. "Would you like some tea?"

Conlon said, "Da is down back of the island, how about we look between here and Tommy's house."

Kathleen shook her head. "Honest? Mostly I don't care anymore what happens to him. I'm so tired of the anxiety he's caused me. But,another part still cares. Why, I can't say."

"It's because of your very good nature." Conlon responded.

As she walked to his car, hair blowing in her eyes, Kathleen saw that Sean had the right of it about the weather. Grey green swells were lashing the shore, the usual quiet shush of the waves on the beach sounding ferocious even from this distance. One rose in a violent froth as it hit the nearer of the Brannocks. Kathleen remembered a nightmare she'd had as a child of a giant wave drowning the two flat islands, demolishing the lighthouse and coming straight for her.

Something felt wrong, so much so that she looked around. But there was nothing to see.

For the next two hours they scoured the countless small lanes that crisscrossed the island between the main roads, stopping at a few houses and asking after Tommy. There was no sign of him. Finally, they went to Conlon's pub for a small meal. The wind pushed strong from the west and light rain was somersaulting in from the ocean. They hung their coats and Conlon ordered Guinness stew for the two of them.

Kathleen took no umbrage at Conlon's next words, as ungracious as they were. "I don't want to speak ill of Tommy, but if he fell, it's likely he had one or two drops over the dozen. There's a million places he could be—we just have to wait for him to show. But Katie, I think you should stay at Aoife's. Or at least let me sleep in your living room tonight."

The sense of wrongness shuddered through her again.

She had to admit she'd be glad for his presence and told him so.

When the window shattered with a loud crash just after 3:00 am she was more than relieved that he was there. It took her a couple moments to clear her head. Then she heard Conlon yelling into the night, and memory tumbled into place. She hurriedly threw on her robe and rushed into the kitchen area. Broken glass was strewn across the floor. One window was broken and a large rock sat near the far wall. The violence, though small by comparison, reminded her of bombs in the North. Conlon closed the back door and turned to her, anger in his eyes.

Kathleen asked, "Did you see him?"

"No, didn't hear anything either, although the wind makes that difficult."

Kathleen got her powerful flashlight, and they went outside under the back awning. There was nothing to see but thick rain in the narrow beam of her light. Frustrated, Kathleen yelled, "You're a coward, Tommy Joyce."

As she took a breath to add something to that, Conlon said quietly, "Katie. Watch your temper now. There's no point to antagonizing the man. Let it be."

Katie had a piece of plywood under the awning that they used to block up the window.

"I'll not sleep, Conlon," Kathleen said as they returned to her living room. She saw the fatigue in his eyes. "Would you like some coffee?"

"Maybe I'll skip coffee. I'm thinking I'll lay down on your couch again. It's not yet four. I might get lucky and get a couple more hours of sleep."

Kathleen listened to him make himself comfortable and a few minutes later heard him lightly snore. Thinking about the day to come, she packed some clothes and other necessities to take to Aoife's.

She woke him gently at six. He drank a quick cup of coffee, although declined breakfast. She promised him she'd leave for Aoife's as soon as he was gone.

Conlon hesitated then nodded his head. "Don't you be wasting any time now, Katie."

Locking the front door behind Conlon, she watched from her living room window as he walked to his car. She was impatient for seven and hopefully a call from Michael.

Kathleen put her head in her hands. Her sensitivities were alert now and the feeling of wrongness was constant. She went to her drawer and got a large knife and took a half-kilo of peas down from the press. To throw at Tommy if he came. She realized the stupidity of her staying and got her coat.

The phone rang. Too early for Michael, but she answered with hope nonetheless. "Michael?"

It was Sean. "Katie, I have the worst possible news. There's no way ta make this easy."

She felt her hands start to shake as she listened in. Everything got quiet as if her body ceased to exist. Only awareness. Floated on a black ocean upheld by the swollen wave of millenia of unjustly shed blood. A sob took her whole body seemed to seize up. Falling to the floor.

She heard Sean's disembodied voice from the receiver. "Katie. Katie, are ya there?" She pulled the receiver to her like a life preserver. But there was no one there to rescue her from this news. Murder. The Garda are called. Turn off your lights and lock your doors. Conlon is coming back with a couple friends.

Colleen and Kevin are dead. Aoife is in a medic helicopter on the way to Galway.

THIRTY

Kathleen had thought she had no more tears. Bereft of feeling, finished with weeping. But as Colleen's coffin was borne out of the gray stone Church of St. Brigid and St. Oliver, Kathleen tore apart from the inside, all that was suppressed breaching the inner keep of her defenses. The pall bearers walked by her, and she reached out with two fingers, almost as if extending a blessing.

"Please stop," she said. They did. Kathleen walked to the coffin, bowed her head and placed her hand on it.

She had attended the wake but it was now, her friend locked and sealed forever to the wild Aran wind, that Kathleen sent forth a keening so suffused with grief that two other women joined her. The six male bearers stood in the immobility of their own grief, honoring Colleen with their stillness until Kathleen bowed her head and kissed the cold wood. She stepped back into the comforting nestle of Conlon's presence.

Kathleen had helped yesterday as the grave was dug at Cill Éinne. Dozens of people had shown up to offer their sweat to the difficult task. When the job was done shovels lay on the ground like branches ripped from trees after a storm. Women gathered in small groups of encircling arms and tight embraces, tears comforting the anxiety and cleansing the stain—Tommy was one of theirs. Men stood in the isolation of their guilt—the Hero in each of them had failed. Many smoked and all eyed the stark and suspicious land spreading around them, desiring secret revenge.

Kathleen's guilt had made her an island apart as she observed the groups form and reform. She gazed at the many crosses in the graveyard, each with their pattern of Gaelic knots circumscribed a path which turned ever back upon itself, again and again, an agony of infinite return. What was, is, and shall be, and this present violence will loom over life like a sword hung overhead by a thread.

So it seemed yesterday and so today. Now, on the drive to Cill Éinne she grew too weary to fight her internal lethargy, at last truly empty of tears.

"'Tis a terrible grief we bear today," Fr. McDarmuid said to those gathered in the wind and light rain. "We worry our heads about small things, and then an earthquake hits and leaves us strewn all about. We all here loved Colleen, and she loved each of us from her deep well of compassion and her strength of character. We are blest to have known her. May she dwell with the Angels and be there to greet us on our own homecomin.'"

"Amen."

When Colleen's coffin was lowered people lined to drop a handful of the rough dirt atop and then three men shoveled until the hole was full. Kathleen stayed as the rain thickened until the last of the earth was laid upon the place of Colleen's final rest. It was nine miles to her home. If Tommy, was out there, she could not care. Leaving her car, she walked, a penitent, a pilgrim asking for she knew not what.

Halfway home and soaked through and through, she remembered. It was six days now, and Michael had not called. Kathleen supposed she could finally get the Juneau operator on the phone and get his mam's number. But she discovered instead that grief has no bottom. Her wet face ran with rain, ran with tears, and she tripped and fell. She needed to smash the tightly woven knot. Somewhere in the world there must be a path to a new dawn. It was not here, not now.

Huddled and shivering against a stone wall, Kathleen resolved to leave Inis Mór.

Four days later found her returning home from Norah's place, accompanied by Conlon and a friend of his, Mick Mullen. Kathleen desperately longed for some time to be alone but was unsure how to ask or exactly what to ask for. She did want them to leave, nor probably would they go even if she requested it.

Tommy remained uncaught. The reality of the murders scratched the edge of her awareness like a dissonant note. She and Mick had checked her small shed and the walls of her property while Conlon looked into every room of her home. The Garda had left two men on the island until he was caught.

"Conlon, I'm going to sit under my back awning. I'd like a little time alone to think a bit."

He was nodding his head before she finished. "Okay. Stay close. We'll be right here."

Kathleen looked up the long rise behind her home, half expecting to see Tommy silhouetted against the far line of the hill. The whole island was on edge, and all were aware by now that Tommy had threatened her.

The murders had been terrible. It appeared Tommy had walked right up to Kevin and stabbed him to death. A blow to the head had knocked Aoife down, then he'd gone upstairs and strangled Colleen. Broken fingernails indicated she had fought hard. It made Kathleen crazy to think of the terror of Kevin's and especially Colleen's last moments.

A boat had been found in Connemara, stolen from off the south beach. The Garda did not think he was on island anymore, but until he was caught no one would be taking chances.

Kathleen took measure of her losses these last weeks. Colleen dead. Kevin, a man she did not know well, also dead. Aoife injured, but (Brigit be praised) recovering in Galway. Her instruments destroyed. Michael, disappeared. The accumulated pressure had shaken loose some foundational stability, and her basic orientation toward the goodness of life teetered on the edge of a crumbling abyss. She had not changed her mind about leaving the island and considered the details about how to do that.

Through the cracked open window into her kitchen she heard Conlon and Mick conversing. They both had businesses to run, and Kathleen knew they could not stay with her indefinitely. She stood up in frustration. Why can't they just catch him? She moved to the edge of the awning that covered her back deck. Every nook and cranny of her property was shadowed now with menace. He could be anywhere.

She despised her fear.

Kathleen turned and gazed back through her window. Conlon was just heading into the bathroom, Mick up at the coffee pot.

Impelled by guilt, helplessness, and anger, her temper flared. She wanted to go to her stone wall, and she was going to go, Tommy be damned. It was only forty feet or so. She made her way around the corner and walked to the edge of the property.

The light was getting away, day slipping fast into the night. Fields and walls lay in subdued shades from gray to almost black, dissolving imperceptibly at their farthest reach into the restless dark of the ocean. Nothing living moved across the blankness, and she felt every good thing she believed slipping into this colorless void.

A shadow disappeared into the deeper shadowed recess of a wall. Kathleen squinted her eyes, but it did not help in the falling darkness. Had she seen something? Remembering how one can better see at night, Kathleen focused her eyes just to the right of where the movement occurred. There it was, the outline of a squatting form. And now it moved, bent at the waist, running fast across the field to disappear behind a wall less than two hundred feet away. Reckless in a suddenly resurging anger Kathleen picked up a hefty stone.

She wanted to yell, "Let's end this now Tommy," but feared to rouse the two men inside. Some part of her brain screamed at her to get help, and as the seconds passed Kathleen began to feel as if she were someone else watching her life. The shadow rose up above the wall and dropped down into the field that ran its course right up to hers.

She lost sight of him. And then the shadow was moving, one hundred fifty feet away, one hundred, coming fast, oh fast.

The vast and ancient love of her ancestors washed over her with the power of words. "Turn back, Katie. Turn back to life."

Tommy was fifty feet away and rising like some ancient reptile. She screamed Conlon's name as she ran. Conlon and Mick were out the door even as she got to it, both with golf clubs in their hands.

"He's here. He's right out there, just past the wall."

Tommy was not visible in the small circle of light from the back awning.

Mick said, "Let's get inside, lock the doors. Call the Garda."

From very close, cutting like the jagged incisors of an incarnate Dark, Tommy laughed.

THIRTY ONE

Once in the house, Katie grabbed another golf club. She went to the telephone, called the number given by the Garda and reported Tommy's presence.

They jumped when a stone smashed through the window. It flew with incredible force to the opposite wall, just missing Mick, who cursed. It crashed into a small shelf full of cookbooks, knocking several of them to the floor. I just replaced that window, Katie thought.

Mick said, "Spread out. If he comes in, we have to attack together. Don't hesitate. Hit. Him. Hard."

Katie quickly closed the curtains in the window and moved to a place some fifteen feet from and directly in front of the door. "I'll stand here. If he comes in, he'll look at me first."

Mick and Conlon nodded and moved to either side of the door, about the same distance away as Katie.

She felt her heart racing and worked to calm her breath. Her eyes moved from the door to the curtains and back again. All was quiet but for the breathing of the three of them. Glass was scattered across the floor, and Katie was shocked to see the size of the stone that Tommy had thrown with such force.

The long seconds turned to minutes and Katie felt herself relax a bit. At last they heard the sound of tires on the gravel of her driveway and the two men of the Garda arrived. They impressed her with their professional calm.

One, Patrick Doolin, went outside with Mick and a large flashlight. They were back in five minutes.

Mick shook his head. "No sign of him."

Kathleen's phone rang. She answered and nodded her head. "I know. No, Mick Mullen and Conlon Conneely are here. So is the Garda. Yes," and she laughed slightly, "I'm the one that called it in. You'll call for me? Thanks, Aileen. It's Old Biddy Derrane. You have her number? Okay, thanks again."

She came back. "That was Aileen McDonough. The phone tree."

"Yes," Officer Doolin said. "We started it right away after your call."

Kathleen said, "Aileen said she'd call for me. It was smart to set that up earlier."

"Ah, I'm sure there's some people that'll be missed, but it's better than naught, so."

The other officer said, "We need to be getting back. We'll drive around some of these side roads first, then it's to Cill Rónain. Going to be a long night for us. You three going to stay together?"

Kathleen looked at the other two. Conlon opened his mouth, looking as if he would offer his place.

She shook her head. "No, I'll probably be heading back to Nora Folan's. She's got two of her adult sons and her husband at home. I'll give her a call."

"Okay then," said Patrick, "just be sure you're not alone."

Again, a boat had been stolen, this time from across North Sound in Connemara. It had been located the next day near Doolin, on the other side of Inis Oirr. Over two days, with the help of dozens of islanders, the Garda had coordinated an exhaustive search of all of Inis Mór. Tommy was not there.

On the morning of the second day, Kathleen took the ferry to Galway. She visited Aoife, who expected to return home in a few days.

It was difficult, but Kathleen kept her plans to herself. She'd gone to a travel agency and picked up several brochures, checked plane prices to a few destinations in Europe, noted ferry times and purchased a plane ticket from Shannon to Paris for day after tomorrow along with a hotel reservation for two nights. Thus equipped she took the bus to Ros á Mhil and caught the ferry back to Inis Mór

It was a cool but dry day, and she sat out on the deck of the ferry. A numbness had crept like a slow tide into her, a response to the repeated gut punches her life had taken. As uncomfortable as it was, perhaps this inner semi-coma was for the best. She believed it would not always be so.

She would start in Paris and take the short train ride down to Chartres. Beauty in any of its forms never failed to fill her cup when it felt empty although she had never faced anything quite like this.

Kathleen decided to sit before the stained glass of Chartres Cathedral, to bring her emptiness to the interior darkness of that great church which played the light of a thousand colors.

As the ferry made its long turn into the dock at Cill Rónain, Kathleen sighed. Norah had become her confidant in her plans and agrees to look in on the house once a week for "as long as it takes ya, love."

She kept Conlon in the dark. She'd simply told him she needed some time off to recover a bit.

Mick had agreed to pick her up at the ferry. When she saw him at the dock and he waved, Kathleen was struck at the abruptness with which her life had changed so much.

"And how is our Aoife, then?" Mick asked her on the drive to her house.

"She's coming home in as soon as four days. She looks good, but it's a dark time she's had, thinking on Colleen and Kevin. My God she's a tough woman. It'll be good for all when she returns, so."

"But you'll not be here."

"No. No, Mick, but it won't be forever."

"Tommy'll probably be caught eventually. It's a mystery where he is then, but he can't hide forever."

Kathleen shrugged. "The Garda have no idea. That uncertainty is hard to bear."

When they arrived, she said to Mick, "I'll probably need a couple hours. Would you like some tea or coffee?"

"Tea would be very lovely. I brought something to read, and if you need help, let me know."

She put on some peaceful music, started a fire and prepared a small tray of cheese and fruit for Mick. Out her window she saw the sky was clearing to the west. She was going to miss this view and all at once wished walk down to the water, to close her eyes and listen to the way of the shore. It hurt something fierce that she could not do so without Mick coming, but the pain reinforced her decision to leave the island.

Into her suitcase went clothes, toiletries, and a couple beloved books. Kathleen thought on taking her new fiddle, but that seemed impractical. She cringed at the thought of being without music. Her eyes fell to the dresser, and she saw Michael's last note to her. Shaking her head, she nonetheless folded it in half and put it one of her books. In no time at all she was packed. She washed the last of the dishes and folded the dish towel over a chair next to the window where the sun would dry it. She asked Mick for a couple minutes alone, and with a nod he headed out to his car.

Kathleen sensed that her return might well be to a changed life. Norah had agreed also to look in on the three women that Kathleen regularly visited. She was certain that Paddy would find someone to sing with him at Conneely's. It felt as if her parting would leave barely a ripple on the daily patterns of life on Inis Mór. Perhaps that was okay, she thought with a shrug.

There was the space where her cello had stood, and its absence mirrored something she hadn't put her finger on until she'd seen Michael's note. Almost forgotten in the disruptions of the last few days, loneliness for him surprised her once again.

Kathleen was in the act of turning away, was already half-turned away, when in the distance a stab of sunlight caught the white feathers of a swan. Kathleen thought in that moment of Fingula from the ancient story of the Children of Lir. Along with her three brothers, fate in the form of a mad stepmother had condemned her to nine hundred years of being a swan. In a single moment of guilty compassion, the stepmother Aoife blessed them with beautiful voices, and the four could sing like no other. But though many loved the sound of their song, the music brought Fingula no joy. After nine hundred years they returned to the castle of their father Lir, but all were long dead, everything fallen to ruin.

Kathleen and Aoife had laughed over the years at the mythical origins of Aoife's name. But now she could not laugh, for she felt as Fingula must have felt, propelled by forces beyond her control. To what would she return?

With a deep sigh she spoke, "Well, and that's it then, Katie."

Double-checking that the front door was locked, Kathleen looked one last time out across the fields of her life to the distant Eeragh Lighthouse. She nodded her head, crossed to the back door and stepped outside.

The phone rang. Indecision. She just wanted to go now. What if it was Conlon? What if it was news that Tommy was caught? Would that change anything?

Kathleen pursed her lips, leaned her head against the doorjamb and listened until the ringing stopped. A few moments more and she reached in her purse or the keys but couldn't find them and realized with a half laugh that they were in her jeans pocket. Distracted by these thoughts she was careless and dropped them. She looked to Mick, who held up his hands as if to say, "not my fault."

Keys in her hand again, she turned the lock. Heard the final click.

The phone rang again.

All right, she thought. She yelled out to Mick, "The phone's ringing, I'm going to get it," and reentered the house.

"This is Katie Flaherty," she said.

"Kathleen? Katie? Um, you don't know me. My name is Marianne Greene, and I'm a friend of Michael Flaherty. You know him? Do I have the right number?"

Kathleen could hear the tension in the woman's voice, and her heart hammered in her chest. "Yes, yes I do know him. Is he—" Fear stopped her voice and her hand shook. As Marianne spoke over the next minute, Kathleen slid to the floor as directionless and dry as a falling autumn leaf.

THIRTY TWO

Rising to awareness of noise. Distant. Like a trumpet hitting low notes. Played with a baffle. In another room. Floating. Drifting. Nothing.

Rising to awareness of noise. Distant. Floating. Memory of this happening before. A sharpening sense. From far back a subtle push. Drifting away.

Noise again. Again—a vertiginous swirling. Almost. Drifting. Floating.

Noise. Noise. A voice. A door opening. "It will be alright." Father. Dad. Memory tumbled into him, as if his being were poured into the vacuity of his brain. A flood of person. Of Michael, and knowing what that meant.

He listened. Breath. A body moved, a sigh. His mother. He waited. Nothing more. He thought to open his eyes, but that seemed so difficult. Sleep.

Later, a voice. "Any change, Mom?" His sister, Linda. What was all this? He tried to think, but something was missing. He had forgotten something. Relax, he thought. Listen.

"No, nothing new, honey. The doctors can't say how long he'll be like this." A pause, then his mom continued, her voice wavering. "Or if there ever will be any change." He heard her sob.

"It's okay, mom. Let the tears come. It's going to be okay." He wanted to do something. He slept.

His mother deserved to be there when he opened his eyes. He tried so hard—he would think, open up eyes, but there was no follow-through. But one day, when his mom was not there, he succeeded— his eyes opened. Slits—it was too bright. So much energy to keep them open. Sleep.

He awoke to voices. Mom. Sis. Again the slits. Then wider and he moved his head the slightest bit. His mom turned her head sharply. She rose, tears forming, reached toward his cheek as if he were a bubble that would pop if she touched too hard. He closed his eyes, felt his own tears. Tried to speak, sounding more like a frog than a man. "Love you."

Followed by, "Water."

The next day he realized he couldn't move his legs. Doctor Akiyama told him this might be temporary. X-rays showed no fracture of the spine. She explained that it had taken a long time to get the swelling down, and this might have resulted in permanent damage in his lower back. It was also possible that the swelling in his brain had caused the paralysis. And then the sobering statement from the doctor—if the paralysis were temporary, she would have expected some sensation to have returned by now. Nothing was definite.

His mom sat holding his hand.

"How are you feeling?" she asked.

He formed his words carefully, as if he were balancing on them like toy blocks on top of each other. "I hurt all over. Can't walk. Other than that, pretty good."

Michael tried to smile. His mom laughed a bit. Truthfully, he was having trouble tracking his thoughts, keeping them lined up correctly. An anxiety had settled in his gut as if someone were pressing a finger from the inside against his stomach. He did not understand why he was in the hospital with no feeling in his legs. There was another question as well, but he couldn't find it.

"Mom, what happened? Why am I here? I'm drawing a blank. Where's Maggie....?"

He stopped speaking, hearing his mom whisper, "Oh my God," seeing the horror in her eyes as memory slammed into him like a rockslide. For an instant quicker than a lightning flash, the reality of Maggie's death was as sharply outlined as the day after it happened. But there, just behind the knowledge his wife was dead, soft and full of peace, was a face framed by lovely hair. In less than a second, everything came back to him. Maggie, Kathleen, Johnny, Evie, Marianne, Vince. A tumbling car in the middle of the freeway. A ferry ride to Inis Mór. Finally talking to Johnny again. Evie's fierce determination to protect her brother. Walking up Marianne's stairway. Marianne?

A full minute passed before he spoke as he remembered. Finally, he said, "Mom, it's okay. I'm okay. I know Maggie died. It's okay." Which was not entirely true—Maggie's death still felt raw as if it happened yesterday, but he thought it would pass.

"What happened? My memory goes blank when I was going up to Marianne's apartment. Did something happen there? Is she okay?"

"She's good. She's good and she wants to see you. You were both attacked—it's a miracle either of you lived. She was shot in the head, but it grazed her; the bullet. Her brain swelled—she can tell you all of it when she sees you. You were hit in the back of the head with a baseball bat, then hard on your lower back." She started to silently cry. "Thank God...oh, Mikie, I was so afraid. The doctors had no idea what was going to happen."

He recognized the sound of approaching footsteps. Entering the room, she looked at him, eyes big. Looking relieved, she went to his mom, kneeling next to her and taking her hands. "There. Your waiting is over, and your son is back," Marianne said.

The three stayed that way as his mom cried. After a few seconds, she raised her eyes to his and smiled. He tried to smile back but had the sense his lips weren't doing what he asked.

After a minute, Marianne rose, kissing his mom's hands and then came to him. Her hair was shorter, and as she pulled it behind one ear, he noticed for the first time a place where the hair was a stubble. A dull red scar was visible under the stubble and extended partway down her forehead above her left eye.

Her eyes commanded his attention. They radiated a peace that he had never experienced before, from her or anyone else. Then, almost as if by a gust of wind, he was hit by joy. Her presence was like a breeze that whispered, "Joy, joy, joy." He did not understand how this could be.

Marianne kissed his cheek gently. "Thank God. Thank God for you, Michael. How lovely you are with us again."

She pulled up a chair, and they gazed at each other. His mom stood up and said, "I'll be back in a minute, I need to get some coffee," and was gone.

Michael looked at her scar. "What happened? The last thing I remember is going up to your apartment."

Marianne said, "We had just got back from our hike. A man was waiting in the apartment. In my bedroom. He came out. You probably never even saw him."

She stopped a moment, and her voice caught. "He killed Skippy."

"Oh, Marianne."

She shivered and wiped at a tear. "I heard a noise and came out to find you on the floor, and he was standing over you holding my brother's bat. He moved to the door, and I went to you." Her voice shook with emotion. "I couldn't even tell if you were alive Michael. He told me to get away from you and when I wouldn't." She closed her eyes. "He shot me."

Marianne took a deep breath and steadied herself. "I actually don't remember that last part, being shot, I mean. And it's only the past couple days I remembered everything else."

"Vince?"

Shaking her head, she answered. "No, it wasn't Vince," and shrugged her shoulders. "He was working the whole time. There is no doubt. The police seem stumped. They asked me questions about my neighbor, but I don't know, he seems like a nice man. There's no arrests. Nothing."

"What day is it?"

"It's Thursday. You were in a coma for thirteen days."

"Thirteen? He thought about that for a moment, speaking the number as if it were scripture. "I...wow. Thirteen days. Are you okay?"

"It's," and she paused, "complicated. I have bad dreams—not horrible, but discomfiting. I haven't slept well. I still have pretty severe headaches. Headaches, unpleasant dreams. But Michael, I feel such deep peace. I'm not afraid. I mean, I don't feel any fear about anything. I thought I was going to die, and right before, I mean right when I told him I wouldn't leave you, my fear disappeared. It's still gone. It's a miracle."

She hesitated, then continued. "We both came so close to being killed, and you, oh, do you...?" He saw where her eyes looked.

"I know about my legs." He felt impatient and didn't want to talk about it.

Marianne reached out and placed her hands on top of them where they lay under the blanket. He felt nothing. She closed her eyes and seemed to be whispering. She was praying. Fuck God, he thought so quickly it startled him.

The words were out of his mouth without a thought. "Stop that. Stop. Stop praying for me."

Marianne looked at him for several seconds, finally saying, "Michael?"

He heard the bitterness in his voice. "So, you're not afraid anymore. Now you can go to El Salvador and get yourself k...." He stopped himself from completing that wretched thought, but his voice was ragged. "And I'm paralyzed. What am I then, your vehicle to freedom, your path to losing your fear?" He was out of control but didn't care.

She looked at him, eyes unwavering, finally shaking her head. "I can't answer that, Michael. I don't pretend to understand the ways of God. Our stories are never written in full, at least not until we die." He stared hard at her as she hesitated as if considering whether to continue. She did. "I try not to lay my faith upon any particular event or outcome."

He didn't need to ask her what she meant, but then the thought intruded, again unexpectedly, where's my damn peace? The intensity shocked him.

He couldn't keep the tension out of his voice as he insisted, "You're going to walk out of here in a while, and I won't. Just don't pray for me. I can't bear that."

How is it that one can read pain in another? By what subtle shift do the inner scars of a life emerge onto the skin of a face, raw and unhidden as if the healing grace of time were an illusion? Michael never forgot this moment when Marianne sat before him like an open wound. Her head lowered just a fraction, eyes glanced momentarily away and then returned to his. It seemed as if nothing in her face moved, but he watched the intimacy between them disappear behind what he suspected was the wall of her own long, dark night of suffering.

Marianne touched her scar as she whispered, "I don't remember him shooting me. I hope I never do. But I remember the moments before. He wanted to rape me, Michael." She shrugged her shoulders. "I'm sure kill me, too. He wanted me to move away from you, but I wouldn't leave you."

He felt unworthy to be under the same roof with her and was suddenly tired, wanting to close his eyes to everything.

"Why did he leave us alive?" He yawned.

Marianne shook her head. "A friend of Mrs. Mahoney was downstairs watering her plants and dropping off her mail. She heard you fall to the floor and then him yelling and called the police. There was a car already very close, right down at the high school. She got beat up but is okay." Her voice slowed. "It's so odd to think that if she'd been ten minutes earlier or later we would be dead. Or if it had taken the police longer to come."

She stood and walked to the north facing window. "Right after we were attacked, Johnny and Evie showed up. When he figured out what happened, Johnny took off after Vince. They fought in his apartment. It was pretty bad I guess. Johnny was in the hospital a couple days. Vince got broken ribs and was pretty banged up, too. Anyway, Johnny was arrested and is at home on bail."

He heard her words, but fatigue slowed his mind. "Johnny. Arrested? Damn. Not Vince. Huh."

"No, and I think someone needs to talk to Vince, to apologize."

"Don't see Johnny...doing that."

"No, I wouldn't think so. So, I am going to find him and talk to him."

"Wait, don't go alone. Wait for...."

When he opened his eyes an hour later, Marianne was gone."

THIRTY THREE

Marianne drove back to town, trying not to cry. She knew it must be hard for Michael. He might never run or hike again. But it had hurt a lot when he attacked her healing as at his expense. She'd almost left right then but stayed to finish answering his questions. It was true her liberation from fear and his paralysis emerged from the same experience. She remembered when he'd said that if God intended her to go to El Salvador, a way would open to loosen the bonds of her fear and anxiety.

Divine irony?

The hardest moment had been when he rejected her prayer. She had wanted hold him and tell him what she knew, that grace could come from suffering.

Marianne intended to go to Vince's apartment to see if he was there but wanted to pray first. For Michael. For Vince. For Johnny—oh heck, she laughed, for the whole hurting world. At the last moment Marianne impulsively turned into Evergreen Bowl after crossing the small Gold Creek bridge. The park appeared empty except for some girls on a swing set. She got out of her car and walked beneath the canopy of trees above the creek, sitting down on one of the large boulders under the forest. She imagined Jesus sitting next to her and talked quietly to him.

"These last few weeks have been hard. The headaches, the nightmares. Worrying about Michael. Wondering who attacked us. Why?"

Marianne closed her eyes and whispered, "I feel so guilty when I see Michael's mom. It's like this wouldn't have happened to him if he hadn't been with me."

The sound of the creek surely drowned out her voice to any but the nearest passerby, but Marianne opened her eyes and looked around to make sure no one was close. She took a deep breath of the cool moist air, sighing with pleasure at the pine smell, remembering as she often did the time she and Michael had climbed Mt. Juneau together in high school, the nearness of him, the easy way their shoulders bumped, his smile when she'd leaned up and kissed his cheek. How nice he had smelled.

She whispered again. "I care about him, Jesus. Too much. I know he cares for Kathleen. I can't help it. I wish it were me." Marianne shook her head and smiled at her silly self. "Some say all is fair in love and war, but I don't want it to be that way. I might need your help with that."

Eyes still closed, she asked to understand this one thing. Michael's paralysis. Hadn't he suffered enough this last year with the death of his wife? Why this. Why now? How much is one supposed to endure?

God?

It smashed into her as if a whole mountain range fell. In an instant out of time she saw and experienced the suffering of every person in the world, as if a series of photos went sliding by infinitesimally crushed to nothingness beneath the burden.

And then it was gone. Marianne looked around, stunned at the way the creek continued its noisy descent toward the Gastineau Channel, at three ravens flying silently by as if nothing had happened, at how the girls on the swings laughed as they had since she'd arrived. Marianne realized she had been shown what Jesus had seen while nailed and stabbed and bleeding on the cross.

What had Michael said? God suffers with us?

Marianne stared across the creek at the forest which rose steeply up the lowest slope of Mt. Juneau and intuited the totality of all human effort and experience, seeing that she was less than the tip of one needle on a vast fir tree in an almost infinite forest of human experience—a *nada,* a nothing, utterly insignificant. Yet impossibly loved and incalculable in worth.

Joy flowed through her as if it were the light of a thousand suns, and in the midst of this flowing light of God she saw anew God's longing—for her to love the poor without reservation as Jesus had, to be the hand of Jesus and the heart of Mary his mother. She heard the echo down two thousand years of the last two Beatitudes in Matthew's Gospel: Blessed are the Peacemakers. Blessed are those who are persecuted for my sake.

Marianne wandered away from the creek toward the three girls swinging. The multiple colors of their clothes and shoes, combined with the long back and forth and opening and closing of their knees as they pumped created three fluid rainbows open to the sky. The girl in the middle leaned her head far back, long hair falling away toward the ground and laughed as she returned to earth and soared again. The laughter surrounded Marianne like wrapping paper, and in the heart of the gift she felt everything in her that was ever tight, knotted, twisted, fearful, loosen and slip away. As it did, absolute clarity bubbled up as naturally as an artesian well, as if it had been waiting her whole life. She was called to minister with the people of El Salvador. Like her namesake Mary saying "yes" to the Angel Gabriel, she recognized that her whole life led to this moment and she spoke the word quietly.

"Yes."

Fifteen minutes later, Marianne sighed upon entering the Cathedral, aware that soon she would be leaving. She breathed the rich smell of this place that had been such a comfort to her. She would return to Portland for whatever time it would take to figure out her specific plans for going to El Salvador. Distracted by her thoughts, Marianne was almost to her pew when she noticed Vince sitting up near the front and stood patiently until he at last became aware and turned in her direction.

Vince jerked back as if lightly struck. Marianne sat down in the pew behind him, staying near the aisle.

"Vince, my name's Marianne. I think you know who I am," she said lightly, resisting the urge to clear her throat.

When he didn't respond, she continued, "Do you know I was attacked a couple weeks ago in my home?"

"I had nothing to do with that, I was working, the police…."

Marianne raised her left hand, palm toward him. "Vince, it's okay, I'm not here for that. I know Johnny Williams attacked you in your home that night. He was under the impression that you were the one who thought to kill me and a friend. He was wrong. I thought someone should apologize to you, and," Marianne shook her head, "I don't see that being Johnny."

"Williams hates me. I hate his guts. And that warhoo…he attacked my mom to get to me. He tied her up. She still has nightmares about him."

Marianne closed her eyes, feeling the grief etch lines in her forehead. She had not known this. "I'm not making excuses for him." She scooted a little closer and looked Vince squarely in the eyes. "But he might have been given reason to think it was you—you have been following me."

He glanced away, then down. "I wasn't following you." He looked up quickly, anger in his eyes. "I never attacked you. What the hell else do you want?"

"I want this war between you and Johnny to stop. I want peace for you. For him."

Vince narrowed his eyes, distrust showing in them. "Screw that. You're lying."

She was unsure how to convince him and decided to let her words stand as they were.

"Nevertheless."

"Why would *you*," he said, practically spitting out the words, "care about *me*?"

Because you are a child of God, she thought. Because now I see you as Jesus does. "It seems like you're trying to make a better life for yourself. To be a better person. I don't want this antagonism with Johnny to mess that up."

His laugh sounded bitter.

Marianne tried another tack. "Isn't her gaze lovely?" she asked him, nodding her head toward Mary. She slid further in until she was just behind his left shoulder.

His head had turned to the statue at her words, and it was several seconds before he looked back.

She continued. "You can do worse than sit in her gaze. We all need to be seen with a look just like that."

He responded slowly. "Just a statue. Ain't real. Anyway, she ain't looking at me. She's looking at the baby." Vince shook his head.

A tremendous compassion flowed into her, and she felt it leave her, almost like goosebumps, flowing in his direction.

"It's real. No one looks at this world with as much compassion as Mary, Jesus' mother."

"Who the hell are you?" His words were harsh, but not the tone.

Marianne looked at Vince for several seconds, feeling his vulnerability. Unable to understand how or why, as if guided through a thick fog by a dim light, she spoke the next words slowly, with no sense of condemnation.

"Seventeen years ago."

Vince jerked back as if she'd shot a gun.

"Was it you, Vince?"

"What the fu…." He stopped speaking, his eyes drawn over and up to the statue of Mary as if she had spoken. She gazed down with love, with love.

His face was turned away as she spoke quietly. "You will never know peace, Vince, unless you speak the truth."

He turned quickly back to her. "Don't fuckin' talk to me about peace. You, you don't know nothin' 'bout me. Don't need you or this fuckin' statue." He started to rise, but she reached out her hand and put it on his arm.

Marianne felt ever present joy surge, and she became aware of tears. Words she would never have thought truly possible to speak fell out into the narrow space between them.

"You need to come here, Vince, and sit in her gaze. Every day. You must come, or you'll never know peace. And when you do, I want you to know this." She took a breath, aware of what the pure divine gift of these words meant for her. And for him.

"I forgive you."

He looked at her, eyes blinking fast. After a few moments, he blurted out, "I ain't goin' back to prison. You can't prove nothin' anymore."

Marianne sighed. "I know that. Don't misunderstand me. You do need to atone for what you did, somehow, Vince. You need to make up for it. But first, come here every day. Sit in her gaze. You asked me who I am. I don't know if you're Catholic." He shrugged, perhaps giving the tiniest nod. "I am named after Ann, Mary's mother, and Mary, who is mother to us all."

She stood, a tall woman at five foot eight, but still diminutive next to him.

"Every day, Vince. Every day. Then you will learn what you need to do." She left the pew. Genuflecting while making the sign of the cross, she looked over at him. He hadn't moved. Nearing the door to the vestibule, the sound of his voice brought her to a stop.

"Marianne." He cleared his throat.

She turned back.

"Look, I'm." He stopped, as if a man who has just come to the base of a cliff and knows he must ascend it unaided.

"This is stupid." He hesitated while she waited. "All right. I'm sorry."

She came halfway back up the aisle. "Now you have a chance to be free." She turned and left without looking back.

After she was gone, Vince felt the emptiness of the room and was left with a vague sense of loneliness. He sat slowly back down. His eyes were drawn not to Mary but to the crucifix up front. He looked around the church, then finally back at Mary's face as she gazed down at her infant son. It had shocked him that Marianne had referred to the rape, and his reaction now shocked him even more. He wished it had never happened. It was as if her words had connected all the dots of his life. The ugliness of his father. The too-passive love of his mom. The anger that would explode out of him. He looked again at Mary and saw the chance he had been given—a job he liked, a boss that treated him good, a mom who looked at him with love. Forgiveness.

For the worst thing he had ever intentionally done.

He wished that he had never raped Marianne. He wished he had not killed Evie's father. He wished his father, who had pounded anger into him like a rusted spike, had not hated him. For a moment he saw his father before him and raised his hand as if to get away from a bright light. His eyes came to rest on the crucifix. A short time later he knew what he had to do.

He rose, left the church and headed toward Johnny William's house.

THIRTY FOUR

Juneau, One Week Later

Michael heard a knock at the door. He yelled out, "Coming," and rolled through the living room into the narrow front hall. There was not room for him to maneuver in the hall, so he said loudly, "You'll have to open it yourself." Probably someone for his mom. At that moment the phone rang. He turned his wheelchair, undecided whether to greet the person who was coming in or get the phone.

Michael heard the door open and someone enter. He started to turn back to explain about the phone, but before he had time to see who it was, the person came quickly to him.

He smelled her hair just before she, from behind, kissed his head and hugged him. He could only close his eyes in the deepest gratitude he had felt in years. Maybe ever.

She sang, "And the seasons, with their turnin' we'll put new seeds down there yearly, and the bloomin' will not end, with our passin' from this mountain, will ye go, lassie, go."

There was a moment of silence. "Michael Flaherty, as Brigit lives it is good to see you then." He could not respond, and she continued, speaking faster, "Oh Michael I have missed you something fierce. I am here to love you. There, I said it. And I've flown six thousand miles to say it so you better well have something nice to say to me."

And Kathleen came around the front of his chair, a miracle, a balm, a wonder. She squatted so her eyes were level with his. A resounding "Yes" echoed through his whole being, months and months of pain released into an ascension of joy that swirled up and up like a release of doves or children's laughter as they ran into the ocean. He still couldn't speak. He reached out to her cheek and then slipped his hand through her thick red hair around the back of her head, pulling her to him. She stumbled a bit and dropped to her knees. "Ouch," she said but laughed.

Their lips touched, opened, and at last they kissed, setting the seal of their hearts.

When they broke the kiss, he buried his nose in her hair as if breathing in the scent of her would fill the black hole of his bitterness.

He laughed and said, "Kathleen, I…."

But she impulsively cut him off with a second kiss.

Michael got himself propped up in the corner of the couch, and Kathleen sat down next to him. He circled her shoulders in the protective arc of his right arm and she leaned in. They sat in silence for a minute. She had placed her right hand on his chest, and he gently reached and pulled it to his lips.

To his surprise, Kathleen began to silently cry.

"Kathleen?"

She told him all that had happened. He reared up himself when she came to Colleen. She'd had so much courage. And Aoife. He realized how much he cared for the older woman.

Kathleen reached the end of her telling. "I was locking my door when the phone rang. It was your friend, Marianne. That was almost a couple weeks ago. Thank God she called. I decided to surprise you, I hope you don't mind."

Michael shook his head in answer.

Kathleen continued. "But Michael, your legs. How are you?"

He closed his eyes. He tried to hide it from his mom and friends, but the reality of his legs was crushing his spirit. How could he be happy without them? Michael thought of never hiking again, never running. Much less walking. Of how hard it would be to simply do the multitude of daily tasks to which he had never given thought. Life's possibilities had narrowed down. Anger and depression were constantly nudging the edge of his consciousness.

But then there was this present happiness. That was what he wanted to share.

"Today is one of the best days ever. Because you're here. Once I could, I called you, but no one answered. I didn't know you weren't there and had no idea what to think. None of it made sense to me, but then I guess I fell into my own pity. To be honest, it hurt so much when I thought you were gone from my life that I don't know how I am now. Without the pain, I mean."

"Michael, I'm so sorry," she whispered.

He shook his head. "I am too, but it's not your fault. It just happened. There's days I feel sorry for myself, then chide myself, lots of people have it way worse than me. But I feel so bleak sometimes, and honestly," and he indicated with his hand his dead legs, "what kind of life is this for you? Would you choose it ahead of time?"

Michael's mom came in, and if she was surprised to see a woman snuggled with her son, she gave no sign. Michael introduced the pair to each other.

His mom asked Kathleen, "When did you get in?"

"This morning." She yawned. "Oh, I'm sorry, I'm exhausted. A long flight, and I think it's about four in the morning for me."

"Would you like some coffee or water?"

"I think some water would be nice. Flying makes me thirsty."

Michael's mom came out a few minutes later with some water, cheese slices and a cut apple on a plate.

"Oh, Mrs. Flaherty, this is nice, thank you," she said after taking a drink of water.

"Good. So now I have to go visit my friend Mary. I'll be back in a couple hours. It's so nice to meet you, Kathleen."

"I'm glad to meet you too."

After she left, Kathleen picked up where they'd left off. "Michael, I know we have a lot ahead of us, not all of it easy. But right now let's just be happy we found each other again."

Michael laughed and took her hand. She snuggled back up to him, lifting her face to be kissed, which Michael was glad to do. After some time, he said, "You'll be glad to know that all is not dead down below."

She yawned deeply and said, "Mmm. That's nice." She yawned again, closed her eyes and said drowsily, "I'm glad. I thought about it. Would have been difficult, what with everything else we have to adjust to."

The ever-ready anger pounced, raking its claws across the skin of his happiness, drawing blood. "Well," he said curtly, "I should probably add that my erections are rather soft at the moment, perhaps not up to your...." His words died out. He was rendered mute by his own petty cruelty. I'm getting good at this, he thought petulantly, first with Marianne and now Kathleen. He waited for her temper to flare. Kathleen had removed her head from his chest and sat up. She appeared to struggle with her emotions and left the couch for the living room window. He could read the tension in the way she held her head higher than usual, shoulders slightly hunched.

Without turning Kathleen said, "I had a boyfriend for two years in Dublin. I think I mentioned him to you." She stopped, as if thinking. "He was difficult. Unable to see things beyond his own little interest. He would take what I said and misconstrue it, time and time again. I thought my wanting to change him was love."

She turned to him. "I don't understand what just happened, but please don't make a puddle into an ocean. Please. I am grateful beyond words that we are together again."

Kathleen came back and sat down. She looked tired and had lost weight. In the months since he'd left Inis Mór her losses had mounted one upon the another, and who could add up to the terrible cost of this multiplicity?

After all that, he thought, she came here.

"Kathleen." She looked at him without moving her head. "I dreamed of you last week. I was on a bicycle, stopped on a narrow road. Nowhere specific, but like Inis Mór. It was a high blue sky but early in the morning, and I began pedaling down this lane. Church bells started to ring. I was pedaling effortless, these beautiful bells sounding all around, practically lifting me into the air with their syncopated harmonies. I came over a rise and looked down to your home, filled with so much joy it was as if the bells resounded from within my own heart. When I awoke, it was crushing. I decided then that as soon as I could I was going to Inis Mór, to find out why you hadn't answered my calls. To tell you that, wheelchair and all, I love you. And now here you are, come six thousand miles for us. I'm sorry for what I said. I was unkind and petty. It's just all my anger at the whole thing."

Katie stood, almost swaying on her feet. "Don't worry your head about it, Michael. I'm falling off my feet. We'll get this all figured out, but I just want to lay down. Near you."

They went into his bedroom, and he laid down on his back on the left side of the bed. She snuggled into the niche of his right shoulder.

Michael wished he could move and hold her more completely. His hatred of his dead lower body surged again. He felt like a ping pong ball in the back and forth of his mood. For an instant Michael felt the future press down like a huge weight and struggled against his anger and self-doubt. How could they adjust to so much change? How would he be able to stop feeling like a hindrance to her? And Inis Mór felt suddenly so small. What would he do with all his days there?

He heard the change in her breath when she fell asleep. She snuggled even closer to him. Kathleen was here, in his arms. For the moment, the negativity slipped away.

THIRTY FOUR

Juneau, One Week Later

Michael heard a knock at the door. He yelled out, "Coming," and rolled through the living room into the narrow front hall. There was not room for him to maneuver in the hall, so he said loudly, "You'll have to open it yourself." Probably someone for his mom. At that moment the phone rang. He turned his wheelchair, undecided whether to greet the person who was coming in or get the phone.

Michael heard the door open and someone enter. He started to turn back to explain about the phone, but before he had time to see who it was, the person came quickly to him.

He smelled her hair just before she, from behind, kissed his head and hugged him. He could only close his eyes in the deepest gratitude he had felt in years. Maybe ever.

She sang, "And the seasons, with their turnin' we'll put new seeds down there yearly, and the bloomin' will not end, with our passin' from this mountain, will ye go, lassie, go."

There was a moment of silence. "Michael Flaherty, as Brigit lives it is good to see you then." He could not respond, and she continued, speaking faster, "Oh Michael I have missed you something fierce. I am here to love you. There, I said it. And I've flown six thousand miles to say it so you better well have something nice to say to me."

And Kathleen came around the front of his chair, a miracle, a balm, a wonder. She squatted so her eyes were level with his. A resounding "Yes" echoed through his whole being, months and months of pain released into an ascension of joy that swirled up and up like a release of doves or children's laughter as they ran into the ocean. He still couldn't speak. He reached out to her cheek and then slipped his hand through her thick red hair around the back of her head, pulling her to him. She stumbled a bit and dropped to her knees. "Ouch," she said but laughed.

Their lips touched, opened, and at last they kissed, setting the seal of their hearts.

When they broke the kiss, he buried his nose in her hair as if breathing in the scent of her would fill the black hole of his bitterness.

He laughed and said, "Kathleen, I…."

But she impulsively cut him off with a second kiss.

Michael got himself propped up in the corner of the couch, and Kathleen sat down next to him. He circled her shoulders in the protective arc of his right arm and she leaned in. They sat in silence for a minute. She had placed her right hand on his chest, and he gently reached and pulled it to his lips.

To his surprise, Kathleen began to silently cry.

"Kathleen?"

She told him all that had happened. He reared up himself when she came to Colleen. She'd had so much courage. And Aoife. He realized how much he cared for the older woman.

Kathleen reached the end of her telling. "I was locking my door when the phone rang. It was your friend, Marianne. That was almost a couple weeks ago. Thank God she called. I decided to surprise you, I hope you don't mind."

Michael shook his head in answer.

Kathleen continued. "But Michael, your legs. How are you?"

He closed his eyes. He tried to hide it from his mom and friends, but the reality of his legs was crushing his spirit. How could he be happy without them? Michael thought of never hiking again, never running. Much less walking. Of how hard it would be to simply do the multitude of daily tasks to which he had never given thought. Life's possibilities had narrowed down. Anger and depression were constantly nudging the edge of his consciousness.

But then there was this present happiness. That was what he wanted to share.

"Today is one of the best days ever. Because you're here. Once I could, I called you, but no one answered. I didn't know you weren't there and had no idea what to think. None of it made sense to me, but then I guess I fell into my own pity. To be honest, it hurt so much when I thought you were gone from my life that I don't know how I am now. Without the pain, I mean."

"Michael, I'm so sorry," she whispered.

He shook his head. "I am too, but it's not your fault. It just happened. There's days I feel sorry for myself, then chide myself, lots of people have it way worse than me. But I feel so bleak sometimes, and honestly," and he indicated with his hand his dead legs, "what kind of life is this for you? Would you choose it ahead of time?"

Michael's mom came in, and if she was surprised to see a woman snuggled with her son, she gave no sign. Michael introduced the pair to each other.

His mom asked Kathleen, "When did you get in?"

"This morning." She yawned. "Oh, I'm sorry, I'm exhausted. A long flight, and I think it's about four in the morning for me."

"Would you like some coffee or water?"

"I think some water would be nice. Flying makes me thirsty."

Michael's mom came out a few minutes later with some water, cheese slices and a cut apple on a plate.

"Oh, Mrs. Flaherty, this is nice, thank you," she said after taking a drink of water.

"Good. So now I have to go visit my friend Mary. I'll be back in a couple hours. It's so nice to meet you, Kathleen."

"I'm glad to meet you too."

After she left, Kathleen picked up where they'd left off. "Michael, I know we have a lot ahead of us, not all of it easy. But right now let's just be happy we found each other again."

Michael laughed and took her hand. She snuggled back up to him, lifting her face to be kissed, which Michael was glad to do. After some time, he said, "You'll be glad to know that all is not dead down below."

She yawned deeply and said, "Mmm. That's nice." She yawned again, closed her eyes and said drowsily, "I'm glad. I thought about it. Would have been difficult, what with everything else we have to adjust to."

The ever-ready anger pounced, raking its claws across the skin of his happiness, drawing blood. "Well," he said curtly, "I should probably add that my erections are rather soft at the moment, perhaps not up to your...." His words died out. He was rendered mute by his own petty cruelty. I'm getting good at this, he thought petulantly, first with Marianne and now Kathleen. He waited for her temper to flare. Kathleen had removed her head from his chest and sat up. She appeared to struggle with her emotions and left the couch for the living room window. He could read the tension in the way she held her head higher than usual, shoulders slightly hunched.

Without turning Kathleen said, "I had a boyfriend for two years in Dublin. I think I mentioned him to you." She stopped, as if thinking. "He was difficult. Unable to see things beyond his own little interest. He would take what I said and misconstrue it, time and time again. I thought my wanting to change him was love."

She turned to him. "I don't understand what just happened, but please don't make a puddle into an ocean. Please. I am grateful beyond words that we are together again."

Kathleen came back and sat down. She looked tired and had lost weight. In the months since he'd left Inis Mór her losses had mounted one upon the another, and who could add up to the terrible cost of this multiplicity?

After all that, he thought, she came here.

"Kathleen." She looked at him without moving her head. "I dreamed of you last week. I was on a bicycle, stopped on a narrow road. Nowhere specific, but like Inis Mór. It was a high blue sky but early in the morning, and I began pedaling down this lane. Church bells started to ring. I was pedaling effortless, these beautiful bells sounding all around, practically lifting me into the air with their syncopated harmonies. I came over a rise and looked down to your home, filled with so much joy it was as if the bells resounded from within my own heart. When I awoke, it was crushing. I decided then that as soon as I could I was going to Inis Mór, to find out why you hadn't answered my calls. To tell you that, wheelchair and all, I love you. And now here you are, come six thousand miles for us. I'm sorry for what I said. I was unkind and petty. It's just all my anger at the whole thing."

Katie stood, almost swaying on her feet. "Don't worry your head about it, Michael. I'm falling off my feet. We'll get this all figured out, but I just want to lay down. Near you."

They went into his bedroom, and he laid down on his back on the left side of the bed. She snuggled into the niche of his right shoulder.

Michael wished he could move and hold her more completely. His hatred of his dead lower body surged again. He felt like a ping pong ball in the back and forth of his mood. For an instant Michael felt the future press down like a huge weight and struggled against his anger and self-doubt. How could they adjust to so much change? How would he be able to stop feeling like a hindrance to her? And Inis Mór felt suddenly so small. What would he do with all his days there?

He heard the change in her breath when she fell asleep. She snuggled even closer to him. Kathleen was here, in his arms. For the moment, the negativity slipped away.

THIRTY SIX

Juneau, Five Weeks Later

Michael looked toward the door with increasing anxiety. His wheelchair had long ago been stored and he could feel the seconds ticking by. What if she didn't come?

The flight attendants were checking and closing the overhead bins when Marianne finally stepped breathlessly through the door. Even while showing her ticket to the flight attendant, her eyes found his and she smiled. Michael shook his head slightly, unable to deny the joy of her presence. Her hair had filled in nicely and the scar was fading. She quickly stowed her carry-on and squeezed past him and exclaimed, "Michael, this is so lovely. I always wanted to travel first class. Thank you."

Marianne had only visited him a few times since that day he had refused her prayer, and they had never been alone together. She'd stayed away almost completely for the six days Katie had been in Juneau and moved out of his mom's home into a co-worker's house who lived only a half mile from the hospital. He missed her presence and had several times chided himself for causing the breach in their friendship. Yet it had been her idea for them to leave Juneau together, and she had waited a few extra weeks for him to be ready. This surprised him and gave Michael hope he might be able to repair some of the damage.

"I kind of had no choice about the first class, what with my legs and all. But I'm glad we can fly down to Seattle together."

"I'm sorry I was late—I wanted to hike back Basin one last time and kind of lost track of how long it would take me to get back home. Oof, the taxi took forever. I was going crazy."

When the Alaska Airlines 727 lifted off, Michael leaned forward to look out the window, and for a moment felt irritation at Marianne for having the window seat. He shook his head, recognizing she had done nothing wrong. This anger was doing him no good, he knew it. It seemed to have a life of its own.

She turned to him and said, "I wish you had the window seat, Michael. I remember how you used to talk about flying with your dad—you must have so many memories."

Well.

"It's okay. Really, it is a lot simpler to sit on the aisle." He leaned toward the window again as the jet finished its long turn back to the south. "Look," he pointed, "you can see Devil's Paw way off there in the distance."

Marianne nodded. Michael noticed the way her hair fell lightly off her right shoulder. He sighed inwardly, wondering what might have happened to them if the rape had never occurred, and they'd gone to Seattle University together. "I see it," she said excitedly.

"My dad took by there once in a Cessna 180. I was nine or ten. I felt like I could reach out and touch its huge cliffs. Then we headed over the Ice Cap to the head of Mendenhall and flew down the long curves of its eight-mile length. I'll never forget."

He said quietly, "Miss you, Dad."

Marianne reached and touched his arm as she nodded her head the slightest bit. "I remember you missing him back then."

It was the look in her eyes and the smell of her hair that sent him spinning back sixteen years to the day he'd told her about his dad's death. They'd driven out to the Shrine and walked across the causeway to a high viewpoint just past the beautiful stone chapel dedicated to St. Thérèse of Lisieux. Twenty miles across Lynn Canal the Chilkats rose to their jagged six thousand foot heights, the cool April suspended above Mt. Golub. He told her of the winter storm and the missing plane and his dad flying out to find it. About his dad's on loss of power and forced landing just offshore in the frigid waters of Peril Straight. How he made it to shore with a first aid kit and food, hiking cold and shivering a couple miles, finding the original crash with two survivors. How he died of hypothermia even as he brought the supplies that allowed the pair to live. Marianne had stepped up on a stone and took him into her arms, and he knew for the first time the comfort of physical touch of a beloved. He remembered the warm feel of her kiss.

That day had been his eighteenth birthday. It was three evenings later that they first made love. Mere weeks from the end of it all. He was filled with melancholy for the untold story of who they would have been. Michael realized he had been resisting his growing feelings for her. He thought of Kathleen and experienced not the slightest hesitation nor doubt. But he could not deny the strength of his affection for Marianne. At exactly that moment she turned toward him, and it was as if her eyes came to his in slow motion. They contained all the joy of friendship and the melancholy of limitation, of what might have been and would never be. Of the kiss last month that had been a benediction. Of the suffering that brought them to this moment. How would he say goodbye? "I like this, Michael. It feels, well," and Marianne shrugged her shoulders, "honestly it feels like our friendship is back. I'm sorry if I did anything wrong. Maybe I came on too strong that day at the hospital."

He was already shaking his head. "You didn't do anything. It's just been difficult. I'm angry, having trouble accepting this. Jesus, I took so much for granted, you know? I'm ashamed to admit I took my anger out on you. But look at you! All happy, full of joy, Christ you radiate it, Marianne."

She shook her head slightly, seeming about to respond. But he continued, "When will we see each other again? I'm glad this gives me a chance to apologize for being an ass. And just to be together one last time."

She laughed and surprised him with her language. "You were a bit of an ass." Then her face turned serious. "But I do know this is easier for me than you."

The stewardess interrupted them, taking their order for two orange juices which she delivered a couple minutes later. Marianne sipped at hers while Michael drank his quickly.

Looking at him over the rim of her glass she said. "So, we're both off to new lives. You must be excited."

Michael smiled. "Oh, I am. A little nervous, too."

"Nervous?"

"Moving to a new place and getting accustomed to these useless legs, and," he took a deep breath, "I mean, at some point I need to figure out what to do with myself."

Michael turned the conversation. "Are you nervous?"

"I don't know. Yeah, a bit. Mostly I just feel so lucky there is a sponsoring parish for El Salvador right in Portland. I looked at the Maryknoll Missionaries, but I'm still praying about being a nun. Sometimes, I'm not…." She stopped and looked quickly away as she said quietly, "I am not so sure." She did not turn back from the window.

In the quiet whisper of her body language, Michael sensed something amiss. He waited a few seconds.

"Marianne?"

"Just a sec." Her voice shook. She wiped at her eyes.

"I'm sorry, Michael, I'm so sorry. It's stupid. It's just these whole last couple months, seeing you again and being attacked and worrying about you, and now having to say goodbye." She choked up and could not continue. For one naked moment, she looked at him fully before she was able to shield her feelings. Closing her eyes, Marianne shook her head and turned briefly back to the window.

"How did I let myself blunder into that," Marianne thought. This is going to be the worst thing ever. And then she remembered where she hoped to be heading in a couple months. She smiled. Okay, maybe not the worst thing ever. The last weeks had been difficult. Michael had withdrawn a bit from her and that had hurt. His evident happiness to be with her now was a wonderful relief but had put her back in touch with her feelings for him. She chastised herself for having let these show even for a few seconds.

Marianne felt suspended from the cord of a complex combination of emotions—happiness, regret, frustration, the loneliness of parting, love. They penetrated her in a way beyond her capacity to fully fathom. The question of how to live, which she'd thought practically settled, had quickened, and her life seemed pregnant with new possibilities.

Marianne thought again of their child. She'd become certain her daughter was also Michael's. It was hard to say nothing to him, and she considered that perhaps Michael's withdrawal these past weeks had been a blessing. But their daughter would be eighteen in just over a year, and maybe then she might try to find her.

Michael touched her shoulder, and she turned back to him, willing her thoughts in a different direction Taking a deep breath and wiping once more at her damp cheeks, she said, "That's better. I hope I don't look a mess."

He shook his head. "And I guess it's not stupid. I'm really grateful we got to meet each other again, but now I'm going to miss you."

If he had understood the look in her eyes from a few seconds ago, Michael gave no sign. He put his hand on her arm and said, "Yeah. Me, too." I'm not looking forward to parting at SeaTac." He changed the subject. "Marianne, I am not sure how to say this, but I worry about you, especially after the murder of those four nuns last month."

Marianne shook her head. "They're heroes to me. One of them, Jean Donovan, was a lay woman," she said, continuing in a whisper, "And Sister Dorothy Kazel, Maura Clarke, Ita Ford. Everything I read talks about what wonderful women they were." Then her voice solidified. "I know it's dangerous, Michael. But this is the only thing in my life I feel certainty about. I do not want to die, but I don't have the capacity any more to say 'no'. I mean, I could, but it would be so wrong. I understand Mary and her improbable 'yes' to the angel Gabriel. I feel like I am living into my name."

The 727 shuddered for a few second in turbulence and settled.

"I don't have the heart any more to turn back."

Michael pursed his lips. "You know that scripture about the grain of wheat that must fall to the ground and die to be reborn? I find myself thinking of that. For both of us."

"My family is so angry—I know I've said this before, but it means so much to me that you get it. It's comforting. "And," she continued, her voice softer, "it doesn't mean I'm going to die."

He reached for her hand, leaned toward her and kissed her hair gently. Oh, Michael, she thought.

"I will pray for your safety every day and that we might see each other again."

He withdrew his hand and putting his palms on the armrests, raised his body up.

Marianne probed gently. "Michael, are you beginning to accept what happened?"

She saw the pain etched in his face.

He said, "I dream almost every night of running. I'm back Basin, between First and Second Bridges. I'm running fast, smoothly. It feels like I'm on the crest of a wave which pushes me along. I'm just flying, my feet light, smooth, almost like I'm soaring. It's so real." He hesitated. "It hurts like hell when I wake up. Every time. For a few seconds it's like crashing back to the first couple days when I first knew I was paralyzed. I guess it's getting a little better with the passing of time."

He wasn't finished. "You know," and he breathed deeply, "sometimes I think I feel something in my legs. But it is always fleeting." He took her hand, and placed it just above his left knee. "Push down."

She did so. Michael shook his head. "Nope. But it's right there that I think I feel a sensation. Like tiny needles. I know it's probably nothing, and the hope it engenders is terrible. It's like I'm caught in a storm and I see the way to shelter, but I keep hoping for the day before when the storm hadn't arrived yet. It freezes me in place."

Marianne physically felt her sympathy, almost like unseen goosebumps and would have taken his pain if it were possible. She said slowly, "There is a gift for you in this somewhere, Michael. A jewel hidden in all the clutter. Christ is forming you into the person you are called to be. I believe that to the core of my being."

He shook his head, but did not disagree. "I said something to you once—that if God intended for you to go to El Salvador, a way would open."

"Yes."

As the 727 hit a little more turbulence, Michael looked briefly irritated and again adjusted his body. "Too much bouncing around today. You know,

I loved flying for Kenmore Air, but sometimes I did dream of becoming a jet pilot. That's not going to happen."

He continued, "I wonder what now?"

There is something else, she thought.

They were the last ones to depart the jet. Marianne saw Michael's relief when the stewardess allowed him to use the bathroom even though the plane was not in flight.

When the two of them emerged into the terminal, they paused a moment, taking in the noisy hubbub. Speaking loudly over the din, Michael asked, "How much time do we have?"

"An hour until I need to check in. Let's find someplace quiet."

Michael agreed and the pair started down the D Concourse toward the main terminal. Their progress was slow, with a couple people staring at Michael. Well, she thought, this was not how I imagined our last hour together.

As they made their way toward the ticket counters, Michael said, "I know a quiet place." He led her past the multiple restaurants and shops which pulled in the waiting passengers, through a huge central hub, past a large piece of abstract statuary and down a narrower corridor that ended at a room with art on the wall and a few people sitting in comfortable chairs, most with their eyes closed. Marianne took a breath of relief as they found a place to sit near each other.

"Much better," she said.

"I found it a few years ago when I had a lot of time to kill. Maggie had a meeting in Tacoma and had to drop me off at the airport three hours early."

They sat quietly for a few moments. Marianne looked at her watch—in about forty-five minutes she'd need to head for her gate to check in. Her stomach hurt at the thought of saying goodbye. Of all that must remain unsaid.

"So, when exactly is your flight to Ireland?"

"A little less than a month. There's a ton of odds and ends to take care of, and I need to decide whether to rent the house or sell it. Plus, more physical therapy. I'll tell you what, first class is expensive to Europe."

They were quiet again. All at once he looked at her and smiled. "When you came on the plane, the look on your face reminded me of when we first met."

"You had just beaten my brother in a race at the old baseball field downtown and David was really surprised. He claimed he stumbled. I laughed that you'd beaten him. You looked at me with an impish smile on your face and kind of won my heart right there."

She felt her heart beat faster. "Well, it took you long enough to ask me out. I said no to two other boys who asked me to Junior Prom. I thought I was going to be reduced to having one of my friends tell one of your friends to tell you...."

They looked at each other and started laughing. Relaxed, the two chatted easily for the next half hour. In the back of her mind, Marianne felt the minutes sliding away. Then Michael surprised her.

"Marianne, I know we have about fifteen minutes left, but I, well, I want to be gone when you board your flight. This is hard enough, and I don't want to be wheeling through the airport." He stopped. "I just, this is too hard. Can we say goodbye now, and I can be out of the airport when your flight boards?"

She pursed her lips, keeping the disappointment off her face but understanding his feelings. "Let's head for the ticket counter and say goodbye there."

He hesitated, saying slowly, "Okay. Go ahead and push me. I think it'll be simpler."

"Your wish, oh master." They both laughed, sounding a little brittle to her. She started to rise, but Michael stopped her with a hand on her arm.

He said, "I never really…." Closed his eyes, sighing. "I think of myself sometimes on that floor, totally helpless. Of you." She saw him struggle to control his emotions, and she was staggered by the intensity of her feelings.

He continued, "Of you standing by me. It's almost like I can see it. You didn't leave me alone, Marianne. You didn't leave me. I suppose we both should have died. I never thanked you."

They looked at each other for a long time. Marianne felt her heart beating. Finally he smiled and nodded.

"So, then," he said.

Marianne struggled to say it. "So, then."

"Maybe I'll just go?"

"Yes." She leaned in and kissed him on the cheek. He did the same, held her hands for a few moments, gave a quick squeeze, and was off. She watched him negotiate around a couple people, approaching the corner. She jumped up and yelled as she ran toward him, "Michael, wait."

THIRTY SEVEN

Seattle

Michael took a cab to his home near Green Lake where he was met by Jake McKiernan, a man he'd hired to take care of the house after he left for Ireland. At his instructions three weeks ago, Jake oversaw some light renovations in the bathroom and kitchen, as well as putting a wheelchair ramp in the garage up the single step needed to get into the house.

That had been hours ago. Michael had eaten some eggs and toast, watched a little television, read the *Times* that Jake had brought him and at one point moved to the couch. It was work to sit in it. His body kept slipping down a bit.

His thoughts shifted like the shapes of clouds. He was so glad Marianne had run up to him at the end, asking if they could write, if she could have his Inis Mór address. She'd laughed delightedly when he took the folded piece of paper out of his coat pocket with Aoifes address already on it, having simply forgotten to give it to her.

He was not blind to Marianne's feelings and would be a liar to deny his for her. As she'd come running up, he was frozen in fear that she'd put them to words and ask something from him he could not give. Or would not.

He hoped for his future with Kathleen. It was what he longed for. Sometimes he felt as if he hadn't chosen Kathleen, but had rather been chosen. He recognized with new clarity that his anxiety lay not with Kathleen, not with them as a couple, but in the newness of everything about to come. It was all so unknown. Michael closed his eyes and allowed himself to feel the anxiety as it came into awareness. Slipping again, he pushed himself up with his hands and ran them through his hair. Getting kind of long, he thought. Tasted his sour breath. Pulling the wheelchair over, Michael set the brake and went to slide himself into it. Carelessly. The chair pivoted away from him on the braked wheel. He missed and tumbled to the floor, banging his hip on the heavy coffee table. Dammit, he thought. This sucks. He angrily pulled himself up and practically threw himself into the chair.

How weird to feel no pain in his hip.

In the interstices of his breathing he noticed the quiet of the house. The fridge hummed subtly, a constant undertone against which the occasional wind-driven patter of rain against the windows would tap, like dead leaves across stony ground. A couple cats screeched outside. A car door slammed. All at once he could see his whole life stretched out before him, a tedious series of struggles to accomplish the smallest tasks.

He hadn't seen Kathleen in nearly four weeks now, and it would be almost as long before he flew to Ireland. They continued to talk on the phone every other day. Women on the island were coming to see her again. She was singing at Conneely's, waiting tables in Kil Ronin.

She seemed happy enough, a turn of phrase that saddened him. Kathleen had shone as a bright star against the firmament of life. Behind the dimming of her light lurked the fear of Tommy, who had somehow eluded capture. Michael had set his one photo of her on the end table and picked it up now. He longed to reach out and brush her curls with his fingers.

Setting the photo back on the end table, he noticed his wallet and used plane ticket. Marianne was certainly home in Portland now. A thought disturbed him profoundly. Whoever had attacked them was still out there, probably planning to harm other people. It made him glad both Marianne and he were out of Juneau, but the evil still lurked, impossible to predict or control.

And Marianne was going to take her gentle heart into the midst of that sort of evil in El Salvador.

Near the end of their flight Marianne had told him about having forgiven Vince, and of the changes she hoped he was undergoing. Vince had been a bad guy for as long as he could remember, and he had kept his skepticism to himself. But he could not refute her hope for Vince nor deny the fact that she was living just as Jesus did.

On impulse he rolled his chair into the small living room and pulled an old photo album off a bookshelf. He turned on a lamp and opened it to his only picture of him and Marianne, from 1964. He couldn't remember who took it. They were in Thibodeau's Market, and she was standing next to him, holding a Tab soda in her hand. It had been on their second or third date, and he'd asked her what she wanted to do with her life.

"I'm not exactly sure. I want to help people as a nurse or even a doctor. I dream about helping the poor, being part of a group who bring medical care to those who can't afford it."

Well, Michael thought, coming back to the present, she's sure making that dream come true.

And what am I to dream now? He thought. His flying days were over. This was what made him most anxious about his upcoming move to Inis Mór—what was he going to do? Kathleen had said she'd be willing to move away for him to have a career, but he found that hard to imagine. Inis Mór was in her marrow. It was her decision whether to stay or leave, but was it only her decision?

"God, it would sure be nice to get some kind of sign," he said out loud into the emptiness.

As a kid he'd prayed for a vision of the Blessed Virgin Mary, but it never happened. He'd been disappointed until about the sixth grade when actual girls had become much more interesting than blessed virgins. He laughed at the thought, speaking again. "So how about it, God? How about a sign? How about some help here?"

The house remained silent. Michael remembered a quote from St. Theresa of Avila, a vivacious and brilliant sixteenth century reforming nun who got frustrated once from her perceived lack of help from Jesus during a difficult time. "If this is the way you treat your friends," she'd written, "no wonder you have so few of them."

He began rolling the chair around the house, looking at all the things he and Maggie had owned, trying to imagine selling most of it. What should he keep? Give away? Everything needed to be packed. He could get help there, but all the upcoming decisions overwhelmed him. Shit, he thought with a rueful smile, I can barely take a crap on my own, and I'm supposed to move to Ireland?

Michael rolled over to the photos on the mantel and stretched to pull down a favorite photo of Maggie. He sighed somewhat contentedly as he looked at the two of them.

A tear fell on the glass covering the photograph, then another and a third. More fell, each tracing the path of fourteen months of grief and guilt down his cheek and falling away like a release. They dropped to the photo album without a hurry.

She came as subtly as a moment between breaths. Michael felt as if he were lifted out of his chair and cradled in the arms of a joy and comfort which whispered, "It will be alright." And then he saw her, in silhouette. The outline of a female figure who turned toward him, and he had to glance away from the radiance behind her.

From nowhere words emerged from his mouth. "Holy shit." And he laughed. The laughter welled up without volition in waves that rolled through his suffering, up and out, up and out, on and on and on, a joy that simply emerged moment after moment. Once he tried to stop, but couldn't, and so he let it come and come until at last it naturally echoed away.

She approached and slowly coalesced into a face that was turned a bit to the side, her eyes looking down and slightly to his right. He thought improbably of one of Marianne's drawings. At that moment she raised her eyes, and Michael saw the contours of a love that probed him with a fathomless compassion. Wordlessly She conveyed to him the certainty that nothing existed more worthy than this compassion.

Sometime later—he would never know exactly how long—Michael had the sense of coming back to himself. The rain had stopped, and the room was subtly lit by the streetlights outside. He kissed the photo he still held of him and Maggie and setting it back on the mantle, rolled over to the phone and dialed Kathleen's number.

She picked up on the fourth ring.

"Hello?"

"Kathleen."

"Michael? But this is as nice as a sunny week in November. I've been thinking of you all morning, wanting ever so to call but knowing it was too late."

Kathleen paused. He was about to respond when she spoke again.

"I feel empty much of the time and missing you is a big part of it."

Michael cleared his throat. "This limbo of not being with you is terrible. I want to simply sit and drink some tea and look at the Atlantic out your window. Hold that hand of yours in mine. I just can't get away from here sooner. I'd forget about the house and let someone else do all of it, but I need to figure out what to keep. And I need more time for therapy. My ticket is in twenty five days. I'll call you every day, twice a day if it helps."

"Is the packing going to be hard? I mean, you know, all of Maggie's and your things. I can't imagine what that will be like."

"No," he said, shaking his head. "No, it won't be easy, but I'm feeling better. It's hard to explain. I'll tell you all about it when I see you. Katie, these twenty five days feel like an eternity."

Her response surprised him and he could almost hear her smile. "You've never called me Katie before."

He laughed lightly into the phone. They spoke happily for twenty minutes, discussing ways he could get help with all he needed to do. Finally it was time to say goodbye.

"Michael, I'm so glad you called. Sweet Jesus, I was missing you. Feeling sorry for myself. I'm singing tonight at Conneely's, just a bit. No fiddle. I miss you most then."

Her last words put Michael in mind of his guitar. He wheeled back into the small family room to where it leaned in its case against the wall. It was such a complicated ritual to play now—getting propped up onto the couch just right with the guitar near enough to pick up. Thank God I can still play, he thought as he reached for the case.

In that instant his eyes fell on something else. Always there, yet never really seen until this moment. He leaned over and touched it as if it were a sacred object. Michael shook his head. It was as if God were laughing at him and saying, "You wanted a sign? It was right in front of you the whole time."

He was pretty sure that when he gave it to Kathleen she would shriek with joy. That it had the potential to change everything for her. And that she would probably give him a really great kiss. He went to bed and slept the good sleep of one anticipating a really great kiss.

THIRTY EIGHT

Connemara

Tommy brooded. He knew his time was limited. Living up in this shack wasn't what he hoped. He had to drive his motorbike long distance to different places each time he needed food, and sometimes saw people looking at him speculatively. Missed his drinking friends.

"Guinness is good for you." He laughed bitterly at the slogan as he opened another. Nothing was good for him anymore. He'd had his moment of glory killing Colleen. Now he could feel everything closing in on him— eventually he would be found. He needed to act first, but he'd had to wait awhile, let things cool off, let people on Inis Mór lower their guard. One person especially.

Soon now, he would go. One last stolen boat. Katie Flaherty, I am coming, he thought.

THIRTY NINE

Michael had asked Katie to not meet him at Inis Mór's airport. She'd objected, but he practically begged her, saying he wanted to see her for the first time at her home. It actually was about keeping his gift secret.

After the landing, Tim of Tim's Taxi, by prearrangement, came up the stairs to the plane. He and the pilot carried Michael down to the tarmac, much to Michael's embarrassment. Better get used to it, he thought. In short order Tim stuffed everything except his wheelchair into the trunk. The chair he folded neatly up and maneuvered into the back seat. At Michael's request Tim gave him the fiddle. Michael had hand carried the fiddle from Seattle to Inis Mór and never let it out of his sight.

"Well, and it's a fine thing to be seeing you, Michael. I bet you're getting good with that fancy chair o' yours—don't worry your head a bit, we'll get you in and out a' this car easy as a warm spring day. Sure and the whole island is gabbing away, the women squawking like a gaggle of geese, the men blummering around like bewildered bulls, wondering how some American caught the prize of the island."

Michael chuckled at Tim's creative language—he's a storyteller for sure. And he felt gratitude that Tim mentioned his wheelchair. Michael found it hard to be seen and yet have the obvious fact of his dead legs ignored in a way that made him feel almost invisible to others.

Tim smiled over at him and laughed out loud. "It's an unexpected thing, then, but you'll be most welcomed here—we love our Katie and after what happened to her, seeing her smile even a wee bit this past week has been a ray of God's bright sun for us all."

Michael frowned slightly at Tim's wording. But then he looked away at the water and beamed with anticipation. Unexpectedly, a picture emerged in his imagination of a seal rising from the sea. The experience was so vivid that Michael shook his head in bewilderment. He thought of Selkies, the seals of Irish myth who come to shore in the form of a beautiful human female.

Tim drove them along the Main Road. Michael and Katie had decided he would live at Aoife's for a while. They needed to reacquaint themselves, and Michael felt, with her agreement, that it would be too much too fast if he were to move in with her.

He worried about sex. They had made love in Juneau. His mother disappeared once for a long walk and a visit with her neighbor. It had been kind of an awkward affair, although Katie had laughed at their incompetence, snuggling up to him after in a way that was, well, really nice. But his erection had been soft, and he'd been aware of his limited ability to move. Katie hadn't seemed bothered, and they hadn't spoken of the physical part of it much. He'd thought about it a lot these last couple weeks.

He held no doubt of his love for her. But that too seemed almost unbelievable—they had really only known each other for a few weeks on Inis Mór and her week in Juneau. He thought of something Marianne had said once. She'd been referring to the incongruity of her desire to go to El Salvador with her still unresolved anxiety about so much in life.

She'd said, "And yet Michael, so it is." Such was the reality of his feelings for Kathleen. So it is.

Tim stopped at Aoife's, who tut-tutted over Michael as they unloaded everything, proud as she showed off the small ramp she'd had put in so that he could cross the threshold of the B and B. And proud of putting him in her only room with a private bathroom, which she had also had renovated a bit for him.

"But this is so good of you, Aoife. Let me know what it cost, please."

"Oh and don't ya be worrying your head over that. I can offer this to others who might also be in the same kettle a fish—good for my business then. And I do it gladly. You're a fine man, and if I may, it's hard to see ya in this chair. But we never control much in life but that how we choose to live."

He'd been inclined to argue the point about money, but the look on her face convinced him otherwise. "Aoife," he'd said in gratitude, "I'm so glad to see you back home."

She shook her head sadly. "And glad I am to be here. It's a great shock, Michael. Who could've imagined it when Tommy was just a tiny lad?" She shrugged her shoulders. "Even last year. You think you know someone down to his little toe. I only wish to God we'd seen it sooner, for Colleen and Kevin." Her face clouded at that.

"But enough with the sadness. You're off to see Katie then, are you not?"

Michael nodded.

"Well and I can say she need to see ya, love. It'll be a bittersweet home-comin' for ya then."

In his anticipation, Michael missed Aoife's caution. It had taken him much longer than hoped to arrive in Inis Mór. He'd had renewed headaches just before he was to leave Seattle back in late January. A brain scan showed no serious problems. Then came the hope—he definitely was sensing something in his right leg and sometimes thought he moved it a fraction of an inch. He'd stayed on through a barrage of inconclusive tests. Sometimes, his doctor said, the workings of the human body remain mysterious. He continued to experience sensation in areas of both legs, like stinging needles. It was not pleasant, but he turned down the doctor's offer of pain medication—he wanted to feel his legs.

The hope had nearly killed him with desperation, and finally he said to himself, I just have to get on with my life. The doctors wanted him to stay, but when he said that to Katie two weeks ago, she immediately replied, "Please come to Inis Mór."

It was evening as the taxi approached Katie's home, and his elation was replaced by a pressure in his gut. Tim pulled into the gravel parking place behind her house. Michael heard the engine ticking. Then the backdoor of her home squeaked, and she was there, opening the car door, looking him in the eyes, kissing him lightly, her lips moist and warm, conveying invitation.

"Michael, *a chara, tá* fáilte *romhat anseo*—Love, you are so welcome here."

Katie pulled back, leaving behind the fresh smell of her hair. She had on a dark blue skirt and green blouse. Her thick uncooperative hair was pulled back in its usual semblance of a ponytail.

As Michael rolled into her living room he stopped short. A beautiful and solid oak chair had replaced one of her paired living room chairs. Katie had it built with movable arms that dropped down so he could easily get in from either side and pull the arm back up. The chair tilted slightly back to help him stay in place.

He looked at her speechlessly thinking on the cost of it all, feeling a need to object. Her eyes held such anticipation that he said instead, "Katie, this is beautiful."

Michael was able to lower an arm and swing himself into the chair without help, and Katie went to pour tea.

He could hear her humming. Eeragh Lighthouse was visible, the sea calm. Michael was struck by the emptiness of the land, reminded of how small the island was. He wondered again what he would do. At that moment, words came into his mind, like a whisper, *"There are only ghosts, now."* He laughed quietly as he looked around, feeling silly. Michael knew no one was there. What was this voice?

Katie came into the living room, set a cup next to him, sat down with her own tea on the couch opposite him and smiled briefly. "So."

"The tea is good. And this chair is amazing. I can relax, not struggle to stay upright. Thank you."

"I'm so glad to hear that. It's what I wanted for you."

Michael heard her clock ticking and caught himself drumming his fingers. "How's the weather been?"

She laughed. "No different than I told you a couple days ago on the phone. Would you like a fire?"

"No, I'm fine."

He yawned, and she followed suit.

"Tired?" he asked, noticing the fatigue around her eyes.

"I was up from the dawn, couldn't sleep much at all."

Katie put her cup on the end table and moved to sit on the floor next to him, leaning her head against his dead legs. "There is no pressure, Michael. Things are different. Sweet Jesus I can only imagine then how your life must feel sometimes, and you're in a strange place altogether. I know you lived her for a couple months, but now you are here for me, for us, and it must be overwhelming. Just so you know, I've been dying for you to be here these three months. It's been, oh, so." She halted and looked away for a minute, shaking her head. Michael instinctively reached his hand, out and gently ran it through her hair.

Kathleen finished, "But now, well, I guess now we find out who we are."

She turned her head and reached her hand to his. He remembered kissing it in Juneau.

"Will you play for me?"

A long moment passed, and a sadness he'd never heard stole her voice. "It seems Tommy killed something in me. I have felt no desire to play since Kevin and Colleen were murdered. I've been waiting for your arrival. I just want to touch you today, to know you're really here."

"I'm here." He did not let his dismay show in his face or tone of voice. All at once the thought of the surprise fiddle made him nervous, and he wondered if he should have brought it. What if it didn't bring her the happiness he had been certain it would? One doubt led to the next until the idea of *them* felt elusive. He spoke simply to get away from his thoughts.

"Kathleen, I'm nervous. I keep asking myself what I'm going to do. I don't just mean for the money, but how will I pass the time?"

She pursed her lips. "I've thought about that, Michael, and wondered, is it any different here than if you were in Juneau or Seattle? You have to find your way into a new life. And I realize that might not be able to happen here on the island, that you might have to move...."

He interrupted her. "Katie, no. Your roots are so deep here, your home, the people, how I could ever ask you to leave?"

She took his hand in hers, interlacing their fingers. "We don't have to solve this now, Michael. Let us just give ourselves the space to be with each other, however that is. Let me just be with you."

What Katie didn't say was how difficult such a choice would be. If it came to it, she would tell him then. As a friend had joked once, we can drive off that bridge when we get to it. Leaving Inis Mór would cut her off from roots so deep that it was almost unimaginable. She'd returned once to the island from Dublin, convinced she would never leave again.

Yet, in a way Katie did not fully understand, the idea of living away from Michael was a thought she could hardly contemplate.

And there was all she had not told him, had not been able to tell him, for she feared he would have left Seattle immediately and come to her when he'd needed to stay and find out if his paralysis might be coming to an end.

All this went through her mind as she held his hand. His eyes were so blue. She loved his dark wavy hair and the way it hung to just below his collar in the back. But the eyes held uncertainty now. She stood, lowered the movable arm, straddled his lap and put her hands on his chest, kissing him. After a few moments he physically lifted her up, lowering her breasts to his mouth, both of which he kissed through her thin blouse. "Michael Flaherty, if we're going to be doing this then, the first time in my home is not going to be in a chair, but on our bed. And," she said mischievously as she watched his eyes, "I've been doing a little reading and have something in mind I think you'll like."

In her room, she lit two scented candles while he went into the bathroom for a couple minutes. Kathleen heard him exclaim, "Kathleen this is too much. You must let me pay for this." She smiled to herself.

"It's a fair offer then. It wasn't that much though. It took Mick only three hours to put in the support arm and the bathtub bench for you."

She had learned in her reading about catheters and supposed he was taking his out. He rolled back in and she pulled his light sweater and T-shirt off his chest.

Michael got on the bed and lay on his back. She straddled him, feeling a little uncertain. Michael helped by unbuttoning her blouse and taking her breasts into his hands. She leaned down and kissed him, then moved up so he could kiss her neck and make his way to her breasts. She had always liked having her nipples kissed and gave a little giggle of pleasure. After a while she shifted and kissed his neck and made her way down to his nipples. He put his hand on the back of her head and gently pushed, so she kissed harder. He made a sound.

She sat up and quickly removed all her clothes. His face was shadowed by the candlelight, and she couldn't read his eyes as she stood naked in front of him. But he reached out his hand as he whispered, "Katie."

She slowly straddled him again and lowered her mouth to his. Michael responded by pulling her tightly to him. A warmth flowed through her, but she broke off the kiss and reached to take off his pants and underwear. His legs had gotten thinner and she felt a moment of sadness for him. He did have a slight erection, and she took it in her hands. It hardened a bit.

Michael suddenly pulled her up and ran his finger into the cleft of her labia, rubbing her clitoris. Her whole body responded in a flush of warmth quickened breath. The orgasm came so quickly it surprised her, and she buried her face in his chest, moaning at the unexpected pleasure. When it was over, Katie lay her face on his shoulder, breathing in the smell of him. She ran her hand through his chest hair and snuggled closer, as if the touch of his body could chase away the....

"Well, Katie Flaherty, that's what I call an Irish welcome."

Katie laughed and kissed his shoulder. "Let me just say, that was damn fine."

"For God's sake, woman, are you going to want conversation every time we have sex? Get me a cigarette and go cook dinner!"

Katie laughed. "The liver and onions are already on the stove."

After a moment, Michael said, "I'm sorry if I got impatient, but I wanted you, your face, near me. And I wish...." Michael sighed.

"We'll do this together. Not just the sex, but the whole thing."

Michael rested his forearm under his head, eyes closed. "I'm getting more used to a lot of this. Sometimes I get almost desperate when I think I'll never run or hike again. Or fly. Shit, I can't even walk across the room.

But most of the rest, it just takes longer to do things. I'm coming to see it's not the end of the world. Still, I've been anxious about bathroom stuff. It's not very romantic having to take out my catheter and make sure I'm clean before we make love."

He sighed again, deeply. "Katie, thank you for fixing up your bathroom. But it's all embarrassing to me. I mean, I know it could be worse."

"Michael," she interrupted. "I've been doing a lot of reading, then, so I can understand better, help in any way I can."

"Everyone says I don't need to be embarrassed, the doctors, other paraplegics I met. But I simply am."

"I know this is hard on you. We'll just work through everything together, okay?"

He opened his eyes and gazed at her. A small tremble of anxiety disturbed her thoughts—what if they couldn't do it? What if, after all this, they didn't work out? Kathleen felt a moment of fear for both of them. After all that happened, how could she bear one more loss?

He said, "Honestly, I feel safe with you. It's just a huge thing. Really hard."

Ah, saved by humor, she thought. Putting aside for the moment her doubts, Katie looked down past his belly button and said, "Well, I can do something about that!"

After dinner they talked some more.

"You know, Michael," she said, "I got a check for twenty thousand pounds for the cello. Insurance money. I don't know what to do."

Michael looked thoughtful, finally saying, "Put it in the bank and wait, I guess."

"I feel such an obligation to the people here. They're the ones who raised the money in the first place. I don't want to let them down, but I just feel empty when I think about playing."

Michael was surprised at the lack of enthusiasm in her voice.

The next day was cold and windy, but no rain. Katie had looked puzzled when he said he'd come late morning but wanted Tim to bring him, assuring her she'd understand when he got there.

When they arrived at her house, Tim brought the wheelchair around. As he moved to swing himself out of the car and into the chair, Michael again had the feeling he moved his legs. He sat there wondering if it had been his imagination as Tim handed him a box which lay the fiddle.

"Shadow flitting among stones, traces of memory." What? He thought. I'm frigging hearing voices in my head. Where the hell are these phrases coming from?

The back door squeaked and Katie stood there. It started to rain lightly as he wheeled himself over, showing off a little by pulling a wheelie. Katie laughed, then saw the box in his lap. The laughter settled into a smile.

"A surprise," she said.

She closed the door until it was only open a crack. "Are you having me on? Let's see how long you can sit out in the rain, then, before you are begging to be let in."

Michael laughed as the light rain dampened his hair. "I grew up in Juneau—this is fine summer weather for us. We had picnics in weather worse than this. But your present might get destroyed in the rain. Better let me in."

Katie waited a moment, then said as she opened the door, "Well, fair play to you, coffee it is. But this surprise had better be good, or you're out on your, well and it's a long wheelchair push back to Kilmurvey."

Michael sat at her round dining room table as Katie made coffee. Setting the two cups down, she exclaimed, "Michael, I can't be waiting any longer then—let me see my present."

He reached into the box and pulled out the fiddle case, setting it on the table. Katie's face froze. He held his breath a full five seconds. She reached out and picked it up, set it back on the table and opened the four clasps. Her hands shook as she took out the fiddle. He couldn't read the look she gave him—could it be fear?

Katie cleared her throat, but still could hardly speak. "But this can't be."

"Grannie Maeve gave it to me on her eightieth birthday—she got it from her mom who got it from her dad, my great-great-grandfather Patrick, the brother of your great-great-grandfather Seamus. It never even occurred to me until I saw it the first night I was back in Seattle."

"Michael, it's identical. This fiddle is the same as the one I had that Tommy destroyed. Seamus and Patrick must have each had the same kind of fiddle." Katie stood. At last she sat back down and laid her hand gently atop the fiddle like a mother touching the cheek of her baby.

Katie stayed in the position so long that Michael asked, "Are you okay?"

She raised her head, shaking it as she pulled her hair away from her eyes. She looks like someone who just received bad news, he thought.

"Katie. Can you play?" He felt a sudden tension in his chest, as in some mysterious way a thought coalesced into apprehension. At the edge of insight he asked himself, what if she refuses?

But she did not. Tucking the fiddle under her chin, Katie stood as still as a rod iron, her eyes closed. Michael thought of a runner just before the starting gun. But then she sighed, set the fiddle on the table, and shook her head. Her eyes seemed to be focused in the distance and a vein pulsed on her temple.

She blinked once. A second time. Looked at him but without really seeing. Turned and walked away, pausing at the opening to the living room, hand touching the wall.

Her voice wavered. "I've been so happy to see you I forgot for a few hours how hard it has all been—my instruments, the ugliness of Tommy, Colleen and Kevin."

As her voice slipped to silence, Michael finally fully saw. He should have noticed, but his own happiness had blinded him.

Michael realized he had kind of half-noticed. He had picked her up with ease yesterday in the chair, thinking it was his increased upper body strength. Now Michael saw Katie had lost weight. She'd smiled and laughed all day, but a few times her eyes slid away, pulled to something unseen out past Eeragh Lighthouse. And a couple times her conversation had stopped unexpectedly. He could see it now.

Katie was not well.

"I needed you here sooner, Michael. It's not your fault, I know you had to stay all that time in Seattle. And I could not tell you over the phone, mores the pity. Tommy did more than take my music. I hardly feel alive half the time. I have not tried to play the fiddle. I have not bought a new cello because I didn't want to hold my fiddle and have no desire to play."

Katie held her hand out to him. She turned as he rolled toward her. Michael would never forget how her face seemed to fold into the slackness of her eyes and how frail Katie looked as she disappeared into the living room, her finger stretching toward him as if reaching desperately up from under the ocean.

FORTY

The weather had turned to rain, the horizon pulled close by dark scudding clouds. Katie turned on the lamps next to her sofa.

Katie herself felt a little uncertain. What she wanted was Michael's touch. Not like the sex from yesterday but the simple solidity of him, his raw physical hereness, the smell of his body, the feel of his hand on her arm or his breath in her hair. It was this for which she'd been dying these many weeks on end now.

Michael's gift of the fiddle was remarkable, and she chided herself for her lethargy, but the truth was she didn't even have the inner energy to pretend. Of late she kept hearing the negative voice of her mother warning her to stop being disagreeable. That of her Dublin boyfriend that she wasn't really interesting. Even of Tommy's that her return from Dublin marked her failure. At the thought of Tommy, she trembled lightly as if her fear were a tiny Banshee running through her veins, headed straight for her heart. Katie began to fall into the now familiar maelstrom of conflicting regrets and guilt. She turned and looked at Michael and could tell he was startled by what he saw.

"I'm not caring then how we do it, but I need you to hold me something fierce."

He hesitated, and for a long moment she thought he was going to decline.

But Michael was only considering how to do it and said. "Let's get me into the corner of the couch, and you can lean up against me."

Her sofa had high arms. Michael wheeled over and with a now habitual deftness locked a wheel and swung himself over onto the couch. Lifting and moving himself with his hands, he slid into the right corner.

"Could you help me get my legs right?"

Katie knelt and carefully moved his legs so they were straight out in front of him and then sat next to him, laying her head inside his shoulder. She could hear his heart. He never said a word, and she was grateful for it. He leaned down and kissed her hair. For the first time in weeks, Katie felt safe enough to let go of the protective layer around her and experience without resistance whatever came.

It flowed a grief that spilled over the rim of her control. She cried, her body occasionally shaking. For Colleen, Kevin, for Aoife's pain, her destroyed instruments. She cried for Michael and the loss of his legs, for her own loss of the dreams that Dublin had held. She pictured them all, and her grief floated as if through a dissipating fog to her ancestors, settling on her great-great-grandfather Tomas and the lifelong pain of his widow Maeve. Others flitted through her mind until she simply lost herself in the immediacy of grief.

At last she raised her head from his chest.

Michael reached over and gave her a couple pieces of tissue. She blew her nose, wiped her damp cheeks and laid down on the couch, the back of her head using his legs as a pillow.

Katie said, "Michael, I'm sorry about the fiddle. It's an incredible gift, and I can imagine you thought I'd be overjoyed. Somewhere in me I am, but it's not easy done finding that part of me right now. I'm in a terrible limbo."

Michael caressed her cheek. She took his hand, kissed it, interlaced the fingers of her right hand in his and held it against her chest, just below her neck.

"I used to think my mother was my biggest problem. It's been three months since Tommy killed Colleen and Kevin. I don't know if I'll have a life until he is caught. I wish to God Colleen had never come back, but I know why she returned—it's home, the smell and sound of the sea, the feel of the wind back of the island. You can't walk this place without knowing firsthand the struggle to live here, how our ancestors fished and farmed with bleeding hands that we might live now. They drug up the stones that made the walls, brought up the seaweed to make soil atop the pavement."

Michael was all at once filled with a deep melancholy. His life in Seattle had been active—running and hiking and sports, attending movies, concerts, visiting with friends, he and Maggie advancing their careers. The island felt suddenly small in comparison.

Michael had listened carefully to Katie and heard perhaps what she hadn't intended—how rooted she was in Inis Mór. How could she leave? She'd closed her eyes, and as he looked at her face, framed as it was by her hair, he saw the place-names of her childhood—the Brannocks, Eeragh Lighthouse, Back of the Island, pavement, seals and selkies and fishing boats rubbing against the dock in Cill Ronan. He saw her as a child, leaping and walking atop and hiding behind the hard-placed stone walls that delineated a border to everything and yet opened to vistas as wide as the universe. He saw her untamed passion for music in the controlled frenzy of her fiddling and the deeper heart of the cello. How her unruly hair was the west wind come to rest for a moment and her eyes the reflection of her ancestors' long dangerous pull of fish from the sea. Her skin was salt-sea-air soft, and she smelled of the sea and fish and honeysuckle and wild roses.

She was a queen.

She was Inis Mór.

Katie sighed deeply and his vision receded. Michael remembered how Johnny Williams told him once that there were days he could see the totem animals alive in the trunks of the gnarled Sitka Spruce, that if you looked just the right way, they might emerge for a second or a minute from behind the veil that hides them, a shift in vision that became an acceptance into rather than a looking at.

That was how he felt now, gazing at Katie. She'd fallen asleep. He let his eyes wander around her living room. There was the place where her cello had stood in its stand, an emptiness into which she had insisted he set his own guitar. It sat now like an interloper in former *anam chara* heart of her life. Michael pondered what that might mean for a moment, but a restlessness drew his eyes away and to her one painting, of the Irish Brigit before her eventual manifestation as the Catholic St. Brigid.

Brigit stood with a long blondish-red hair, a full moon behind her left shoulder, a just-beginning-to-bud tree to the right. Her hands reached out as if in invitation, from the palms of which flowed flames. She was one of the Triple Goddesses, and her influence was complex, including being the Goddess of Poetry and Healing.

How perfect for you, Katie, he thought.

On the mantle below the painting he noticed the small container of pepper spray. As it was illegal in Ireland, he had snuck in two from Seattle. Their presence a reminder and a wound. He thought of his Juneau friends, of Johnny and his battle against the inner demons of his war, of Evie and how much hurt her love for Johnny cost her, and Marianne and her long struggle with fear. Of his mom who had been living a long loneliness since the death of his dad. Looking again at Katie, he so wished he could feel her head as it pillowed against his legs. Again the stab of grief almost overwhelmed him. He could put on a mask, but even after these months, he sometimes could hardly bear to think about a legless future. Jesus Christ, how much are we supposed to endure?

Katie turned onto her side, and he let go of her hand. All he saw now was how thin she was, and her thick fall of hair. He gentled it with his fingers, moving it away from her mouth. The depth of his feeling for her flowed out in silent tears on his cheeks.

"Katie," he quietly said.

She reached for his hand, kissed his palm again and sat up.

"Michael, I dreamed. Brigit came to me. Flames flowed out from her hands and formed the shape of a fiddle and guitar. She looked at me—I'm not having you on—she looked at me with so much love and I felt it flow into me. She backed away and disappeared into the forest behind her as if it were fog. I heard you call my name, and I still feel her love and peace, right now, this moment. Waking up with you next to me feels like the ending of the dream and the beginning of something new and beautiful. Like I have been waiting all my born days for you."

Michael had no idea what exactly to say. I love you too, he thought. Not good enough. It came to him.

"*A rúnsearc.*" My deep beloved.

Katie smiled, nodding her head. She leaned in and kissed him on the mouth.

"*M'fhíorghrá.*" Meergrah.

He did not know what that meant, but heard the intent in her voice. Like what he'd said, but more.

She stood and went to his guitar. "Will you play for me?"

Michael began doodling almost mindlessly in the key of G. She closed her eyes and listened, swaying slightly to the music. He let his fingers slide into the key of D and after a minute went into The Beatle's "Here Comes the Sun." She opened her eyes, and he really began playing, showing off a little.

Unexpectedly she began to sing the lyrics. At first her voice wavered a bit but firmed up into its beautiful soprano as she came to the refrain. The meaning of the words were not lost on Michael. When he came to the end of the song, by some indefinable intuition, he knew to keep playing as she sang. He watched the subtlest shift occur, a scarcely discernable transition, as if the thinnest veil of fog lifted her left hand a few inches from her lap as she sung.

Katie stood as she said, "Keep playing," and went into the kitchen. Michael heard the clicks and knew before she returned that Katie had gotten out the fiddle.

Michael had no idea how long it had been since it'd been played. It took her a bit of effort to get it tuned up.

Finally, eyes closed, Katie started playing with him, fingers dancing easily up and down the instrument. He simplified his picking as she played a happy harmony above the melody. With the seeming exuberance of a child at play she ran off a series of quick trills, one after the other, higher and higher on the fiddle's neck. She stood and swayed to the music, some hairs of the old bow breaking and floating around the quick movements of her arm.

As he returned to the D-chord sequence that opened the song, Michael impulsively grabbed a pick and strummed out a reel pattern. Seamlessly, Katie switched her tempo to match his as she opened her eyes and smiled. They played fast, a well matched pair. At some point a couple minutes later Michael abruptly stopped playing, but Katie continued on, her fingers now in full flight across the playing board. Sweat formed on her brow, and finally she ended with a little hop and a quick final note.

Breathing hard, she said, "Oh, Michael, it's a little deeper than old Tomas' fiddle, but it's the same. I never thought something like this could be, that what Tommy destroyed could be so perfectly returned. Our great-great-grandfathers must have played together, and now here we are. Although," and here she slowed her voice as she looked at him with an impish smile, "you're playing that inferior instrument known as the guitar."

She laughed. He sat there, unable to speak at the return of her joy.

But he had his own reason as well. He could scarcely form the words, but managed to get them out.

"Katie, when you played, without even knowing I was doing it, I moved my legs to the rhythm of the reel. Katie, I moved my legs!"

FORTY ONE

Michael and Katie had laughed tears of happiness for each other—she for his hope of active legs, he for the freedom of her music-heart emerging from the long night of her loss. For the sweet forgetfulness of a day they lived in the abandonment of such promise, and Michael forgot how hemmed in Inis Mór he felt, and Katie forgot that the monster was out there, and neither wanted to think about Michael leaving.

But leave he must—he knew it, she knew it, and on the second day he spoke of it, just after a late breakfast.

"Would you like another cup of coffee, love?" she asked him.

He nodded his head, taking a sip as she returned the pot to the counter.

"Katie."

Katie came to the table, nodded her head and sat with a sigh, taking his hand.

Steeling himself, he said, "I think I have to return to Seattle to work on rehab. They know my history. They're really good at Swedish Hospital. I guess I could go to Limerick or Dublin, but is that really any better? I still wouldn't be here."

"I know," she answered in scarcely more than a whisper. "It's had me on the dangle these last couple days, so."

"I don't know how long it'll be. Maybe they can get me started, and I can figure out a way to continue here."

He stopped speaking, considering his next words carefully. "Tommy is still out there. I'd like it if you came with me. Tommy doesn't even matter, really, I want you to be with me." He took a breath, feeling the import of his question. "I wouldn't ask you to leave but for Tommy."

When she didn't reply right away, he felt his gut tighten.

"Michael, I feel stuck. I realized a couple days ago that you might need to go. But I have been helping Aoife, she can't really run the place by herself." She sighed and shook her head. "Tommy is like a ghost in the fog and laid a wound on me I'm tired of. I feel like I'm on the side road of a suspended life."

Katie stood up and walked to her back door. She kept her back to him for a few seconds, then returned to the table. He had the feeling she'd made a decision.

"I want to stay here right off. I'll never be without the pepper spray you brought me. I'll sleep at Norah's. You go and find out how long it will be. We'll decide then what to do. If it's just a couple weeks I'll stay here and wait, but if it's longer, maybe I'll come to Seattle."

Maybe. Meaning no. Michael looked down at his coffee so she would not see his irritation. But he heard the edge in his voice. "I'll worry so much. It's dangerous. Katie, please."

She said in a somewhat curt voice, "I don't think there's much danger. It's been three months. Even the Garda think he probably is in Dublin or Limerick, disappeared into a large city. They say it's just a matter of time until they get him. There's still two Garda here on the island. I promise I'll be careful, why wouldn't I? I will never go anywhere without my pepper spray. I'll never go out at night alone."

Michael gave a snort of frustration. He began shaking his head.

"Michael."

He heard the tension in her voice. But he had slipped into a powerful vortex of anxiety that swirled with the power of having lost Maggie and fearing to lose her. A buzzing rose in his ears, a high flat tone that reminded him of a bad electric organ. Michael knew he was whipped around by inner forces that were reacting to a past not of the present moment and strove to calm himself. He heard her voice as if it came from another room.

"Michael, we need to leave off for now. I'm going for a walk. I'll be back and we can talk about this some more."

He heard the back door close, and he thought, "shit, this sucks." Do the best moments in life always come with a shadow hanging over them?

His eyes went to the mantle. She'd taken the pepper spray.

Katie headed uphill. Energy fed her fast ascent, and she moved for some time without thought. At last she slowed and took stock of her situation.

She was frustrated with herself and her temper. It wasn't Michael she was angry at, it was the feeling of helplessness that pervaded every day, the endless waiting, the sense of having lost control of life, of putting everything on hold. And she knew she had been unfair to Michael. Maybe she should go to Seattle just to get away from everything. Surely Aoife could find someone to help her, or maybe she would need to close her B and B for a few weeks?

In that moment she heard what she'd missed in what Michael had asked—come to Seattle with me. He'd said that, hadn't he? She decided herself for her refusal. It would be a few days before he left anyway, and she could help Aoife make arrangements in the interim. The idea of getting relief from the constant tension sounded actually nice.

But a part of her felt like she would be abandoning the island, Aoife and all the others who felt anxiety. She was tired of running.

Katie sat down on a nearby wall and looked out at the view. For a moment she felt uneasy, as if hearing a scream in the far distance. The feeling faded.

She could see across North Sound to Connemara, and to her left the ocean rain in by the Brannocks. Kite clouds dotted the sky, their shadows laying on the fields like napping cows. She could mutely hear the waves pounding into the south side of the island and realized how far she'd come—the walls of Dún Aonghasa were only a few hundred feet away. She decided to take a quick look, no more than five minutes, for Michael was waiting and was owed an apology. And an answer. But Katie knew it might help to sit near the cliff edge, feel the ocean air and pounding of the sea. It might give her clarity.

In a couple minutes she dropped down to the narrow ledge and entered the inner sanctum of the ancient fort.

She guessed there were fifty tourists milling around. A few wandered slowly along the back wall, but most were near the cliff, some brave kids sitting right on its edge, legs dangling over the side. She'd never been able to make herself do that and shook her head at their apparent cavalier attitude at perching three hundred feet above the sea. There's no surviving that fall, she thought. Katie walked further in and sat down some distance from the closest tourists, a few feet from the edge. Closing her eyes with a soft sigh, she listened to the sea as it frothed up from far below.

Michael sat and waited, hating his immobility. He checked again—yes, he could move both legs just a little bit. He did this fifty times a day, maybe more, each time afraid he'd lost the power, each time relieved to see that connection between mind and body still functioned. Yesterday he'd tried to go an hour between attempts to move his legs and hadn't made ten minutes.

He concentrated on his right leg to see how far he could lift it and was shocked when it rose about six inches. Excitement coursed through him like a swollen river overrunning its banks. In a moment of forgetfulness, he started to call Katie to show her and realized she wasn't there. Her mantle clock indicated it had been a half hour since she'd gone. He felt irritated that she'd left him here, but he expected her back soon.

One thing after another worked to keep them apart, starting with him having to leave Inis Mór so unexpectedly because of his mother's heart attack. If they could just get clear of everything that kept getting in the way, he believed they would discover real happiness with each other. In Juneau, Katie had told him that his paralysis would take some getting used to, that she would need time, but that she really didn't think in the end it would prove to be much of a problem for her. And now he at last had returned and needed to leave again already.

Going now was in so many ways the worst thing for them. But he didn't see a choice.

Or?

He considered more seriously looking into what kind of care he could get in Limerick, perhaps even Galway. He still had most of the life insurance money, but suspected it would go quickly to medical bills. Okay, he thought, I'll look into rehab here in Ireland and only return to Seattle as a last resort. He felt content, believing that somehow this idea would bear fruit, and he would not have to go so far away.

Michael looked at the clock. To distract himself he concentrated and lifted his right leg again.

He heard her coming up the front stairs and relaxed, eager to share his decision with her.

Instead there was a knock.

"Who is it?"

"It's Conlon Conneely. Michael? I need to see you and Katie," he said even as he opened the door and came in without invitation. Michael recoiled from the look on Conlon's face.

"She's not here, she headed up the hill. She's on her way back, I think."

Conlon's face went white. "Michael, the Garda found a boat past Bun Ghabla. There was no attempt to hide it. They fear Tommy is on the island."

Clarity came quickly to Katie. If they were to have a future, she needed to choose for Michael, for them. It was not as if they'd just met. She'd told him weeks ago in Juneau she loved him and believed those words today more than then. Now the season of choice had arrived, no longer a distant spring from the vantage of a long winter but right in front of her, her equinox of hope.

"You can run, lass, but if you do, there's a man down in your house in a wheelchair, and I'll kill him."

She exploded up even as her mind processed Tommy's words. He stood between her and the way home. It was not possible to get by him, and if she tried to run back to her home where Michael waited in a wheelchair, if she ran all the way across the inner field of Dún Aonghasa and out the other entrance she would never beat Tommy home. It was too far.

She said, "If you come at me, I'll scream and run to the others."

"Ah yes, you might well do that Katie Flaherty, but then some of them will die too."

Katie heard his absolute conviction and knew he spoke a simple vile truth. In these, what she knew were likely last moments of her life, she chose to face him alone, not to endanger those nearby.

A moment of inner peace flowed into her whole body, feeling like subtle goosebumps over every inch of her skin. *Ah, my sweet loved ones, thank you for coming to me now. I will not be alone.*

Even as she remembered the pepper spray in her pocket, she noticed the stone in his hand, taken she assumed from the wall. With a smile that ran across his face like a badly stitched scar, he threw it. It hit her shin and bounced away. Pain lanced up her leg, and she cried out involuntarily.

Let him get close. Do not let pain get in the way.

She heard some people in the distance yelling and thought a few are coming—too late. Tommy loomed over her like the massive shoulder of a nightmare, reached to lift her, and she knew his intent.

FORTY TWO

As Tommy leaned over her, Katie gathered her legs under him. Bent at the knees, she shut out the pain and pushed as quickly and hard as she could. Fueled by a massive infusion of adrenaline, her legs hit him just below the sternum and propelled him up and away.

He laughed at her effort, certain he would easily find his balance. But before he did, he stumbled over the very stone with which he had smashed her leg. Katie watched him plant a foot right at the edge of the cliff to regain balance. His foot slipped on some loose rocks.

He pin-wheeled his arms and seemed to be catching his balance.

Aware that her life depended on what happened next Katie rose onto her good leg. She thought of the pepper spray but instead scrambled to the stone, lifted and threw it at his head. Tommy reflexively went to block it. The quick movement of his arms threw off his balance. She saw in his eyes the moment he realized he was going over the cliff. Another second and he was gone.

Katie sat down, stunned into an emptiness of feeling and thought.

She heard the cry of a gull and another, became aware of the people running up and the cacophony of their concerned and confused voices. Her leg started to hurt, and she saw blood where the large stone had struck.

Months of grief, fear and anger, lodged in her breast, hit like a storm wave smashing the cliffs below and burst out her throat with so much force she was convulsed into a fetal position. She was no longer herself as the torrent burst forth.

"Katie. Katie."

She heard her name, felt lips at her ear. His lips. Mike's lips.

"Michael."

She felt his hand and opened her tightly closed palm, clung to him like to a rock in a heaving ocean.

Later she sat up. A few tourists remained, but most were gone. Conlon stood next to Mike, hands on his wheelchair.

Mike said, "Katie, oh God."

Katie laughed through her tears. "Some pair we make. Ooohh. Mike." She could not finish. "Mike, I need to look."

She stood and winced but was able to put weight on her leg. She shook her head, lay down on her stomach and inched to the rim of the drop-off.

Did what she had never before done—she looked down the cliff face. Waves heaved mightily, froth shooting up. The boom of their collision was a constant undercurrent. Birds flew dizzyingly below her.

She knew with certainty. Tommy was dead.

Katie watched Mike walk carefully down the stairs and onto the small tarmac. He glanced across the short distance to her. He'd been gone seven weeks. Looking at her the whole time he seemed to take a moment to carefully balance himself, then lifted his arms into the sky, the cane in his right hand reaching even higher. She walked quickly toward him.

"Don't run me over, love," he humorously said as she neared.

"Oh for Brigit's sake, Mike, I'm not as dumb as a sack of dirt." Then her arms were around him, and she did almost knock him over.

"I have missed you so damn much, Katie, I never want you out of my sight again."

She stepped back, her smile big as a balloon. "Oh, and you are a sight for lonely eyes. But what then, already with only the one cane? Just a couple or three days ago you said you needed two. Have you been having me on?"

"It might be a wee bit of a lie took place." She laughed at his exaggerated idiom. "About three weeks ago I started walking with the aid of only one cane. The doctors said that my progress has been faster than most, but I can't walk unaided yet."

Back in March, after Tommy's death, it had been easier to make the decision that he would return to Seattle. They also decided that, difficult as it was, she would remain at home in Inis Mór.

Now the long loneliness is over, she thought with gratitude as they slowly made the way to her car.

On June 17th he walked unaided for the first time.

A week later, Katie was making sandwiches while he made a second pot of coffee. They sat and chatted a few minutes about "what and what", as she liked to say.

"Katie, it's a lovely day, how about a walk down to the shore and a look at the Brannocks?"

She was surprised at his ambition. "Is it a bit far?"

He laughed. "Only one way to find out."

Fifteen minutes later, they set out. He put his arm in hers, and they slowly made their way down the narrow road past several cottages toward the water. Michael walked on the cracked pavement, Katie on the grassy verge next to the three-foot stone wall. Eeragh Lighthouse probed the sky from Rock Island, opening to the calm, infinite-seeming Atlantic beyond. Katie glanced at her watch as they arrived and found a log to sit on. The normal twenty minute walk had taken almost three quarters of an hour.

Michael sighed as they sat down. "Well, made it, but I'm pretty pooped."

Katie laughed. "I know now what that means, but every time you say 'pooped' I'm thinking of the bathroom, not being tired."

He smiled and shook his head. Then she saw his face turn serious.

"Michael?"

He took a deep breath. "Katie, I'll just say this, like you did when you came to Juneau and said you loved me. I want to move in, to be together."

Katie leaned over and kissed his hair above his ear. It smelled of him and of the sea, and she inhaled deeply. "I've been waiting, then, for you to ask. I was thinking it needed to come from you, although I wasn't going to wait long. Yes, Michael, it is time."

He said, "I'm seeing how much Maggie's death made me cautious. The pain was almost too much, you know?"

I remember, Katie thought but did not say. "Oh I have a good idea what you are about, love, and so didn't want to push. I knew you couldn't resist my charms forever."

"You have no charms whatsoever, Katie. It's just that you cook ever so much better than Aoife."

"And sure it is you're in a winter storm of trouble— if I ever tell her what you just said, you'll not be leaving this island alive."

He laughed with her, but she wondered if he noticed it was a little forced. She was worried.

She loved being near Michael, seeing in him at last what she had always intuited— that he possessed a generosity of heart that was wonderful to be around. She had seen it in his coming up with the idea for flying Colleen from the island and in the kind way he spoke of Aoife. Even in the way he had defused that ugly scene with Tommy outside Aoife's. More than anything, she'd sensed it when he sang. From the first time they sang together, Katie had almost physically felt a wall fall away from him, and the real Michael, being freed from his grief. The happiness of their one afternoon in Galway, after he'd flown Colleen off the island, and the ferry ride back to Inis Mór that evening, had been the hope she had held to in those lonely days after he left the island the first time.

He came with her now on her every other day visits to three elderly women who lived alone up on the narrow tracks which spidered off the Main Road. She discovered that in high school he had done much the same thing for four women in Juneau. They sang together with a couple of her friends two nights a week at Conneely's, and few people had started boating in from off island to hear them. A call had come from a large pub in Galway, and in a couple weeks they would head there for a weekend and four performances. She was happy.

But she also noticed how he often sat outside, looking down the Main Road past Eeragh to the Atlantic, and wondered where his thoughts were taking him. Last week he had walked to the shore alone, and now he took the walk daily, sometimes by himself. Yesterday he'd been gone almost four hours, so long she had gotten worried. He'd looked somber when he returned, but had smiled and assured her he was okay.

The next day Katie remembered what she always ended up saying to the women who came to her. Don't be afraid. Don't let fear dictate your actions. She resolved to speak to him and put on a pot of tea.

Some books Michael had ordered from Galway had arrived. He sat on the couch, reading. She brought him a cup of tea, placed it on the end table and sat next to him, pulling her feet up under his legs.

"Thanks for the tea, love."

"What are you reading?"

"It's a new book by a theologian I really like, Karl Rahner." He looked at her more closely and put the book down.

"How are you doing, Michael?"

His eyes narrowed a bit, and he nodded slightly. "Pretty good. Every day feels like a miracle— to think I may run and hike again, and fly." He closed his eyes a moment. "And you. My God, Katie, you are more to me than my own life. As I said yesterday, it scares me." He looked away, and then back. "Nobody tells you growing up that to love is to suffer."

She moved closer, so their shoulders and thighs touched. He reached and took her hand. "Yes, we do suffer when we love," she said. "But is not some of it unnecessary? Fearing what we can't control?"

He slowly nodded his head.

Katie took a deep breath. "And Inis Mór, Michael, is it enough for you? I mean, this island is a small place altogether."

"I never will ask you to leave, Katie. Your roots are too deep here. You are not like some tree that can be transplanted."

She nodded her head. "And I thank you for saying it, sure I do. But you didn't answer my question."

Now it was his turn to take a deep breath. "You know, I've had this idea for a while, even before I left after mom's heart attack, that I would get a job flying for Aer Arann. But these past few months in Seattle, as I got my strength under me, I felt restless."

He gave her hand a squeeze, got up and walked slowly to the large window. "My old life of flying doesn't seem so fulfilling any more. You know I met with Marianne when I was in Seattle."

Katie nodded.

"She came up to Seattle one day. God, she has this joy. It's amazing. But more, she is doing something good. Important. And courageous."

He shook his head. "I don't know, I just have this sense, this feeling, that I want to do more, to do something that makes a difference. It's strong."

He returned to the couch and took her hand.

"I don't know what it is. Sometimes I think it's going back to school, becoming a Professor of Philosophy or Theology. Or something else. I just don't know. And then there's you, us. I'm not a tree either and can't be transplanted. My roots are...."

"Not here. I know."

He smiled. "You misunderstand. It's true enough I am not from here, but what I meant to say was, my roots are so deeply intertwined with yours now that it'll never do to be without you. Hell, it's more than that. If I can wax poetic, you are like a full moon rising into a dark night, casting a subtle and beautiful light over everything it touches. My whole being shines in your soft light. 'O Sole Mio.'"

"Sure, and what woman wouldn't like a poem written for her?"

She reached for his face and pulled him to her, kissing him fiercely, hugging him tightly, their damp cheeks touching. She eased back. He looked pensive.

"Well, and this is a fine mess altogether. There's that old joke, men, can't live with them, can't live without them. I would never want to hold you here. You would slowly wither. Your days would become narrow and bitter. Michael," she whispered, "I don't know if I could leave Inis Mór and be happy."

Mike fell asleep that night before she did. Katie rose quietly, pulled on her robe and went into their living room. A full moon floated low in the sky, its dim reflection trailing in the water toward her. The land seemed to glow from within with a pale light, crisscrossed by the darker lines of the stone walls. Fog lay like wisps of memory in two isolated spots. She thought of Mike's words.

Katie stepped out the back door, a blanket from the couch over her shoulders, barefoot like she had often wandered as a child. The grass was damp with dew on her feet, but the night was pleasant. She walked carefully to the three foot wall at the edge of her property. Every stone seemed familiar. Tommy came to mind and she shivered. As good as it felt to have him gone, she did not bear her part in his death lightly.

She thought about walls as she lightly ran her hand across the top, remembering a time as a little girl when she'd been afraid to climb it and wander beyond its protection.

The moon worked its peaceful grace. A light breeze wafted in subtle sounds—the occasional bell of a distant buoy, the endless lapping of the sea as it ran past the Brannocks and onto shore. A car drove by, heading down the back of the island. A small animal rustled on the other side of her stone wall.

She found herself thinking of the myth of a Deirdre. At her birth, Druids predicted that she would be the cause of much death. She dreamed of, then met and fell in love with Naoise, but she was so beautiful, King Connor MacNess swore he'd marry her. Deirdre and Naoise escaped to an island where they lived happily for five years, but Connor tricked them back and had Naoise and his brothers killed. When Deirdre saw the body of the man she loved, she fell dead on his corpse. Their love could not overcome the harsh dictates of fate. She wondered if life would treat her and Michael in so cold a fashion?

Is there not a choice?

She heard the door quietly open and close, felt his approach.

Wordlessly she offered him half her blanket, which he wrapped around his shoulders. She leaned into him, and he kissed the top of her head. They listened to the night sounds together. In the sweep of the long mile to the ocean there was not a square inch she hadn't run over and played in as a little girl. She knew the name of every family who lived in every house she could see. She knew their lives, the tragedies and difficulties, and joys of them all.

"Ah, Michael, you don't always know what you have until it's not there altogether. Wherever I go on the island, I feel like I'm moving through space shot through with stories, like radio waves, you know? Sure and I've always felt our present lives float on the ocean of a past that is teeming still with life. I remember thinking once when I was just a girl that the gardens on the island are fertilized by the bodies of the dead."

She turned and smiled up at him. "My mom was horrified when I told her that. She was always after telling me to not speak so. But they have never been dead to me—they live in the tears and laughter of stories and songs half-anchored in a mythological past—selkies, the Tuatha Dé Danaan, their battle with Firblog. The great Druids and heroes and heroines that at some point in history became actual people, our great heroes who fought for our land. Do you know that Brigit, who was one of the Tuatha Dé, is the patroness of poetry? I thought you'd like that."

"Well, and I did at that, Katie."

She felt his smile and continued, "And all this flows into the story of our own family. Our twice-great-grandparents, two tragic deaths, the third leaving in grief for America. They are alive to me, Michael. I feel them and their love when it is quiet at the back of the island, when the water is running smooth past the Brannocks, and in the storms as well.

"It's all somehow one, the whole story of our people. It's like a single moment that seems thousands of years long. And now we are here, and I trust you enough to be saying it aloud. We are as tightly bound together as this island and the sea that surrounds it. I believe this as much as I believe any ever thing at all. We have been brought here to this moment. You and I are knit by more than our love. Our pasts are woven on a loom that has twined us in a pattern of healing that we may never understand altogether."

"Or maybe, the weave is part of our love."

"Ah Michael, of course and you have it right, so."

Mike whispered, "That was so beautifully said. You are becoming a bit of a poet yourself."

The silence of the night enveloped them. Katie closed her eyes, smelling the sea and him. She wished they could stay in this moment forever.

He sang quietly. *"And the seasons, with their turning, we'll put new seeds down there yearly, and the blooming will not end, with our passing from this mountain."*

She joined him as he came to the refrain. *"Will you go, lassie, go? And we'll all go together, to plant wild mountain thyme all around the blooming heather, will you go, lassie go?"* When they were done, it felt to her as if their singing floated like a gentle breeze across the land in front of them and our over the waters, blessing every square inch over which it hovered.

"It's come on fair, Michael."

Katie shivered and the pair went inside. Mike made tea while she dried her feet and started a fire. It was 2:40 in the morning.

They sat together, gazing silently at the fire.

She laughed as she spoke. "I'm always after telling women who visit me to not be afraid. Well and I'm a great one for words. But I'm losing my fear, Mike. When you go, if you must, I will come with you." She shook her head as he started to speak, reaching out and putting a finger to his lips. "There is no other choice I would make but to be with you. I'll not try to put one by you. It will be hard. Perhaps I need to step over the walls of my own fear."

He kissed the top of her head again and answered after a few seconds. "Ah, Katie, what was it you said yesterday? To try not to fear what we can't control? If I must go, I thank you right now for the freedom of knowing you'll come with me. Whatever comes, I can't help but think if we just hold onto our love, life will see us through. Oh, I'm not saying that well. It's what I thought about as I fell asleep. I will choose you every day, and God will bless that choice."

She nodded her head, taking a sip of the tea, and nearly choked. "Whoa, stop the ferry," she said, grimacing. "Sure and if you don't learn to brew a better cup, there'll be no choosing me." She smiled and moved closer to him, laying her head on his shoulder. The fire crackled quietly. The clock ticked quietly. She felt Michael's quiet breathing slow and drifted herself toward sleep.

He shook his head. She felt it, and woke up. "Are you all right?"

He yawned. "Katie, for weeks, even before I went back to Seattle, I have been, well, not exactly hearing voices, but it's like lines of poetry are being whispered in my mind. I've been writing them down, changing them a bit. And I think it's done—I've heard the same lines now three times in a row, nothing new. It goes like this: *'No island can save us, nor cliff deny the sea or hold the wild Aran wind. Even Inisfree recedes.'* It's an odd sensation, like I am the one being spoken, rather than the one who speaks. As if I am the one being written." He fell silent. "There's the better part of a whole poem that's come to me."

She turned to him with a look of wonder and nodded her head. "It's makes perfect sense. Our whole family, torn apart by tragedy all those years ago, is whole again in us, and a little of the *seanachie* in you is coming out. Now that you're here, it is emerging like a whale from the ocean."

He laughed out loud. "I love that image. Sure, and you've got a bit of the poet in you as well. But I have a question. I think I knew once but have forgotten. Do you know what Inisfree is? It's a place, no? I keep meaning to look it up, but always forget."

"It's a small island in a lake just east of Sligo—a favorite of the poet Yeats."

He seemed to ponder that a moment. "The poem's about the past and how everything lovely is gone from families who are now dead. But it feels not quite done. Not yet right. I think it's for me to finish."

"Do you know how you'll end it?"

"However else? I am thinking with you."

FORTY THREE

Juneau, Late July, 1981

Johnny rose when his clock hit 3:00 and dressed silently in the clothes he had set out some hours earlier. He pulled out his daypack, already stuffed with the things he'd need, tiptoed down the stairs and left his mother's home. He was especially quiet as he went by Evie's room.

It was dark. The town was quiet. One car came his direction on Sixth Street as he made his way down the stairs on Starr Hill. A few birds roused with their tentative first notes, but he was so focused he scarcely noticed.

Reaching the last streetlight on Basin Road, Johnny relaxed as he passed into the black of the night. He stopped at the end of First Bridge, looking across the deep ravine down which Gold Creek tumbled through and up toward the peak of Mt. Juneau invisible in the dark. He thought of Mike, with whom he'd climbed it three or four times in high school. Word from Mike's mom was that he was back in Ireland. Johnny wondered about his paralysis and how hard that must be. For sure he couldn't imagine a life without legs. Evie had heard that he might be getting better and had returned to Seattle for treatment. He deeply hoped that it would work out for Mike.

Johnny had lost hope that he himself could heal. At that thought, he felt the weight on his hip of his Browning. It was a semi-automatic, seven plus one in the chamber. He'd purchased it after his release from the army. In Angoon, he frequently used to head out to the rifle range and sight in both his 30-06 and the Browning. He hadn't done that since returning to Juneau. Well, Johnny thought, I won't be able to miss today.

Turning back toward Second Bridge, he continued on as much by intuition as his eyes. It took him a few minutes to reach the Stump. He sat on his favorite stone, waiting, eyes closed. He jerked awake sometime later. There was a hint of light, just enough to see. With a brief intake of breath, he waded right into the creek, remembering how his teeth used to hurt from the cold when he'd drink from it as a kid. He turned left, headed upstream a couple hundred yards and crossed it at a sharp bend where a small pool of calm water formed in the eddy of a huge stone. It was still too dark to see the bathroom, although it was only two or three feet deep.

Johnny set the pack on the bank right next to the creek and stood for a minute. Reached in, took out a pair of scissors and sheared his shoulder-length hair short. Watched it float away on the water. Closed his eyes, thought of Uncle Walter. If you were ever with me, let it be now. Thought of his mom with sadness for the pain he'd caused her. Remembered his sister's deep love for him. Remembered camping with Rock down at the south end of Douglas Island when they were in high school, and the salmon they'd caught and fried up. How frustrating it had been trying to catch Mike in track when they were seniors.

Uncle had taught him how his ancestors, before a challenging task, would sit in the icy water of a creek. The steely determination needed to do so strengthened one for the task and granted the approval of one's ancestors.

He reeled in every good memory and pulled out his gun as he stepped toward the water. To his surprise Marianne floated into his thoughts. He'd seen her once when he went to visit Mike in the hospital, and they'd chatted for a few minutes just outside the main doors. The change in her was startling, especially the happiness that seemed to radiate off her. He still found it incomprehensible that she, who had seemed so timid to him, was actually in El Salvador. Or that she had forgiven Vince.

"Johnny," she'd said to him, referring to Vince, "I'm not exactly telling you what to do, but what is there to hold onto that can be good for you? It's been almost seventeen years. Besides, not that it excuses what he did, but violence was all he ever knew as a child, I'm sure of it. His life, just as mine, is always open to possibility."

He had shaken his head, angry. She read his body language perfectly.

"Even you, Johnny. I've gotten to know you a bit and know you are haunted by something. I am not saying there's an easy cure, but I remember like it was yesterday that day on the Knoll.

"I don't even remember walking up there. But I will never forget your kindness."

All this passed through his mind in the half second before his feet entered the water. As the cold again bit into him, he saw Marianne as she'd looked at him, her eyes steady on his as she crossed the short distance between them, placed her hands on his shoulders, and kissed him on the cheek. It was a moment of intimacy that startled him. And she hadn't pulled back but kept her hands on him.

"Your kindness was the very first step in my long journey toward healing. It started with you. You were a true warrior that day, Johnny. With all my heart, I thank you."

Coming back to the present, Johnny sat down in the water, all thought briefly shocked away by the cold. Holy shit, he thought, the ancestors were nuts to do this. Gathering his courage and good memories, he lifted the Browning. Pulling out the clip, he unloaded it one bullet at a time, throwing them into the creek, until all that remained was the single bullet in the chamber. He looked at it for a long moment, considering other options, but finally fully rejecting them. He had come here with a plan, and he was going to stick to it. Held the pistol with both hands. Extended his arms. Shot it into the sky.

Already shivering, Johnny set the handgun on the bank and, with a deep breath, leaned all the way back into the water.

And he thought he'd been cold before. He opened his eyes. The light still a little too dim to see anything. Johnny sensed a presence that seemed to disappear into a far distance. He would later think of the infinite reflection of a person in side-by-side mirrors. When his breath ran out, he came up out of the water with a rush and let out his pain, his fear, his hope, his gratitude, and the shock of the cold in a scream that echoed up the slopes of Roberts and Juneau and into the heavens beyond. Stunned, he sat for a few seconds. Then, with a "Holy shit, this is cold," he left the water. Stripping, he pulled out two large towels, standing on one and drying himself with the other. It was hard to dry his skin, it was so cold. He hurried into clean clothes, including a ski cap and heavy winter sweater he'd brought along. Wool socks and hiking boots.

Johnny heard the thwap, thwap of wings and looked down the creek. Raven flew toward him in long beautiful strokes, bringing daylight. As he came abreast of Johnny, Raven turned his head and looked Johnny in the eyes. For a moment less than a microsecond, for an instant shorter than time itself, he saw Uncle's eyes looking back. Raven looked away and disappeared around a bend. Johnny looked a long time after it disappeared. At last he said, "Thank you."

Johnny moved quickly along the bank of the creek. He turned away from it through a dense stand of alder and scrambled up a high rocky outcrop that wasn't quite a cliff. Cross country, Johnny wended his way uphill for twenty minutes until he intersected Mt. Roberts trail. Up and up he quickly hiked, his body warming. Past tree line, on by the Cross, up and over the three rounded ridges, then across the small arête to the stony section that led to the top. So great was his speed that he stood at Robert's Peak in just over ninety minutes. The sun floated low in the morning sky. It was lucky timing.

The beauty of the soft light across the peaks to the east and the contrast of the deep shadows between them brought goosebumps to his skin.

He received the beauty.

Johnny rolled his shoulders a bit, picked up several stones and threw them, each farther than the last. Finally, he took out the Browning. Facing the sun, he reached back and heaved the gun as far as he could. He watched it arc out and down, down, down until it smashed on stone far below with a clatter that he heard a couple seconds later.

"Amen."

Three hours later he arrived home. His hope felt as fragile as a baby grouse. He knew he was not out of the water, that difficult experiences lay in front of him, that he might still fail. But a new, deeper determination seemed to lay in his guts. He would try to find the man who had sat for hours with Mike in his sadness and confusion after Marianne left Juneau. He would try to find the man who had helped a deeply wounded Marianne off the Knoll. He would try to find the man he saw in Evie's eyes. He would try to forgive.

Not Vince. Himself.

FORTY FOUR

Inis Mór, August 29, 1981

Aoife had called and said she had two letters from America for Michael. Katie dropped him off so he could stay and visit with Aoife while she ran into Cill Rónáin on some errands. She picked him up after a couple hours. He was quiet as they drove home.

"What is it you say, a cat has your tongue?"

He looked at her and said, "Got. You say 'cat got your tongue?'"

"What a strange language you Americans speak. I remember once you told me it was 'windy as all get out.' I had no idea what that meant. How does that mean ever anything at all?"

"You're one to speak. Half the time I wish I had subtitles when I'm listening to Tim or Aoife."

"Mmm. But why were you quiet? Who are the letters from?"

"Evie, you remember her? And Marianne."

Mike opened one of the letters. "I won't read you the whole letter, but this is what Evie said:

It's difficult. Johnny went for thirty days to treatment. But his nightmares never stop. He has shared with me some of what he had to in the war.

It's awful. He doesn't want drugs, although lately he seems more open to the possibility. You know what a good man he could be, Mike, but I sometimes think his guilt is too deep, the memories too horrible. He tries with everything he has—he's been more determined these last few weeks, and that gives me some hope. I wish Uncle were alive. I wish you could be here—he has so few friends. There's Rock, me, and a man named Jake he met at some meeting or other. He tries hard, Mike. You would be proud of him. I got him a beautiful set of carving tools for Christmas, but he doesn't use them. He says he will. But he does hug me every day, and tells me he loves me. I am okay. I will be starting at the Auk Bay campus in September. I want to become a counselor—yes, you guessed it, to help veterans suffering from war. It'll take me several years, and I don't know yet how it'll go for Mom and Johnny when I have to leave Juneau to finish my education. I'm just going one day at a time now. Hey, Mike, do you remember that time you took Marianne to the Prom or Homecoming, and I was there with Rock? I asked you to dance, and Marianne danced with Rock. You and me laughed so hard at Rock, he looked so afraid he was going to make a mistake with Marianne, step on her feet or some-thing, like she was some fragile flower. It was fun dancing with you. You were one of the good guys, Mike, and I never forgot that. I hope things are good in Ireland—I'm real glad I got to meet Katie. Remember us in your prayers, especially Johnny, okay?

Evie

They drove the last mile to their home in silence. As they approached the driveway, Mike turned to Kathleen. "Love, would you mind if I walk down to the beach for a while?"

She sighed, looking at him with a small smile. "Weight of the world?"

He smiled back. "Something like that, I just want to think. I'll be back by 4:00 for sure, okay?" Then he thought a moment. "Why don't you come down in say an hour and a half? I'd love to sit a while."

He took his time walking. Walking. Every day was a wonder of bodily movement. Every step seemed an occasion for gratitude. He lifted his heart to the heavens.

A light breeze blew in across the Brannocks. Mike left the road and walked close to the water, which shushed in and back out in a quiet, constant motion.

Mike read Evie's letter again. Johnny's situation was hard to hear. Johnny had gone to Vietnam, he to Seattle University. Johnny had lived the book of violence, while he'd read and fallen in love with Wordsworth's poem "Tintern Abbey." He thought of the great lyric poet's return to the beautiful Wye river valley and the Abbey after five years away. About how much Wordsworth loved his talented sister Dorothy, and she him. Would there be any return to beauty and peace for Johnny and Evie? He closed his eyes, picturing them in imagination and lifted his hopes for them to God.

A couple birds squawking at each other drew his attention. They fought over the carcass of a dead fish. Not much of a fight, actually. One bird, probably the latecomer, simply bullied the other into submission. The strong dominating the weak. He thought again of Johnny, who was the most fearless kid he'd known when they were young, quick with his fists when provoked, the undefeated middleweight of Sixth Street and Starr Hill.

He cried for him, his prayer reaching into the deepest part of his being. The view comforted him, and the sound of the sea. He thought of John Masefield's "Sea Fever."

I must go down to the seas again
to the lonely sea and the sky,
and all I ask is a tall ship

And a start to steer her by.

Jesus, he prayed, help Johnny find his star.

He took out Marianne's letter.

Dearest Michael,

I have been in El Salvador for eleven weeks now. It is the hardest thing I have ever done, but the best. My days are long and exhausting. You'll laugh, but I'm up really early each morning—it is quiet and cool, and I pray for an hour or so. Every day is different, although I spend more and more time tending to the physical needs of the people here—word has gotten around, I guess, that there is a nurse in the area. I often wish I had more medicine to help, and the parishioners back in Portland had several fundraisers so they could send me packets of antibiotics and bandages, pain medicine, all sorts of stuff. The poverty is overwhelming. Their lives revolve around their children and would be immeasurably better without the violence.

Michael stopped reading. Marianne never really mentioned it, but she was in danger. Catholic men and women were being brutalized, accused of supporting the FMLN, an insurgency fighting the oppressive government.

It was a wonder to him that he hadn't fallen in love with her. Truth was, he had half-fallen—she was funny, playful, and had such a deep faith. She was no dummy, either. And beautiful. They had their past together. But through it all, Katie had never waned for him. He thought of Katie as the light of the full moon soft in the night. The moon was *an ghealach* in Irish. He loved the Greek word for the moon—"Selene." If they ever had a daughter, he'd like to name her that, although Katie would probably want something Irish.

After a few minutes, he looked toward the end of the letter, the only place Marianne made even an oblique reference to the danger.

Michael, there's something I want to say in case I never get a chance to. I am so glad we met and got the opportunity to get to know each other again. You are so fun to be with, and I'll never forget that day we just drove around, looking for the sun, and ended up on the beach where we went once in high school. It was lovely to be with you again. I thought back in high school you were someone special, and I was right. I think Katie is the luckiest woman in Ireland. But you're really lucky, too—tell her I said that!
So, here's lookin' at ya, kid!

Marianne

He heard the car and turned as Katie got out. She carried two light folding beach chairs down to where he sat. They remained in silence for a minute, both content to watch the sea running in. Mike looked over at her. The wind lightly ruffled hair into her eyes. He reached over and moved it behind her ear. Mike knew she didn't like the small bend in her nose. She referred to it as her beak. But he liked it, that and the light freckling that ran across it and onto her cheeks.

"So."

"I'm wondering why I get this great life here with you while Johnny suffers so deeply and Evie with him. Why there are people in El Salvador being murdered by their own government, and I got to grow up in the US."

Katie reached for his hand. "Do you want to go to Juneau, to see Johnny?"

"I do, but I don't want to be separated from you."

"Oh, and you'll not be getting away from me that easy, Michael Flaherty. If you go to Juneau, I'll be coming with you."

He smiled and the pair sat in comfortable silence for a couple more minutes after which she asked, "And how is Marianne?"

He handed her the letter, which she read through.

"She's brave. I admire what she's doing altogether."

Katie snorted in derision. "Luckiest woman in Ireland." She started to say more, and stopped.

Then continued, "She's a beautiful woman, no?" She was smiling as she said it, an impish look in her eyes.

Mike leaned forward and looked back at her. "Yes, she is. She's the, well, the third most beautiful woman I ever met."

A slow smile crossed her face. A question occurred to her, but she did not ask it. The answer did not matter.

"And what must I do to keep you, Kathleen Flaherty?"

"Oh Mike. Just breathe."

"Is that all, then? But I have something for you, two things actually."

"Sure, and the last gift you gave me was a wonder, but it was complicated, no? Maybe you should stop while you're ahead."

"Ah, well, when you put it that way, I don't know what I was thinking. Give away!"

He pulled the poem out of his pocket and handed it to her. She read it through, looked up at him and read it a second time.

"Michael Flaherty, and you are a wonder then. So, this just came to you?"

"More or less, I made some small changes. And the verses didn't all come in the order I put them. And the last stroph is all mine."

"Fiddles don't whisper."

He raised his eyebrow. "Ah, lassie, but you did, right to my heart."

She smiled at his words, shaking her head. He held his fists out to her. "I was planning on waiting until tomorrow for this, but I just can't anymore. Not another minute. Guess which hand."

She had her first inkling what he was about as she reached and touched his left hand. He laughed as he opened his right—a simple silver ring lay in his palm.

"I like this ring a lot. If you want a diamond, we can pick it together. You know it's been almost exactly a year since we met? And sweet Jesus, what a year altogether. I can't imagine life without you, Katie Flaherty."

She laughed at what he said next. "I won't even ask you to change your last name. Will you marry me?"

She was silent for a moment, her eyes on the ring, then on his eyes. "The ring is perfect, Mike, and I want you to wear one just like it."

"Ah. Well. That's a yes."

"Sure, and if you don't know the answer to that, you truly are dumber than a sack of dirt. Yes, Mike, I really, really want to marry you."

That evening Katie's cousin Seamus and his wife Fiona met the pair at Conneely's. Seamus was known on the island as the Bassman, as he both played the upright bass and sang bass as well. Fiona had a sweet soprano voice and played the Irish pipes as well as the bodhrán. They had been together a month, had already performed several times at Conneely's, and were known as *The Four Flahertys*.

Seamus brought incredible news. A music agent had heard them perform and wanted to meet with them and discuss a contract to make an album and tour Ireland. They discussed the matter over dinner and decided to go for it.

Then the instruments came out, and the four warmed up as the pub started to fill. Katie knew she was an outstanding fiddle player, and Michael was nearly her equal on guitar. But their voices, she thought. It was as if God had created them to sing together. And truth to tell, Seamus and Fiona were also talented.

Katie had the intuition that in the end, Mike would need to leave Inis Mór. Perhaps it lay in the genes of his great-grandfather Tomas, the one who left the island in the first place. He had that American quality of needing something, to make a difference. She'd resolved to enjoy every moment here in her home, to feel as deeply as she could every clod of dirt, every gust of wind, every rainstorm, so that nothing would be regretted when they left. But now a new possibility opened—that the music itself would be their future, and that this could happen right here. She was content to let the future become what they built together. She thought of the poem he had given her. Dedicated to her. She wondered what kind of songwriter Mike might become.

They were well into their performance and started a reel. Mike had never played for a group as talented as this. Seamus laid down the bassline with authority, and Fiona did things with the bodhrán he'd not known were possible.

He felt Katie's gaze and knew to pick up the pace. She closed her eyes and set the bow to flying across the strings. Faster and faster she played until Mike and Seamus simply stopped playing. The two women picked it up even faster, and the crowd started clapping to the beat, and yelling their approval. Fiona had moved up next to Katie, and her hand was a blur on the bodhrán. "All Ireland, All Ireland," people began to yell out, and finally Katie indicated the end by trilling on a high note for four or five seconds. She finished it with a dramatic flourish of a down-stroke of the bow as Fiona hit the drum one last time. The crowd raised to their feet.

She looked at Mike and thought, how wonderful to be swaying to music on a Friday night out on the west of Ireland.

In that moment Katie felt the presence of all her deceased loved ones and knew with certainty that they approved.

While Gazing At A Ruined Farmhouse

For Katie

There are only ghosts now
shadow-flitting among the stones,
traces of memory
tumbling out these half-walls.
An echo of a question
sweeps through the high grass
as if voices long forgotten
sigh in their bones.

What these walls, roof, doors
crumbling from stone to sand?
What they who breathed this place?
All laughter and weeping silent beneath Gaelic crosses
which stand in rows to the long horizon.

No island can save us,
no cliff deny the sea
or hold the wild Aran wind.
Even Inisfree recedes.

Then, just there
a small melody of air
fiddle-whispers through
an unseen crevice,
swirling up a fallen leaf

or a bird—I cannot tell—
and I follow
its ascending curve
into infinite blue.

FORTY FIVE

Diocese of Santa Ana, El Salvador
August 31, 1981

She was up before the rooster called down the day.

Marianne stretched in her cot, glad as always to be up early, an hour before dawn. In the quiet and dark, she loved to pray. And God knows, she thought as she sat up, there is enough to pray for.

She habitually ran her hands through her hair, laughing inside. It was the same every morning, realizing as if for the first time that her hair was now too short to put in a ponytail. Tomorrow would be hair-washing day, and she'd be glad of it—her hair was all she remained vain about and hated how greasy it got.

With long habit she groped under her cot and pulled out her piece of *ocote*, from the core of a pine-like tree that was damp with sap. She felt for her small square of corrugated metal and lay it in the middle of the dark room, setting the *ocote* on top of the metal. Reaching unerringly to the matches, Marianne set one to the wood, which quickly lit, burning with a small brightness that still surprised her. She got dressed by its light and poured some water into a wood bowl, rinsing her face, cleaning her underarms and then poured herself a small cup of water. She had learned to be fast. A quick trip to the outhouse to pee, and she was back to her cot as the fire died out, leaving behind its pleasant, pine-sweet smell. For the next hour she prayed, starting first by picturing the local villagers, raising their grief to God, praying especially for the men, women, and children she knew of who had disappeared or been killed. She especially prayed for Alejandra Martinez, whose husband Santiago and son Jesus had been murdered just after her arrival, their bodies left by the road less than a mile away, and who Alejandra had been forbidden to bury as the two had been suspected—falsely—of being members of the FLNA. After all this, she placed her mind on the attack in Juneau last year, especially the moment in which, having decided to die with Michael, all fear fled. She thanked God for this second chance to give her life in service to the poor. She prayed for her daughter. As always, she hoped that the girl—she'd be almost seventeen now—might someday find it in her heart to contact her. And then she asked for inner peace.

A half hour later Marianne sighed and opened her eyes. She could hear two companions in service, as she thought of them, beginning to stir. Mary Francis and Julia were both Maryknoll sisters, a few years older than she. Mary Francis was a charm of with and joy who also possessed a piercing intellect. With her psychiatric background, she was a gift of prayerful listening to the suffering of the villagers of the area. Julia was quieter than Mary Francis, but had a steely courage that inspired Marianne.

Mary Francis greeted her. "And a beautiful morning to you, Marianne."

"And also to you, MF." They laughed, as always, at their morning ritual. Julia came in and said without preamble, "Marianne, could you go see Alejandra this morning? She was really depressed yesterday and seems to respond to you the best of the three of us."

"Yes. Do you think late morning will be fine? I was planning to read bible stories to some children at the Rodrigues' home after their breakfast visit with Elena. There's also a few people I want to see before lunch who are sick." And so the trio planned their day, parceling out who would do what, aware as always that the need was greater than what help they could offer. The sisters would be away at nearby villages much of the afternoon, leaving Marianne alone.

A couple hours later Marianne approached Alejandra's fragile looking *champa,* always amazed that the small home—built of sticks, corrugated metal, and a couple ratty pieces of plywood—held together. She was glad the hottest part of the year was over, but the damp of the roads from yesterday's thunderstorms followed her into the humid interior of Alejandra's home. It was dark and dense with the smell of human habitation. Alejandra sat on a stool near the door, praying with a rosary.

"*Hola, Alejandra,*" she greeted her friend.

"*Ah, angelita mía. Buenos dias.*"

"Can I sit and help you with the *pupusas?*"

"*Si, si, gracias.*"

Alejandra had already made the masa. Marianne began forming them into small balls, which Alejandra flattened into round tortilla shells, to be cooked later and stuffed with pickled carrots, cabbages, onions cheese, meat if they had it. They didn't talk much as they worked, Marianne content to let Alejandra have her company in quiet. What was there to say, after all?

After twenty minutes, the tortillas were made. Alejandra looked at Marianne almost shyly and asked, "*Angelita,* could you go to the field and bring me a cabbage and an onion? I'll need them for tomorrow."

"*Si, puedo.* I'll bring them this afternoon."

"*¿Come conmigo?* Will you eat with me?"

"*Si, mi amiga, gracias.*"

Marianne took her time making way to the edge of the village, beyond which lay a small garden patch where Alejandra worked. She stopped by several *champas* to greet people, visiting a small time with each, and looking in on several people who were sick. In a shed bordering the *selva*, the forest, lay a wounded man from a nearby village who was hiding here. The story was that soldiers had tried to force him and a few other local young men into the army. He'd fled on foot and was shot in the arm, but escaped into the thick *selva*. An infection had developed. Marianne had given him antibiotics and changed his dressing regularly. He was improving. Marianne did not care if his story was true or not. He was a human being who asked her help and she gave it. She was aware, however, the risk she and the others took.

The man, little more than a boy really, was ready at a moment's notice to flee into the *selva*, but he was still weak.

An hour or so after leaving Alejandra, Marianne headed out past the end of the village to pull the onion and cut a cabbage for Alejandra. A few children, accompanied as always by two women from the village, played nearby, running around and laughing. Marianne had sliced a cabbage head and was just leaning over to pull up an onion when she heard the approaching vehicle. She stood, lowering the bill of her hat to see despite the bright sun. A jeep had appeared at a distant corner of the dirt road which led to the village. The road sloped down a couple hundred yards to where the jeep now slowly made its way up the long hill.

Marianne felt her heart begin to pound. The two women gathered the children and rushed them back to the relative safety of their homes and to get the injured man away. One of them gave her a long, fearful look at the last moment. Marianne turned back to the jeep, intending to slow their arrival in the village in any way she could. It stopped a short distance away.

Four men got out. Marianne had trouble seeing them clearly because of the sun. Two of them carried what looked to be machine guns. Their leader approached.

"*Ven acá, puta.*"

Marianne decided to pretend she didn't understand the insult—he'd called her something between a bitch and a cunt. Legs feeling wobbly the first few steps, but following his order, she walked slowly toward him, stopping a few feet away.

"So, you are the golden angel everyone talks about," he said, looking her up and down, his eyes hesitating at her breasts. When she didn't reply, he continued. "*¿Cual es tu nombre, puta? Me llamo Capitán Rojas. Respóndeme,*" he ordered, harsh at the end.

She took a deep breath, "Mari…" She stopped to swallow. "Marianne Greene," she answered.

He continued in decent English. "You are not wanted here, *puta*. You should go back home."

"I am just here to help. I am a nurse, and there are a lot of sick people."

He shook his head. "I lived a little time in your land, training. Not even your own government wants you here. Your *Presidente* is saying you are helping communists. We are hearing you hide a man in this village right now."

She shook her head. "There is no one. *No hay nada.* As for President Reagan, I like to think if he came here and saw the reality, he would know we are here only to serve the poor."

The *Capitán* barked a laugh. "You live in a world of dreams if you are believing that, *puta.*"

"Captain Rojas, we help the people, the children of this village. I read to the children from the Bible every day and help with the sick."

He leisurely reached to his side, putting his hand on the pistol holstered there. Marianne followed his hand and looked back to his face, seeing the coldness. She pulled her rosary from her left jeans pocket, while touching to fingers of her right hand to her lips.

Rojas laughed, his eyes narrowing. "Go ahead, *puta*, put that *rosario* like armor over your pretty breasts. Then we'll make an experiment. I will shoot you through the heart and see if your *Santa Maria* saves you."

He pulled the snap that kept the pistol in its holster, seeming to be waiting for something. Marianne realized he searched her face for tears, perhaps looking to hear her plead. His eyes narrowed.

The words came, not as if she spoke them, but as if she were spoken.

"Do you have a mother, *Capitán*? A wife, children? If they needed me, I would help them."

His eyes narrowed further. "*Mi madre* is safe. She lives under my protection."

"And does she pray, *Capitán*? Does she pray for her son and for her people? Does she hold a *rosaria*?"

He stepped forward. Reaching out quickly he ripped the rosary from her loose grip, holding it up in both hands and yanking it apart. Beads flew out in all directions, as if caught briefly in the twisting turbulence of an exploding bomb. He dropped the detritus in front of her.

Now tears did emerge in her eyes, but she beheld him with no fear, finally kneeling down, picking up the crucifix and a few beads.

Rising up, she asked, "And *hijos, Capitán,* do you have children, a family?"

He pursed his lips, looking past her shoulders up the long slope. Marianne followed his gaze. A couple women stood at the furthest visible distance.

"*Capitán Rojas,* I read to their children. I teach them to read, about *Jesus.* When they are sick, I help them. There is a very sick woman in the village, I give her medicine every day. People from my home in the United States send me money and medicine. I sit with villagers daily who have loved ones missing, or killed. That is what I do. If your *madre* ever needed my help, I would give it. If you came to me shot, I would help you, for it is as Jesus would do."

And she offered him all that was left to her, the ruins of the small *rosario*, the crucifix. She put it in the palm of her left hand and held it out to him.

His eyes never left hers. Seconds passed.

"You cannot survive, woman." He nodded in the direction of the hills in the distance. "Is it not beautiful from here, when the hills light up with bombs at night?"

She said nothing, thinking about the acrid smell from the bombs that sometimes wafted through the air.

He continued. "We are killing men who hate and murder. They say they fight for your precious villagers, but it will be no different if they win their revolution. You, you give them hope. You are not innocent." She sensed his fingers tighten on the gun, but he did not pull it out.

Marianne's arm grew tired. He finally looked down for a few seconds, then back away toward the hills as he spoke. He sighed.

"Keep your *crucifijo, señorita.* You will need it. You cannot survive here."

A long moment stretched into two, then three. Marianne felt the sweat forming under her t-shirt, her underarms wet.

At last, still not looking at her, he reached his hand beneath his outer coat, taking out a piece of paper and the stub of a pencil. Marianne watched in curiosity as he drew lines on it, but she could not tell what it was. Finally, he handed the paper to her as he named a village about three miles away.

"*Mi madre* lives here," he said, pointing to an "x" on what she realized was a map. "When you come into the village, you must take that first road to the left. It is easy to miss. It is really just a trail. Her *casa* has a red door, and a window next to it—it is the fourth house. No other is like it. If you ever have a need, go there and tell her I have sent you, and she will protect you. You can pray your *rosaria* with her."

His eyes looked quickly over her shoulder again, and Marianne turned to see a large group of women from the village striding quickly toward them.

"Ah, they come to protect you. Or die with you. Well, you can tell them to go home. I am in a good mood today. So, I offer you no harm. Do you know, *señorita,* you are called the Angel of Santa Ana? Even *mi madre* knows of you. She tells me to look out for you. It is said that you always come with a smile, like the sun."

Marianne held up her hand, yelling to the women that she was okay. The women came to a stop a hundred feet away but did not retreat.

"*Gracias, Capitán.* If your mother ever needs help, I will go to her. Just as I would before our conversation."

He clearly sighed as he nodded his head. He pivoted and walked back toward the jeep. It turned around and headed away.

Marianne watched the back of the receding vehicle for a few moments. "You cannot survive here," he'd said. She hoped his words were not true, but she knew too that her rosary would not have stopped his bullet. The women came and circled her in the womb of their love. They walked almost wordlessly back up the hill, at the top of which the children ran to her full of innocent chatter of the young.

She stopped and picked up one of her favorites, three-year-old Angelina, kissed her hair and set her on her right hip. The child's eyes rose to the sky where she pointed. The contrail of a jet painted a cloud-like line across the sky, leading to where the aircraft raced toward an unknown destination.

She thought of Michael and Kathleen, together in Ireland and allowed herself to feel her love for him. How wonderful, how infinite the human heart, she thought as she followed the trail of the jet, that I can love him and also be genuinely happy for them. That I love these people so much I find it impossible to leave. That I can love *el Capitán.* Vince. My daughter.

Her being filled, and she experienced with wonderful immediacy, with a certainty beyond all reasoning, that love never reaches a limit, that it flows from and into an infinity beyond any capacity to contain.

"*Angelita, te quiere,*" the girl said.

"Oh, I love you too, my little Angelina, *te quiere.*"

POETRY BY TIM MILNES

Gabriel's Rose part 2

Late Apple Tree Visit

The high grass stands tanned with autumn.
Dim shadowed evening arrives on
an intaken breath of surprise.
Out where apples in their dozens
have fallen unpicked, unwanted
a short antlered bull elk chews.
Three years old, big as a mountain—
this one who last week shrugged aside
my carefully built deer-net fence
behind which plans of green gardens
had dreamed and dreamed and dreamed me.
I'm willing to give insects their part
but good-god-damn that trampling elk
that bastard buck . . . (I measured once
on a rime-frosted day the place
a hoof crunched through to the soft damp
belly of earth—seven inches
by six. By God I swear this true)
. . . once in the garden the beast broke
branches, crushed two squash leaving me
stunned, then a-rage, my careful plans
become a scattered detritus.
It devoured every string bean.

Now in darkening dusk it chews
rotting apples but hesitates,
thirteen billion years of instinct
turning its head.
                    I, from behind
a bush still bearing summer leaves,
step into the clear.

Chewing stops.
From the recess of cervid skull
where two pinholes of blackest black
obscure its eyes something uncanny
spills out hard-set boundaries. He takes
two cautious probing steps my way
half-emerging from the shadows
uncertain as a timid cat.
Head chuffs up, an agitation
trembling in his rounded haunch
and deep-recessed sinews of leg.
He negotiates one slow sideways step
and in a spasm of quick strides
head swiveling my direction
seeks the forest rimming the light,
there to pause at the edge of dark
with one long last backwards look
before returning to the night.

— January 2016 (last revision November 2016)

winter walk

all animals are snuggled
around their hearts and blood
the very air
withdrawn
into the vacancy of earth's great lung
the dark morning

suspended

in that moment before
the sun is exhaled
rosy-hued into the sky

last night's snow falls
from laden boughs
in clumps
and I arrive late
a fine mist on my face
a thousand cold kisslets
like love   no
it is love

coyote prints lead off
through the ghostly snow
and I follow
under trees into darkness
toward the tinkle of a creek
half frozen   but
running yet

— July 2015

Dusk

Evening, and a low September sun
spilling long shadows from the trees.
Lost in a pensive memory of spring
when from the top of an evergreen
a bird sings, as if the sky unleashed
from autumnal blue and cirrus white
this counterpointal melody.

Searching with uplifted eyes
I just catch from their corner
the faintest and farthest flutter
of wing, subtle as a faded dream
bubbling into consciousness,
the limits of language sundered
while hinting at some deep impress—

I feel the expanding robin breast
preceding the exhalation,
an excitation meant not least for me?
Down through the feet the breath,
through twig and branch, limb and trunk
deep and deeper to that dark
where moisture moves like the tide
of an unfathomed ocean

surging back up the probing root,
woody capillaries and pulsing throat—
blessed be the robin singing,
a blessing on the coming night
its sweetness to a silence fading
into an unheard melody

softer than this half-moon light
now out upon the earth cascading.

— May 2014

Forest Nymph at Sunset

Breathless, topping a steep ravine,
a gleam appeared on the opposite hill
a sunbeam slipping down between
branches and trunks, a bright and still
luster, floating near the dark forest floor
like the moon soon will sit against the sky,
or the return of an unremembered joy,
or one unlived, if there is a difference—
T'was all the while a coy coalescence
lit by its own inner light; a fine-featured,
translucent-winged creature
took in my surprise with impish eyes,
whispering across the intervening air:
You see? You do not know all of it.
I laughed, what was lost coming clear,
a child's forgotten, sweet secret
running unburdened into arms opened wide,
lifted up and up into a wild sky.

— January 2014

Incoming Tide

in memory: my friend Jimmy Sundberg

I picture you at mid-day
after a morning of maul-swinging,
rolling your shoulders a bit,
sharing a laugh at lunch.
Did you eat from a box or a bag?
Did you sit on a stack of lumber,
or wander to the Coastal Terminal,
watch the seaplanes come and go
as we did all those years ago?
I do not know where to put you,
or even, to call you Jimmy, or Jim?

But those who knew you as Jim
remembered with a broken laugh:
a comrade in the carpenter's craft,
a belt of stories always at hand,
your word a true-struck nail.
You knew a man's measure,
about your two best days, exact;
one when Cindy became your wife,
then Jenny floating a sunbeam
through Love's pane into life.
These are my greatest treasures.

I wonder what building, what room,
what wall it was betrayed your lungs?
I want to smash, burn it to the ground.
Now your clock has wound down,
a quiet I cannot encompass.
My thoughts edge to an angry abyss—

but though all knew your mind was sharp
you were loved for your honest heart—
so to tenderness I'll acquiesce
and say it straight: I loved the boy
who never left the man. Jimmy,

husband, father, son, brother, friend—
I am the child tagging at the end.
But I still see, when we were eight,
pigeon poop landing on your hand,
you laughing out that's just great,
chasing me down Franklin Street!
and your unfailing determination—
we can do it this time, Tim—
summer after summer, never giving in,
piling up sand, side by side,
trying to hold back the incoming tide.

— August 2013

Tina's Left Hand

I laid the Buddha head
in a garden excavation
gently as a newborn in a crib.
Messy business on a rainy day,
hands smeared with mud
leaving smudges on his face.
Half out of the soil he lay,
slight curve of a smile,
eyes shut, long-lobed ears
reaching to the earth.

After three days of sun I knelt
before his dirt-caked face,
adjusting the nozzle to mist—
right hand holding the hose,
left in soft circular motions
caressing the dark accumulation.
I started to sing. A moment . . .

Tender love lifted into memory,
my father, still in new death.
Only moments before he had
opened his eyes, held each of us
in the cradle of his final breaths.
And Tina reached to him
Oh dad . . . dad . . . it's alright
you did it . . . you did it . . . oh dad . . .
her fingers caressing his hair,
his cheek, his face.

June 2013 (last revised May 2014)

Moment

I envied those poets their special places,
who live by, say, an ocean and beach,
waves foaming and floating-in flotsam-traces
from rim of a world just beyond reach.
I had no pond nestled silent and deep
in its crook of earth, pale as milk,
while the world dreamed its last hour of sleep
tucked under a blanket of fog-thin silk.

I had no New England. No Amherst nooks,
no home holding Emily's room,
the window of her terse observation,
the Garden of Wither and Bloom.
No New Hampshire farm, no cow-licking-calf,
no laughing tramps or half-frozen brooks—
the unflawed stones of Frost's excavation
unearthing a wordless creation.

    But here,
drowsing in a dim pre-dawn,
Kinnell's
"The Last Hidden Places of Snow"
open in my lap,
partway through a poem—an indrawn breath,

taken up by the wings of imagination
through layer after layer into the unhidden—
an oncoming night, deep-shadowed with
death   a blizzard falling   forlorn
winds sighing   bare winter
branches skyward sway-

ing, trembling with
spring's green
surging
deeply
with
in

— August 2009, last revised October 2013

The Right Hand Chair

At rest,
that "fat old tub" bobbed like a boat
but was no boat, and my father
no sea captain when he fired those
twin Pratt and Whitney radials—
barking and belching blue-black smoke
dissipated in the which propwash.
"Bucket a' bolts" my father said,
but with affection, like tousling
an eager eight year-older's hair,
making him think he was needed
fidgeting in the right hand chair.

Eight passengers buckled in back,
me in the front, propped up atop
two Sears catalogues, dad revving
first the right engine, then the left—
the Goose hopscotching one pontoon
to the other, slewing slighty
in a curve that bumped me against
the dry-cracking leather armrest.
The radio squacked, dad talked back
while searching the water for logs,
giving me a part—"You look too."

My nose stuck to the side window,
I peered with all my child's heart
to help dad, proud to be his son.
A half mile out he swung us south.
I craned my neck to see over
all the instruments of his craft,

watched the line of mainland mountains
and Douglas Island's lower peaks
a mile east, rotate into view
as if parallel railroad tracks
vanishing at eternity.

Gastineau Channel lay between.
"Juneau Dispatch, Coastal 30,
Oh-9-40 for Haines, Skagway."
He tapped the altimeter twice,
"for luck," with a look and a wink,
then, reaching up his right hand
he eased the throttles forward
into 10 knot-choppy seas .
Engines roared. The boy in me
whispered "go go go" as we
bounced through water sluggishly.

The tether rope on the wing
swung back and suddenly
the old Grumman rose
like a dog's nose to the wind,
up on step, spitting speed.
 "Go, go, go." "Go… go… go,"
a racing pulse through the waves
until, catching one last crest,
dad laughing at my full-moon eyes
let loose in the boundless blue—
I want to shout it still! We flew!

My stomach unsure of the lift
houses and cars suddenly small
two quick miles, at five hundred feet,

dad dipped the wing of the Grumman
turning in space between mountains
back over the steep, narrow streets
of childhood, and the long replaced
steel-girdered Juneau-Douglas bridge.
Beyond high-country peaks we flew,
diminishing dot through the sky,
until, one breath to the next,
we were gone.

— April 2013 (later revision?)

Mountain Spring

Life flows thickly
within this small trickle,
too nothing to name.

Leaning low, my hands
curve into a drinking bowl,
a beggars empty space.

Water drips down my beard.
Quiet as a passing doe,
a breeze chills my lips.

— January 2013

While Gazing At A Ruined Farmhouse

There are only ghosts now
shadow-flitting among stones,
traces of memory
tumbling out these half-walls.
An echo of question
sweeps through the high grass
as if voices long forgotten
sigh in our bones.

What of walls, roof, doors
crumbling to stone and sand?
What of they who
breathed this place?
All is done and all are dead,
all laughter and weeping silent
beneath Gaelic crosses
which stand in rows
to the long horizon.

No Island can save us.
No Cliff deny the sea
or hold the wild Aran wind.
Even Inisfree recedes.

Then, just there
a small melody of air
flute-whispers through
an unseen crevice,
swirling up a fallen leaf
or a bird—I cannot tell—
just my eyes following

an ascending curve
toward infinite blue.

— December 2012

Inisfree: a favorite place of William Butler Yeats

Capitol Lake Circuit

October has arrived
with an unexpected run—
lingering days of sun.
My feet feel quick and light
like water flowing over stone—
or so I imagine it.

I elevate like a
banner behind a plane.
A half century ago
this was not possible—
I ran relentlessly
but never soared.

Last year the air
solidified in front of a bird
and it lay gasping, dazed
below the offending window.
Compassion welled into
a cupped hand

bodhisattva eyes
gazing into mine until
arose the slightest twitch
of tail and whir of wing—
a bit of how it is, at 56,
to run and feel 18.

— October 2012

The Way Back

One windless, silent night,
guided by my darker sight,
placing feet in crystal snow,
the crunch of crust letting go
into the hidden white below,
feeling the cold at fingers, toes,
at ears, at nose, feeling the threat
of cold which wasn't finished yet,
stopping by a creek amid a frozen field

interspersed with random trees
bare branched and dark, and under these,
silhouetted in the barely white
of a fragile moon which fought the night
to illumine with a half-moon light,
the narrow arms of some bare bush
which dared to push up through the snow;
later, buried beneath a blow,
blank-whitened storm across the world.

Immobile in the flurried black
and certain there was no way back
without a light, and I'd not thought—
or perhaps I had thought not—
(more complex than I just forgot)
to bring one to this frozen dark
of bare and stark, immobile fear
this darkest evening of the year
by frozen creek and frosted field.

And then I heard a horse's breath,
blades upon on an unseen path,
creak of sleigh stop by the trees,
a quiet voice upon the breeze—
these dropped me weeping to my knees.
They never saw the man alone
cold to bone, heart-hardening chill—
now to leave this frozen field,
risk the lonely road, and live.

— September 2012

Evening in the Garden

Lush red and green
after a late, cool spring
the trees sway like a line dance
beneath a bass-whistle wind,
ruff of fingers through my hair.

I have seen Japanese maples
glow with a secret light
beneath a full moon.
Their leaves tremble now.
While I was reading a poem

robins left the tree-tops
for their hidden nests.
In the silence I hear you
on the outer stair,
my heart beating to your steps.

— August 2012

Sunrise, July 7, 2012

for Mark Hart

The impression of your patient art
is rising with this new-lit day, and you
already writing from that place apart—
fertile soil of mind's service to the heart

with words your tool to excavate the true,
leave exposed the open-wounded cavity
which seems bottomless. This is your due—
I write again with energy renewed,

step in where I have stepped so timidly,
where thought reduces all to the absurd,
unredeemed by God, or poetry...
and yet, the pencil nestles patiently

in my hand, eager as when a child
I woke to *something* beyond mere measure,
the way a flower feeds a hummingbird—
again the open book, the honest word.

— July 2013 (last revision)

Prayer After Hearing

For Jim Sundberg

1

Your words clutched, and clenched, and twisted
my guts—an acid bitter on my tongue.
I could not bear to be so bared alone,
driven from my corner chair, that so-called
"powerful place of prayer," to Capitol Lake

where I have run a thousand times. My feet
know every step. People even greet me.
I need their faces—owners walking dogs,
runners straining like horses at their bits,
parents a protective wing for their kids.

I find a familiar bench, lightly groan,
tears locked behind the shutter of my lids,
still as stone until my eyes rise to where
three ducks descend a diagonal line,
releasing like a sigh into the water.

2

Beyond, across the Lake and Puget Sound,
the Olympics, still snow-topped this July,
crag up against the sky—remind me of
touching, at ten, Mt. Juneau's peak with you.
Memory rolls then like an avalanche

and I slide as if into a dream—one
clean moment—I was five—when your voice
became my childhood refrain—can Timmy

come out and play? A million times, yes.
Jimmy—what am I now to say? To pray?

3

Someone laughs. Long shadows pattern the grass.
Birds murmur unseen in the shadowed trees.
Caressing breeze... like a sudden, indrawn breath
the ducks leap into the air, furious wings
beating, turning north, up and up, toward you.

July 13, 2012

Before Dawn

Silence.
In the full dark
a long canine howl.

Alert,
I feel the rooster
fill his bellows with breath
craw-crawing light
down upon all things.

— April 2013

Unexpected

Last night, infinitely irritating.
It was April 18, for God's sake,
cherry tree blooming pink these three weeks,
plum petals opened white with invitation
to the bees. Damned Canadian north,
coming in cold, colliding with the moist
Pacific, concocting a high altitude slush
dropping down wet and shivery,
making a muddle of my plans
to garden today in shorts and a T-shirt.

But then I woke to the finest
feather snow falling like piano notes
played for lovers—the child in me running
outside. Staring into the swirling flakes
they suddenly seemed stars, and I, light itself
weaving back and forth between them
across a vast expanse of universe.
I picked a point fifty feet up, danced
beneath its slow unsteady descent,
and felt it sparkle on my tongue, like laughter.

— April 2012 (last reivision December 2012)

Light At The Edge Of The Earth

For a few unexpected moments
I caught a glimpse of an infant's face,
when, as if playing peek-a-boo,
it dissolved back to gray and white.
The profile of a dog briefly coalesced,
looking like our beloved Pinto,
his front legs rotating as if to sidle
in his one-eyed, half-sideways gait--
then, quick as a bubble-burst, he was gone!

When I was a child I did such as this
on dreamy, lay-away-afternoons, leaning
into that niche on Helicopter Rock
letting my imagination be shaped
in the lower crowns of cumulus,
in which joy as surprising as the next
shifting shape emerged like a shout.
If Jimmy were there, I might exclaim,
"See that king, that car, that bear?" "Where?"
"By the break where you can see the sky!"

Two figures formed, vaguely like my parents
as they appear in a photo from 1948,
walking hand-in-hand, looking in love,
not seeing, not yet, their future gathering.
I know my father dreamed of flight,
landing in Juneau in bouncing, fragile
Grumman Gooses, and mother loved us but
hated the rain. Then, in a creek flowing west
of Mendenhall glacier, she saw salmon running,
at last sharing her hopeful poems with me.

Like dreams disappearing, their forms withdrew.

Just then you stepped in the door,
I again amazed at your smile for me,
like the sun probing through parted clouds
chasing the gray that once had gathered here.
I look at your face, and I know, I know
lines have grown I do not see, and cannot,
for there is no calculation by which
to set before me merely proof of them.
You are luminous! You are luminous,
your love the light in which I am seen,
as we too float on ever-turning clouds.

— April 2011

Girl Flying a Kite

There's a girl running
in the median on Pacific Avenue.
When I first saw her, I thought,
that's no place to be flying a kite!
But I was wrong, for each time
I drive by, I root for her,
feel the air flowing underneath,
my spirits rising up the string
strung diagonally behind her.

A large jumble of sharply curved shapes
lies along Tumwater Avenue,
as if someone had cut the punctuation
from a complex sentence—
a comma, one or two question marks,
an exclamation missing the point—
and dropped them beside the street.
They're an eye-catching red, rusted a bit,
and I whistle when I see them.

In the Seattle Art Museum
hangs a solid white painting,
utterly plain, a wall-in-a-frame.
Puzzled people shake their heads,
seeming to think, "Hell, I could do that."
What is it to submit to the wheel
of any art, then give it away—
hoping the curve of a question emerge
to bend another's box of rigid lines?

At an intersection on Capitol Avenue

Mark Twain is bronzed on a bench,
arm flung across the bench's back
in open invitation—"Come sit with me!"
My wife swears she will do it one day.
Oh, I can hardly wait to see it—
the two of them, grins on their faces,
leaning toward the blue like a bird
just before flight, and she will point
to the sky and exclaim in delight,
"Look, Mark, look at the kite!"

— November 2008 (last revision November 2010)

Musings on a Late Autumn Afternoon

There will come a time
of last things.
The final time I hike
these hills, up and down
deep-welled ravines,
the forest and
slow tide of night
enshrouding me.
The last time I look
into my children's eyes,
those of my wife—
and if I am lucky,
I will know it.

Mist floats the trees,
a pale, translucent scarf
woven among the trunks.
Rain tap-taps
the forest floor,
a rhythm evoking eternity.
Too rarely! vision
clears. Far far away,
beyond an ocean of
wind-swept waves tossing
like wild horses running free,
I glimpse a distant land
shining as if its own moon,
as if its own rising dawn.

Do I dream?

— September 2010

A Blue-Jean Kind Of Awakening

As I gazed upon a rain swept street
from my restaurant seat, coffee cup
half-empty near to hand,
Buddha and Christ happened in—
as the place was full,
they asked to share with me
the near-bare table and empty chairs.
How could I decline what was sure
to be an excellent conversation?
A pitcher was ordered up, with three
pints; I prepared for illumination.
So Gotama goes: I teach only this,
the cessation of suffering.
So Jesus says: I teach only this,
the divine suffers with you.
Wow, I thought, this is it…
each looked a long moment
into the other's eyes, and
one moment more, then both
burst out belly-laughing. The beer
arrived—Jesus poured while
Gotama looked to me and asked,
Aren't you drinking?

— April 2010

Birth of Poetry

Somewhere, ago,
waking up
from ocean to
unfailing flame,
a creature
(bi-pedal with
opposable thumbs)
experienced
dark-starred sky
rich-veined venison
breeze caress
robin song
fragrance of flower
and bubbling up,
a spring named Word,
for stars are
never just light,
the dark not
encompassed
by night.

— April 2010

Christmas Dinner

We have gathered across a thousand miles,
all roads converging on home.
Grown a quiet pair to a noisy seven
and now, two more—a husband and a wife-to-be.
No grandkids, but three great big grand-dogs!
The night before we'd dressed the tree with
store-bought bulbs and glowing glass shapes,
remembering years with branches bare
but for rough-cut cloth circles and stars
bought and sewn on the cheap, and always, ours.
Now, in the dark spaces between bulbs
we laugh and hang memories in paper
cut with second-grade fingers, mangers
and pull-out Jesus babies, names scrawled
on the back—"Joel" with a backwards "e",
"Rachel" lettered as if walking down stairs.
Santa riding a dragon—James' favorite still.

Our elbows rub in the tightened space
of a table meant at most for eight.
David leans to Esther's ear, Robbie calls
Bekah by her middle name, "Hey, Claire."
Then we roll into the living room and
one by one unwrap the secret in the gift.
Cosby croons hymns as we settle
into the soft pillow of our history—
until someone mentions "pie!"
Like obligation we moan and rise
to the moment of pecan and pumpkin.
There are dishes to be done, and one by one
children disappear downstairs to sleep.

Later, a perfect half-moon drops toward
the ridge of trees opposite our home.
I turn off the lights on the tree. In our
darkened room, I hear your breathing,
reach unerringly and touch your hair—
you stir and settle, unaware
of this moment when
gratitude washes
life clean, like
a baptism.

— April 2010

Book of Revelation

I was walking in the shadowed canyon
Of majestic, heaven-reaching firs,
The cool crispness of early morning
Filling my lungs with all the breath that I
Could hold, when of a sudden I stopped
And gazed up to the distant pale blue
To see if any threat of judgment
Ripped through the sky like a meteorite.

Then I saw it plummeting a preacher's
Venom, cloaked in piteous protest—
It's in the Book, and truth is Truth is TRUTH—
As if message and messenger were distinct,
Shrink-drying Presence to parchment pages.
A god as like to burn us as embrace.
We build righteous bombs arcing down the sky,
Or strapped to chests, just a divine day's work.

It seemed that Satan fell a closing fist
In that moment between breaths, where fear
Compresses in its paralyzing grip
The air right from the lungs; compassion dies.
But then it swerved aside—instead of Death
A robin curved to a branch, craned its neck
And sang as grace will ever sing, filling
The forest like fall of water on stone,
Pooling in the lowest, driest places.

— April 2010?

After

After the debacle with the sliver
impaled in her paw,
after telling her
as we wrapped her other claws
within a towel,
"It's OK, it's OK, it's OK,"
after her frantic fight
to win back her freedom,
after we painfully pulled it out,
after this she has made us
outsiders to her life,
camped on the porch railing
licking herself clean,
coming in only for food
and then right back out
to her secret cat-life.
We are stuck standing next to
windows, hoping to catch
just a glimpse of that
which she used to give freely.

If I looked, would I see God's face
peeking through a hole in the clouds?

— December 2009

Kathy's Gift To Tim

Twenty-five years now, your face ebbing away,
like sand-smoothed, ancient sea-glass,
the receding tide of an ocean of days.
This is the terrible mercy of memory.

I have dreamed of you only once,
rising from some great deep,
or perhaps from some great height
you fell into my sleep.
I awoke, unsure, this very night.

Four words you spoke
through the just-ajar door—
that moment of turning,
as when sparrows hesitate in flight,
that instant when they are still
balancing lift and pull, energies

between

where dreams are and no dream is.
Your face, light-echo on my iris,
lingers…

"It will be alright."

These I take to heart as a universe-prayer,
star-fire, pulsing, aware, gathering.
The universe-axis lifts,
whole galaxies of grace
brought close in the lens of this sleep-gift—
my mothers voice, my mother's face.

— November 2009 (later revision?)

Star Dreams

Fortress clouds closed the sky,
incessantly pounding down,
jabbing in hanging tendrils,
fists of snow. Snow piling on snow.

And snow. And snow, until at last
an evening star appears, and a slipping moon
in the scarcely light of a waning day.

I walk stooped under this sealed horizon
knife-edging a pale, too-near sky.
Silhouettes of shattered, stone-still trees
and under these
and indecipherable sameness, gray-white.

A single scratch of crow stirs,
fading in abrupt, uncertain curves.
Night spills darkly seeping from my bones.

I wander with this one hope—
that it would be enough
to raise my eyes to the light
of some distant star,
and tremble if you gazed there too
and wished, and caused to disappear
these intervening miles
and this far loneliness.
As if were poured down
these long light-years
an overflowing of moment,
somehow and fully,

You.

— November 2009 (later revisiiom?)

Face to Face to Face

I desired to draw old barns
so I learned to let the eye lead
the hand—but what guides the eye?
I cherished character; cracked planks,
missing shingles, a dip in the rough
roof ridge, hay hoist crookedly hanging
from one last rusted bolt. Darkness
deeply shadowing the eaves.
Once I parked below a barn
which rose up like a Parthenon.
I approached as a supplicant
through a bee-buzzing orchard
of knot-gnarled, wind-twisted trees.
I liked the lean of its walls,
the jagged hole in the roof—
a place where ghosts might come and go,
if such there are, though some say
walls and roof do not hinder them.

I pulled out pad, ink and pen,
sat on a stone, and with my eye
took measure of its crooked lines,
a latitude and longitude askew
like a crumpled map, reflattened.
Two broken panes peered a blank face,
as if life had fled and left a corpse.
Evening shadows probed my vision
in long dark tendrils. Wind hissed
like a snake through the dry August grass.
My gaze was suddenly raised to an owl
encompassing me in a silent circle

of measuring eyes. A feather-flick
and he curved away, beyond my paper's edge,
backlit wings glowing in the setting sun.

The bees were busy in the raw pulp
of fallen, skin-split plums. Warm juice
wet on my beard, sweet on my tongue.

— June 2008 (revision November 2009—one after this?)

Writing Icons at Mary Queen of Angels Convent

The bells from Mount Angel Abby
pulse down the hill in repeating waves—
pealing Compline, evening prayer.
At my table, Jesus' eyes take shape
under my anxious hand, but at the sound
I settle intention and raise my head.
The bells are ringing and ringing—
on and on until I feel a lightness
lift like the birds in evening flight.
That my brush might feather so,
as if the very breath of God.
The bells echo down to one moment,
balanced forever between breaths,
and silence draws across the Willamette.

— July 2009 (last revised April 2010)

Smooth Landing

It poured earlier, hammering the walls.
Sat on the porch, a buck-shot of coffee
jump-starting my jittery heart.
Just "one of those days," as I like to say.
I rocked, considering aspirin, or sleep—you'd
think I'd been drunk, or fought and lost, lost bad.
But was none of these, just the way it goes
some days, and there ain't nothin' can be done.

Looked across water—at least there was that,
quiet cove, anchored boat, tall trees beyond
massing darkly up the opposite hill.
Over there, two early morning joggers
traced the rise and run of a dead-end road—
ten minutes later they returned, faster now,
one pulling away. Will it matter, back
at their car? Bet the same one always wins.

Sipping cold coffee when three ducks dropped a
diagonal line across my drained eyes,
left to right. They curved, slewed back, web-feet down,
bodies beak-up, long necks arcing to wings'
furious beat, then settling softly,
as if coming home, into the water.
Memory flared like breath on dark coals—
nineteen-sixty-six, just me and my dad

in a Cessena 180, bouncing between
precipitous, tree-shouldered mountains, pearls
of two narrow creeks falling a necklace
to the dark sapphire-gem of Jim's Lake

nestled completely still, gray edged, but bright
in the middle, a flat mirror with mountains
dropping deeply into the hole of the sky.
Engine feathered, we fell as into a well

leveling off tree-top high, running down
past the end of the lake where, wing on end,
my father slipped us low to the water,
and I watched our mirror-image rise.
We touched so gently—floats, water, eyes…

.   .   .   .

The sun leapt through a hole in the clouds.
Ducks bobbed in the cove, diving for food,
feathers shining as they surfaced in the light.

— March 2009 (last revised June 2009)

Raven Returns Daylight
A Tlingit Legend Retold

In memory of Walter Williams

Dignity furrowed your broad, totem face
where the chisel slipped and the mallet fell—
"None of my children know their Tlingit names."
In your rough, raven-pebbled voice
you storied the midnight Kush Ta Ka—
danger drifting down a Wrangell street—
bespoke a broken-clamshelled Taku beach
over which grandparents ran, soles unscarred.
My ears lay in the palm of your memory—

winters, women twisted soaked spruce roots,
tightly wove the basket of their village names;
springs, men bent branches into river weirs
summer-trapping the thick-running salmon
massing the mouths of the Stikine and Taku—
"you could walk across the river on their backs."
Your face mirrored the cracked, carved totems
which bound and separated, Raven, Eagle, Frog,
weft and warp of war canoes and high-shouldered poles.

You paddled a land of deep-misted silence,
hidden in your bays beside overgrown paths,
grieving the sugar and alcohol of Lituya Bay.
Look down today to summer language camps
outside Angoon, and hear the children laughing—
your elder's face transformed into the sky
and Raven comes returning to its dawn
the stolen sun, stippling the forest floor

which ripples in response—it breathes again
your people.

"Yéi áyá yándei shukgwatáan"
"This is how I'll end it"

        — January 2009 (last revised June 2009)

Tlingit—pronounced "klinkit," with a guttural feel on the "kl" Kush Ta
Ka—a threatening phantom Wrangell, Angoon—towns in southeast Alaska
Taku—an abandoned village, a river. Stikine—a river

Lituya Bay—where the Tlingit first encountered Russian explorers

Truth At 3:17 A.M.

When I was seventeen my mother
three years removed from death
smoking her killing cancer to birth
crushed her cigarette into an ashtray
I had gifted one childhood Christmas
set her blue-green eyes on mine and asked,
"Do you remember the breakfasts
I used to get up early to cook you?"
I thought a moment and thoughtless said,
"No, not really." It was the truth.

That cuts a serrated blade this night
when I have woken moist-eyed from a dream
of bacon sizzling and eggs popping
a humming from the next room and
the small nestle of her in my breast.
Something kept me locked in place
although I longed to rise and peek
around the dreaming doorway's edge.
In dark I whisper through the just ajar door
"I remember, mom, I remember."

—January 2009

Dark Mirror

In the morning with your Mary beads,
breath of bread still on your tongue,
a longing grew to live as Jesus lived.
You chose his thin love-lighted way,
creeping quiet feet into Calcutta
and the dark holes of the poor.

Ah, but he is an absentee lover
setting you up in the apartment of your trust
then withdrawing, taking every lamp and
locking you in darkness.
Click.

We avert our eyes, we demand some
redeeming corner-candle—
against this Unspeakable.
Sixteen thousand days you bent your back,
your touch his touch, your voice his voice
but the door stayed closed.

Dark. No idea, no line of thought
sheds even the slightest light.
Hope is crucified, heart sliced open—
blood makes the hand slippery,
and nothing can be grasped, clung to.

You put your hands to the face
of a shell-shocked boy in Beruit
trembling and moaning with fear
who quieted at your touch.
You softly sang and held him close,

absorbing his dark into your own.
In the silence between bombs
he smiled, eyes shining twin stars,
teeth a luminous quarter-moon
against the firmament of your night—
shone forth a One who abandoned heaven
and so abandoned you—
Sacred Heart of Gonxha Bojaxhiu.

— January 2009 (may have a later revision—see Dark Mirror2)

There and Here

I envied those poets their special places,
who live by, say, an ocean and beach,
waves foaming and floating-in flotsam-traces
from rim of a world just beyond reach.
I had no pond nestled silent and deep
in its crook of earth, water pale as milk
while world dreams its last hour of sleep
tucked under a blanket of dense fog-silk.

I had no New England, no Amherst streets
I could walk to see Emily's room,
the glass through which she observed,
sparsely expressing life's wither and bloom.
No New Hampshire farm, cows licking calves,
stone walls and tramps and crystalline streams
with which Robert unearthed winter and spring
with seemingly effortless rhythm and rhyme.

I was here, sipping coffee in pre-dawn light,
Kinnell's "The Last Hidden Places of Snow"
open in my lap. To be halfway through a poem
and breathe a sudden, rising breath of gratitude—
images igniting a slow alchemy
burning its way to a minor transformation.
All day now, everything shimmers a
metaphor and more. Shadowed
with death, blizzard falling,
distant winds sighing,
bare winter branches
skyward reaching
trembling with

lift of spring
hidden
deeply
with
in.

— January 2009

Afternoon

Not a breath of air stirs the still trees
bowing under snow-weight, as if praying.

The forest breathes. Piled white powder
sighs off long fir branches. Birds spurt
around trunks, claws clacking as they
probe bark-cracks. Flakes hiss swirling down
to their final rest. A coyote howls,
its single note settling like dusk.
Its prints cut across my trail
wandering into a rising ravine—
I follow its meander by the dark of dense
de-snowed salal. Nothing
but shades of grey and white, bewildering
horizontal of trunk and cross-hatching of
branch, like one of those impossible puzzles.

Below, white-weighted fern
lay crushed to the ground, looking like
a holocaust of marble gods and saints
broken and strewn across the forest floor.
No witness to my ascent up the final ridge
where wind cuts through all my layers,
vortexing small tornadoes of snow up toward
the pale metal grey sky. A hawk circles,
considering. At the peak, prints of
another solitary figure track up from   in the snow   greeting
the next valley, snow pushed aside where
he sat atop a boulder. I place my feet
inside the larger depression of his, and sit,
simply that, and look off where earlier

he had looked.

— December 2008

Searching For William Conklin

Alki Beach, October, 2007

I

There would have been the usual concern—
he had a wife and five young children—
"Poor Mary," many must have said, tsk-tsking
with a down, dour turn of lips.
(He might have been drinking, goes family lore,
though no one can say for sure anymore).
Probably some newspaper blurb noted

his passing.
"William Conklin drowned off Alki beach last night."
For a few months, passersby maybe shook their heads,
but came a day when not a single passing person
lifted the smallest pebble of thought in
his direction. Still, memory lingers.
Like water leaking from cupped hands,

we who hold him barely hold him—
a wedding day photograph from 1900,
the sketchy story of his death.
Behind him, veiled by time's long mist,
faceless, deep-shadowed names
etched at the base of Gaelic crosses
recede into death's dark unknown.

II

A ball skips by, children giving noisy chase,
laughter flowing a flute and oboe descant
all around them. The wave of their joy

breaks over me in memory— I tumble
into a day walking this very sand,
tugging on mama and gramma like a
puppy, eager to get God knows where—

maybe they'd made me a promise of ice cream.
But they, immune to my pleas, plodded
a chatty, mother-daughter pace.
Did gramma look north over Elliot bay,
wondering… was it there? Over there?
It came a whispered moment, as when wind
whisps away the sound of children playing,

like silence between one wave and the next,
when their conversation faltered, enough
that I turned to see a tear in gramma's eye
and my mother cupping her cheek in hand,
the softest, softest gaze I have ever seen
floating between them. I think it was then
the better bit of me was born.

III

Laughter brushes against this remembering.
Rising a bubble back to the surface where
children kick balls and run, my eyes settle
far out on a wave which flashes briefly
in the sun, then slides back to the sea.
Just so you, William, slid into the deep
ninety three years ago. I slide too

toward time my life is etched in rock—
a name, two dates, wife nearby, some saying,
hopeful like the one my mother chose—

"Into your hands I commend my soul."
So we die, carved in stone, so briefly scribed,
yet you live! A memory-moment from
when I was five, a love-loss which flowed—

through gramma, through mom, into me, waves of
suffering compassion, that for which Buddha
sat the night and Jesus bled the afternoon...
Sometimes, when I hold your picture just so,
I catch a glimpse of children glancing back—
our five I love with an impossible love
and never well express nor really get right.

IV

A soccer ball skims my head, Elliot-bound—
these children won't leave me alone!
I bounce on legs suddenly young
to water's edge, turn with moderate skill,
knee bent as I taught a thousand times,
laces dropping to the curve of play, and launch
a returning arc to a leaping, laughing

pony-tailed head-of-a-girl, who neatly drops
the ball to the sand, a boy chasing her
down the beach, their play receding
to the near-nothingness of distance.
Then, emerging through their laughter,
I see my own children, older now,
walking with their mother my direction,

their love for each other a grace
gripping my breath. I know not, William,
what really brought me here—that you

might look upon them, no matter the dust
your bones have lain? Or they, somehow, you?
On the bay, sunlight gleams in long lines
of low waves ceaselessly flowing beachward.

— December 2008

Picking Blueberries With Jimmy

We parked at the end of North Douglas Highway
before a bank of bushes and a clearing
pushing into the dark border of
soft-needled hemlock and gnarly
arthritic-branched Sitka spruce.
A sweet August afternoon, the high sun,
untroubled by the usual clouds,
warming our shoulders—at least as much
as it can here in the cool of the north,
up at the end of Douglas Island.

Jimmy and I tumbled out, buckets in hand,
our moms emerging more languidly,
putting out their cigarettes and perhaps
finishing a story that one or the other
had started with a laugh some minutes before.
We never really listened to their tales,
not knowing then how one day
we might wish we had them in memory
that the train-whistle of their lives
would never stop echoing in our own.

Blueberries waited at the top of the rise
where trees shadowed much of the day,
leaking liquid-purple onto our fingers
which we licked as we picked our way
from bush to bush, filling the buckets.
Jimmy and I, like errant moons, slowly
slid away from our moms, until their presence
came in distant, short staccatos of laughter.
I turned from one bush to the next, and saw

how it lay crushed, really crushed, to the ground.

"Jimmy," I whispered. You turned and you saw
what I had seen, and quieted too, and peered,
as I, into the dark, rising deep of the forest,
looming now with the unseen presence
of the bear which had slept here last night.
This was the last bravado of childhood—for what
can really happen when your mothers are near?
We became in an instant bear hunters,
eyes piercing the gloom, undaunted, waiting
for it to return, and then, the poor bear

would fall to our courage—you'd draw his
attention away, and I'd whack him hard
with a rock or a branch, and we'd finish him off
as always, the world safe once again from bears,
or Indians, Commie spies, every man or beast
that we'd chased and fought and defeated
all the way down our years of imagination.
Our mothers came up just at the end,
(so the bear ran off, limping badly), asking
why their buckets were full, but not ours?
Mothers! Why couldn't they see what we'd done?

So we went back to plucking blueberries
and they to their chat, chat, chatting,
but we looked at each other with a secret smile,
that sweet secret smile I still remember,
racing twigs in a gutter gullywasher,
or building a stone bridge across Gold Creek

(which half-held until the spring runoff),
or stopping the tide with a sandcastle wall—
but you never can hold the whole ocean.

Sometimes now I phone you, Jim, recall your
knock at my door. "Can Tim come out and play?"
No voice like your voice slides these years
back to summer, 1967,
astride a bike high on Seward Street
heart pumping along its narrow, steep line
and with a glance to you, pushing off
drawn down by some unseen exhilaration
of balance, speed and air, lifting us
as if winged into infinite, endless blue.

So it was and always was with you
flying down Seward, beside the wet gutters,
astride Gold Creek, piling beach sand
out Thane Road, and there among blueberries
where bears slept and forests rose a dark dream
to high, steep ridges and peaks beyond.
They called, and we went, on separate trails.
I wonder, never asking, if you remember as I
days so long and lovely that I would be happy
to trade them forever for heaven.

— December 2008

The Walk

I often wonder what
ideas I'll miss in all these
half-read books I've bought,
semi-tomes with serious themes,
sitting in shelves like second-graders
vying for attention with the raised
waving hands of their titles—
"The Church!" "The Meaning of History!!"
"Buddha and Jesus!!!" "Fire in the Mind!!!!"

Sometimes, puttering at my desk,
I'll glance over to see one book
eyeing me like a dog at rest,
tail wagging and peeking through his paws,
a raised quizzical brow asking,
"What are we waiting for?"

More rarely, I might reach to
pat him on the neck
and head out for a walk,
watching with interest
where he wanders, nose to the ground.

Rarest and loveliest of all,
unleashed,
I might follow his lead into woods
and some unexpected wonder;
sun slanting through trees
at the curve of a creek—
where he barks and bends
to lap from water glistening

like diamonds.

— December 2008

Into Evening

--For Helli and Eero

Inbound, east of Shelter Island,
Racing pink in cloud and sky,
Plunging deep into a swelling sea
Pregnant with whale and tide.

Sun slips behind the Chilkats'
Ragged ridge of snow-freshened peaks,
Darkening to a fire-edged silhouette
Receding toward night's infinite shore.
Venus beckons, a distant lighthouse.

Slowing, water nodding pink behind us,
You nudge our boat back on its wake,
Swing the Chilkat's darkened heights
Astern to port, and now afore the bow,
And leaning, dip your hand in liquid light.

We run like salmon beneath a shoulder-moon,
Spray misting air and salting tongue.
Sea-child, lift your face into the tang,
Nestle your shoulder inside mine,
Tee Harbor bound—port, anchorage, home.

— January 2008

Into The Quiet

For Mary Lou, on Jesse's 18th Birthday

Into the quiet, this resting place
Of grass, of stone, of final words
In which we trace old memories,
Fingering a chiseled litany of loss.
All about these, some overgrown,
Some newly sown, a breeze whispers
Softly. Birds do not stir in the trees.
What art of life, held so long and so true?

And you.

All around and about and within,
Uncontained, unrestrained.
To feel just once your fingers brush my cheek,
To hear your voice, oh, to seek your eyes…
But breathes the whisper of this breeze.
I soar the silence, speak this wild choice,
Lift, feeling sun upon my face,
Into the quiet, this resting place.

— January 2008

Who Let The Elephants In?

The problem with opening windows and doors
Is the air gets all puffed up with arrogance,
Micro-storms punching and gusting the room
A mini-disaster remaining behind.
Books open to an intentional page
Riffle and turn so you lose your place,
And don't even mention neatly stacked papers
Blown like a card-deck thrown in the air
Strewn cattywampus all over the floor.

And it's not just the papers. All manner of
Things in place fall out of place, scattered
Like elephants had tromped through the room.
Elephants do serious damage—think of the dents
In the floor, and one of them could smash
A hole in the wall, falling right through and
Onto the ground—the absolute end of the lawn.
The roof would be leaning most likely—
Why, the whole thing might fall all the way down!

It is a matter of some delicacy (prompt, don't provoke!)
Convincing elephants to leave the house.
Far better to keep them out from the start.
Then, simply shut the windows and doors,
Lock down the shutters if you think it right.
Everything put in its proper place.
Though, who was the first to see elephants?
I only felt a sense-freshening breeze,
Elephant-energy run through stale air.

— December 2007

Rising To Hawk

Arc of wing, silent, still,
Curving through the unseen
Across this pale dawn.
I see every filament
Of every feather,
Every finely felt line,
Trembling.

Hawk's eyes
Gazing down at a gazing up.
Rise, rise to intricate wings
Feel them blaze with each
Breath-breeze.

Oh, great, vast Empty!
For an infinite sum of moment
Floating out across time,
Whisp of dream
Spiraling this airy stream.

— November 2007

Running the Bases

I remember dad squatting sixty feet away,
Glove up, encouraging me to
                    Whing it in there
                              —atta boy!
Alas, I was no pitcher.

Oh, I could throw it at 15
                    Vacuuming
              grounders to my left
The long
              clean throw to first
Bang-bang play, "Y'er out!" from the ump
Exhilaration.

I heard my name called on that field,
"atta boys" aplenty.
Eighteen times that year
              I'd led off from first and
                         Lit out for second.
Eighteen times   I made it.
              (and three more to third)
Concentration narrowed to pitcher's eyes
Peering under his cap like a hurt child,
              His left knee, his shoulders,
                    And that twitch
                              From fear and a will to win
This confrontation.
The twitch, turn of ankle and hips, and
                         I'm gone
Glorying in a
              three

        second

              spurt

Of genetic gift,

Sliding safe, every time,

Rising from the base a god   —atta boy!

dusting off pants   —way to go

Too cool to smile, (as I'd been taught)

Deified in their voices, (or so I thought)

staring intensely instead (as I'd been taught)

To third base,

That possession and part time place, last turn

                     before home.

Then came a late inning call.

None on

        None out

             One run lead

                  Pitchers used up

Standing surprised on the mound

Peering down a

        long tunnel

To a real catcher's mitt, nodding my head

As if I actually had

            Two pitches

        I could throw,

A curve   maybe

        To go with my so-so fastball—

        "Y'er the best we got"

        My Manager's motivation. He spit

              some seeds

        Out his chipmunk cheek,

About-faced to the dugout.

Two grounders later I was one out away
When to the plate

             Strode…

      Well, walked

      S l o w l y walked

"Waterbucket" Wally Thompson. He was no

                 Casey At Bat—rumor had it he was

                   Worst

In the league.

        Easy out, I thought
        And would have been

But that

        the plate

            repelled

Like same-poled magnets
Pitches that felt perfect when

            leaving my hand.

            At 3-and-0

I took something

           Off

Just to get a strike.

Wally swung, shooting a line drive

            It had eyes

Just over first and
Under the diving right fielder
Who gave chase toward the wall.
After, Manager called me over.

        "Whatcha hell ya doin? (spit)

he meant the slower pitch

"I didn't want to walk him."

      (spit)   "Really"   (spit)

(Spit)

He looked to third, (where Wally stood panting)

      Contemptuously

He looked to first, then

      Pointedly (spit)

Glared at me.

And (spit) spit on my shoes.

I thought, I didn't

Put me

      here

          Looked longingly to third,

          Where Wally waited

Grin on his face as

          Big as the Babe

But a certain uncertainty   (Interloper?)

      Not sure

      Which direction to look.

No matter

My manager's stare,

It was Wally who'd waited

Laying off three close pitches—had he not earned

          His one

          Perfect swing,

The excellent crack, the pumping

      Of arms

        Of legs

          Of heart

     And tearing 'round second

For third,

Knowing the ball

Is coming

Is coming

Is coming

Faster than you're running

And the sliding dusty

Convergence

The "Safe," relief and elation, eyes shining

Knowing this once what it's like, a Triple?

Had he not earned it?

"You want to win too much," I told

the

manager

And turned to the mound.

He left me in.

Their leadoff batter stepped to the plate

And after five pitches it stood 3-and-2.

I heard the cheering and jeering abate

Unleashing the last pitch I ever threw

For someone else's reason to throw.

No longer a god, and glad of it, I sensed

How the batter dropped his wrists down low,

And dig off his heel to reach for the fence.

Did he hope with this blow, divinity claim?

Last pitch approaching, long ago game.

— November 2007

Symphony and Coda

Early, intentioned with pruner and spade
I slipped down the garden path, pausing
Where the first crocus tip of spring
Peeked through the dark earth.
Bending close to see its intricate veins,
Arose a subtle invitation.   "Listen"
Then I heard the soft sibilance of fog
Feather-floating down the trees.
I heard a spider unravel its first silken thread,
Send it probing into the all-unknown.
I heard the moment the first delicate rose of dawn
Blushed the eastern bark of a hundred thousand trees,
And a million drops of dew burst into mirrored suns…
Soon, all was silent.
But there!—one long slender thread of light,
A spider balanced halfway along,
And the crocus, promise of purple or yellow or blue,
One half-inch higher toward the sun.
Oh! And forgotten pruner and spade
As I sat to the slow spinning-probe of the spider
And the patient push of crocus toward the light.

— October 2007

Nestucca Eight-Day Retreat

The days float by as the Nestucca
Slowly flows toward the ocean.
Walking in the morning,
Sun leaping into the sky.
Sitting in the evening,
Sun falling into the sea.

Between, deer gaze into our eyes
Unafraid.
Fawns skid and skitter amid
Massive-boled Sitka spruce,
Scattering their energy in youthful circles
Curving ever back to their mothers
Who lick them with their tongues,
Erasing their scent from coyotes.

When the tide moves in
Filling this delta like a bowl,
Salt mingles with fresh
And the river-run ebbs toward the middle.
Here by the shore
Incoming and outgoing merge
Into quiet water, an unlikely mirror.
Someone floats a canoe, gently on oars,
Projecting a double-seeming image,
Two canoes, two oars, two faces.
A moment of perfect stillness
And a startling recognition

That I have left the shore,
Left the ancient spruce

And mother-searching fawns.
There is no fine-atomed edge,
No subtle line of demarcation between,
To separate what is one—
Above, eyes raised to the sun
Below, eyes lowered to the deep
Where water flows mysteriously.

— June 2007 (last revised January 2008)

First Light

Early,
Intentioned with pruner and spade
I slipped down the garden path, stopping
Where the first crocus tip of spring
Peeked through the dark earth.
Bending close to see its intricate veins,
Arose a subtle invitation.   "Listen"
Then I heard the soft sibilance of fog
Feather-floating down the trees.
I heard a spider unravel its first silken thread,
Send it probing into the all-unknown.
I heard the moment the first delicate rose of dawn
Blushed the eastern bark of a hundred thousand trees,
And a million drops of dew burst into mirrored song…
Within an hour all was silent
But one long slender thread of light
A spider balanced halfway along,
And the crocus, promise of purple or yellow or blue,
One half-inch higher toward the sun.
Oh!
Oh! And my spade, pruner, intentions, all,
Lying on the ground, forgotten, unused.

— June 2007

Well Spoken

After, how strange my heart raced,
A cirrus-pulse which warmed my face.
In your eyes, I saw a love of flight,
This place in which you soar aloft
As if the light, not air, upheld our wings.

You spoke so seldom of such things.

But on this low and gray and rain-drenched day,
Seventy miles up Lynn Canal,
In an instant
The sun pierced the laden sky and cast
Between two jagged Chilkat peaks
A prismed, blinding beam
Down and down upon a beach.

I watched the graceful curve which formed
And flung against the misted gray
Its outstretched hues—and here you had your say.
"Son," you said, and swung our craft
Beneath.

Rainbow-ends curved on themselves and touched
And through the circle's heart we flew, and you
You turned and laughed, your voice and eyes
Starburst of my inner light. We flew, we soared,
We laughed and laughed this unexpected arc of flight.

— June 2007

The Tao

Eyes and nostrils peer from the sea
Crocodile intense.
Pulling up and out,
Muscles rippling, striding erect
In illusion of height and strength.
Blocking our own radiance,
Casting long sunset-shadows
Across our umbilical cord,
Metaphor emerges our stumbling attempt
To walk in light.
See in water
Breathe without thought
Breathe water water water.

— May 2007

Gentle This Rain

Today you are my Spring.
You come as of an April rain
Singing-falling in your eyes
And in your eyes I am falling.
As with the morning's light the dew
Transforms, so I am freshly born
Emerging in this brush of rain
Creek-gathering and falling-flowing
Over some high precipice
Soaring out, white foaming arc
Shattering into ten thousand weightless
Pearl-droplets
Throwing off ten thousand rainbows—
Tiny sun-lit gems, prisms of grace
Floating a scarcely whispered breeze.
In these, my fingers, gentle rain,
Caress your cheek your hair your face.

— April 2007

Just A Little Resurrection

It poured earlier, hammering the walls.
Sat on the porch, a buck-shot of coffee
Pull-starting the pounding of my heart.
Just "one of those days," as I like to say.
I rocked, considering aspirin, or sleep—you'd
Think I'd been drunk, or fought and lost, lost bad.
But was none of these, just the way it goes
Some days, and there ain't nothin' can be done.

Looked across water—at least there was that,
Quiet cove, anchored boat, tall trees beyond
Massing darkly up the opposite hill.
Over there, two early morning joggers
Traced the rise and run of a dead-end road—
Ten minutes later they returned, faster now,
One pulling away. Will it matter, back
At their car? Bet the same one always wins.

Sipping cold coffee when three ducks dropped a
Diagonal line across my dulled eyes,
Left to right. They curved, slewed back, web-feet down,
Bodies beak-up, long necks arcing to wings'
Furious beat, then settling softly,
As if coming home, into the sea.
Memory flared like breath on dark coals—
1966, just me and my dad

In a Cessena 180, sliding past
Precipitious, tree-shouldered mountains, the pearls
Of two narrow creeks falling a necklace
To the dark sapphire-gem of Jim's Lake.

It lay completely still, gray edged, but bright
In the middle, flat mirror of mountains
Dropping deeply into the hole of the sky.
Engine feathered, we fell as into a well

Leveling off tree-top high, racing down
Past the end of the lake where, wing on end,
My father slipped us low to the lake,
And I watched our water-image rise
And we touched so gently—floats, water, eyes…

.   .   .   .

Sun leapt through an opening in the clouds;
The ducks bobbed in the cove, diving for food,
Feathers shining as they surfaced in the light.

— February 2007

The Kiss

Somewhere beneath perception whispers
Your heart-breeze. Branches stir as
One lone leaf falls at my feet.
Swelling now, airy, infinite,
Floating down the trees, rain so delicate
Upon my cheek, I open, unaware.

And then, oh then, the storm unleashes,
Lashing branches in fury-dance
Madness of leaves twist and tumble
Vortex-spiraling up and ever up
whirling, swirling, twirling,
Flung out, away, jumbled, upended…

One long suspended moment penetrates,
Hesitates,
Then settles, so softly settles.
All Prediction, all Custom, all Knowing
Crumble.

Breeze-breath hushes
Between breaths, where no life is
Nor death, nor mine, nor yours.
Trembling,
One heart, one beat,
One heart, one beat,
One heart, one beat,
One.

— January 2007

Christmas Eve

We carry these gifts,
Old World recipes (with secret spices),
In paper bags wrinkled like an aged face.
Carefully we carry with hands
That stirred and mixed and measured—
A tablespoon of this, a cup of that, and
With long intuition,
A kind of dash of this. Then we sit,
Relieving our backs and fallen arches.

After knocking, we give them to your hands.
Lingering over coffee and your own secret
Christmas delicacy, the sun
Seemingly slows in the sky. Soon enough,
Children will tumble laughing through the door
Faces sunset-glowing with winter's chill
Snow sticking to boots and mittens
And falling from its matting in their hair—
But not before we have our fill
And leaving, take our mingled body scents.

— Christmas Eve 1988

Child Games

You walked in
        Slanted
Ordering specialty coffee, sitting
Beside a well-manicured lithograph
Of pastel colors of some
Out of perspective coffee shop scene
With a river running through the center
Washing all away, sitting
Under a trimmed and potted plant
Stair-stepping down a pastel pink wall,
And from the corner piped-piano music soothed.
At the counter you sat, you set your strained,
Lined face in your left palm, and you—
Maybe all of twenty-one—turned the
New York Times pages with your right,
Grinding teeth and drumming fingers
Spilling like fear as you raised the shaking cup
To your lips, sipping from shouted black over white.

How like a child you looked,
Dressing up and playing house.
It wouldn't surprise me if in tomorrow's Times
I read that you'd walked out the door
And found some high bridge with which to play
Leap-frog.

                  — sometime in the 1980s

Requiem

Standing in aisles and along walls,
Shifting from foot to foot,
Faint from too much perfume and compression.
At last the minister finished preaching
The organ silenced its tinny prelude
The real movement began.

Men did uncommon things:
Weeping, weeping, in this moment
Sweeping away fear of male body—
Chest to chest, cheek to damp cheek,
Holding on unaware of their quivering chins.

Women loosed tears to drown the world,
Handkerchiefs tight to stifle staccato sobs
Lining their faces with an intensity of
Question which aged each fifteen years.

And this, this last.
The long fingers of an older sister reaching
And touching, touching, staying
Staying, oh, staying.
Head bowed, three fingers of her left hand
Resting and resting on velvet covered casket.

The smell of extinguished candles
And a hint of flowers
Remained.

— sometime in the 1980s

The Death Of Poetry

The restless earth of this place
Heaves flecks and shards
As if millions of gravestones,
Repulsing singular, skinless traces of bone.
Brick walls have crumbled, weeds overgrown.
Freight Car One-two-five-six-eight,
Capacity ten thousand and twenty-three
Jews
Gypsies
Homosexuals
Handicapped
Undesirables
(what meticulous records)
Sits a rusted dagger on rusted rails reaching
West to the Urquelle of Goethe und Schiller.

Some scream—did you hear?   you must hear
(or did I dream?)
Perhaps trapped in an air bubble
All these years   (you)
Arcs like a woman dying in labor
              (must)
And settles
              (listen)
In the dust, disturbing my vision.
There is more—Zyklon-B gas pellets,
A mountain of shoes…

Birds do not sing here.

              — sometime in the 1980s

What I Learned From Hans Georg Gadamer

Reality is intelligible. I do not know what is meant by "God." If there is a God, this reality is present in, incarnate in, reality. Meaning is inherent in reality. Nothing exists by itself, distinct, but everything is rather a tapestry, a continuium, a unity. "Thingness" (ie, a tree) is essentially a conceptual construct, an intellectual pulling of certain noted qualities out of their unitive reality.

The material and spiritual "world(s)" are not separate. This is a conceptual distinction. All of reality is expansive, processive, transformative, in a process of becoming. So it is with human consciousness/awareness/mind. Humanity has the potential to move from particularity to unity.

Finitude means context, means particularity. Interpretation is an effort to transcend particularity.

Particularity in human awareness/consciousness is enculturation, it is the social/psychological context in which our inherent freedom and drive for understanding come to life, are animated. There is an intertia which pulls against the transformative push in reality. This inertia is the comfort of the known, the predictable. It is the gravity of and attraction to that context in which our whole person was woven. It wants to contain, rather than grow. Psychologically it exhibits itself as fear, as anxiety, as the need to be right, as pride that accompanies the boost of ego. These have their existential counterparts--trying to quiet the unease that comes with our inner existential restlessness and sense of incompleteness. This inertia is closed to the moment of "Eureka!" It will never say "Aha" with humility.

The more shrill the speaker, the greater their fear.

Human understanding has the possibility of expanding, of transforming. This requires an attitude of dialogue—with another person, a text, a religious or philosophical tradition. Allowing one's ideas to be put at risk. As your thought grows, you grow. As your thinking changes, you become a new person.

Truth is not the mind thinking the correct things about realities outside oneself. Truth is living one's commitments/convictions in a life shot through with possibility, growth, willingness to change, desire to share.

There are 3 septillion stars in the universe. That is 100 billion squared, times three. Abundance. An estimated 30,000,000 earth-like planets. Do you think we are alone? The upswelling of consciousness is the universe becoming aware of itself all over the place. This is the deepest insight of the process of evolution.

Hold to this paradox: the material world is not primary, with the spiritual secondary. Nor is the other way around true. Matter and Spirit are not separate realities. This is the deepest insight of quantum physics.

Here is one of the most important verses in the bible: "Go forth from the land of your kinsfolk and from your father's house to a land that I will show you." (Genesis 12:1)

Here is one essential question: Is it so?

Have this attitude: Listen.

Do this: Love.

— January 2011